The DISSOLUTION Of Eastern European Jewry

WALTER N. SANNING

1990
INSTITUTE FOR HISTORICAL REVIEW

The Dissolution of Eastern European Jewry
By Walter N. Sanning

Copyright © 1983 by Walter N. Sanning

Published by the
Institute for Historical Review
1822½ Newport Blvd., Suite 191
Costa Mesa, California 92627
Under license from
Grabert-Verlag
Tübingen/Germany

The German language edition
Die Auflösung des osteuropäischen Judentums
Published by
Grabert-Verlag
Tübingen/Germany

Manufactured in the United States of America

First printing July 1983
Second printing May 1985
Third printing November 1990

Library of Congress Cataloging in Publication Data:

Sanning, Walter N., 1935-
   The dissolution of Eastern European Jewry.

   Bibliography: p.
   Includes index.
   1. Jews—Europe, Eastern—History. 2. Europe,
   Eastern—Ethnic relations. I. Title.
   DS135.E83S33 1983   947'.0004924   83-81042
   ISBN 0-939484-11-0

Table of Contents

APPENDIX AND TABLES

"... it is questionable whether one should accept improbable figures supplied by a not overly friendly source."

American Jewish Year Book

Foreword

It is understatement to say that the study of 20th century Jewish population changes presents us with irresolvable problems, but there is much that can be reliably observed. The principal background developments were the rise of Zionism as a significant international political force and the rise of anti-Jewish movements in Europe, notably in Germany. Implicit in both developments were policies, however differently motivated, that would have relocated European Jews in great numbers. Indeed this common objective was the basis for a not negligible amount of cooperation between Zionist and German authorities in the 1933-1939 period.

Other background developments were the adoption of pro-Jewish policies by the USA and the USSR, the latter maintaining those policies through 1948 (the year of Israel's establishment). These victors in World War II continued, also from various motivations, processes of relocating Jews that had been carried on by Germany, while Germany in turn had not been the first in the field, as large relocations of Jews had been carried out earlier under Zionist and Soviet auspices.

As these massive movements subsided to trickles in the postwar period, the broad outlines of what had happened were clear. Jewish communities had drastically shrunk or even virtually disappeared in much of central and eastern Europe, particularly Poland. Correspondingly, there had been great transfers of Jews to Palestine, the USA and other countries, employing means provided by Jewish organizations or by the US controlled UNRRA, whose Directors had been New York Zionists Herbert Lehman and Fiorello LaGuardia. There had also been a large dispersion of Jews, especially Polish Jews, into the Soviet Union. Thus the excellent title of this book.

While such broad outlines were clear, many details remain obscure, shrouded or inaccessible. Particularly troublesome are quantitative aspects. We do not know how many were absorbed into the Soviet Union, how many emigrated to the USA or other specific countries, or how many remained or resumed living in central or eastern Europe, and the not

9

insignificant number of those who perished has not been firmly reckoned. On the last matter, only propagandists and uninformed people come forward with a purported accurate number.

Reasons for this ignorance are not difficult to give. The movements of Jews through the UNRRA camps were camouflaged as much as was possible under the circumstances, for the excellent reasons, among others, that the subsequent movements to Palestine were illegal and in any case UNRRA was supposed to be for "United Nations Relief and Rehabilitation" in a war ravaged continent, not for conquest of non-European territory by indigenous European populations.

Useful data on postwar migration and resettlement is difficult to impossible to obtain. Since 1943 the US Immigration and Naturalization Service has made no attempt to count immigrant Jews as such, and Soviet dominated eastern Europe does not welcome foreign or scholarly curiosity on politically sensitive matters.

Census data is not of much help. In the USA, which is today the leading center of Jewish population, "Jews" are not a category for census purposes, and indeed Jews do not like being counted. The ongoing controversy in Britain on this point is a current illustration of this aversion.* The Soviet census attempts to count Jews, but the procedure of the census takers is to accept the word of individuals on this question. When to that observation is added the aforementioned Jewish aversion (operating in a state encouraged climate of anti-Zionism) and the usual skepticism appropriate to evaluating Soviet claims, the Soviet census figures are seen to be of little value. Jewish spokesmen in the West claim that the Soviet figures are unrealistically low.**

To these considerations should be added the difficulty of producing an operationally useful definition of a "Jew". This is an especially grave problem in the western liberal democracies, on account of the large extent of intermarriage and the larger extent of religious apostasy.

This book jumps squarely into the uninviting waters of 20th century Jewish demography and migration and attempts to reconstruct these Jewish population changes, especially in their quantitative aspects. One immediate consequence of this choice of subject is that the person

---

* *Jewish Chronicle*, 28 Dec 79, p. 5; 7 Mar 80, p. 9; 11 Feb 83, p. 4; *Patterns of Prejudice*, Jan 80, p. 24+.
** *American Jewish Year Book 1981*, p. 239f.

looking for light reading is advised to look elsewhere; this book is difficult to read even for somebody who is accustomed, as I am, to reading texts with high quantitative components. Another consequence is that the reader looking for final and definitive answers to "how many?" type questions, as distinct from at best provisional estimates, will be disappointed. There is scarcely an estimate arrived at in this book that cannot be challenged on some plausible grounds.

Such limitations of this book are not the author's fault. There is no way his subject can be served adequately with easily readable text, and there is no way to determine the more important numbers involved with the accuracy and reliability of, say, a total population census in a contemporary western country. The author is well aware of such constraints and limitations, and specifically cautions the reader that one vitally important estimate "has no claim on absolute certainty." If I were to select only one respect in which I wish the author had done something differently, it would be that I wish he had been more emphatic on the rather tentative nature of most of the quantitative conclusions reached here.

Such negative features of this book having been conceded at the outset, what are the positive features that excited my admiration for this work when it was in manuscript, and caused me to strongly urge its publication?

This book is the first full length serious study of World War II related Jewish population changes. Its esoteric air is perhaps on the perceptual level the perfect antidote to the vulgar idiocies that are today monotonously peddled by the media, for whom recent Jewish population changes are also of major interest, although such dry terminology is rarely employed by them.

This book presents the fundamentally correct account of the subject. While the basic structure of that account is not original with this book, the scope and depth of the study are great enough that I daresay that, barring the miraculous release of hitherto confidential data, especially by Zionist and Soviet controlled sources, the treatment has been carried here about as far as it can be.

While the complexity of the subject may disturb some, it is important to learn, as we do from this book better than from any other, why this complexity exists. While many of the numerical estimates are not conclusive, it is important to learn, as we do from this study better than from any other by examining its sources, that such estimates can be made by conscientious deduction from widely accepted, accurately cited and, on very important points, mostly Jewish literature.

11

The result is that the simplistic legends that have petrified postwar thought on the Jewish aspect of World War II are dealt another of the many blows they have received in recent years.

February 1983   *Arthur R. Butz*
                                                       Evanston, Illinois

Introduction

Just one hundred years ago eastern Europe – Galicia, Ukraine, Hungary – was the center of the world's Jewish population, but today that center has moved overseas to the Western Hemisphere and Israel. Whereas previously there was little doubt as to who was a Jew, today it is much more difficult to arrive at a satisfactory definition; the increasing secularization of industrial society in the recent past affected the Jewish people in particular. No wonder that today the question of the numerical size of the world Jewish population is one of the most controversial of demographic statistics. Nowhere does one encounter as many contradictions as in the attempt to assess the world's Jewish population even within the margin of error of a million. The reputable *American Jewish Year Book*, for example, lists the size of the world's Jewish population in 1979 as 14.5 million; looking a little closer, the surprised layman will find that this number includes several hundreds of thousands of gentiles. Other highly regarded experts such Dr. Nahum Goldmann, for example, believe that Israel's almost 3.3 million Jews constitute almost one-fifth of World Jewry; in effect, he has put the figure for the world's Jewish population at 16½ million.

Also, if one learns that only eleven million Jews are supposed to have survived World War Two and that this decimated remnant – with the exception of the Israelis – experienced a very slow natural growth in the post-war period due to over-aging, small families, rising assimilation tendencies and widespread mixed marriages, both of the above figures for the world's Jewish population become questionable.

Any attempt to trace the flow of migration of the Jewish people during the past fifty years and to narrow down the size of the Jewish population – then and now – can only be successful if the enigmatic demographic characteristics of the Jews in their areas of departure – i.e. eastern Europe – become unravelled and, furthermore, if the migration movements are seen in the historical framework.

Unquestionably, the Second World War had by far the largest impact on the numerical development of the Jews in modern times. For this reason, especially the German-Soviet confrontation until 1945 and, thereafter, the determined effort of the Jews to leave the devastated historical countries of origin deserve to be paid the utmost attention.

Primarily in order to meet possible objections, this analysis is based almost entirely on Allied, Zionist and other "sympathetic" sources. The significance of the statistical accountings in this study is also in the demonstration that they at least *can* be made on the basis of allegedly authoritative and largely Jewish sources. The most striking findings of this study are:

A. The world's Jewish population faced a serious demographic crisis even before World War Two. This was also true of the Jews in eastern Europe.
B. During the 1930's roughly one million Jews left the historic places in central and eastern Europe for North and South America, Palestine, western Europe and several other minor recipient countries.
C. At the beginning of World War Two there were fewer than 16 million Jews in the world (Zionist data are listed in parentheses):

United States	5.0	(4.8) mio.
USSR (incl. Baltic states)	5.3	(3.3) mio.
Palestine	0.4	(0.4) mio.
European countries occupied by Germany during WWII	2.9	(6.0) mio.
Rest of the world	2.4	(2.2) mio.
	16.0	(16.6) mio.

D. Of the 5½ million Jews in the Soviet Union at the outbreak of WWII, by far the largest part was evacuated to Siberia; less than 15 % fell into German hands.
E. One million Jews died while fighting in the Red Army or in Siberian labor camps; this aspect is generally passed over in Zionist accounts.
F. 14¾ million Jews survived the last war (Zionist data in parentheses):

United States	5.2	(5.0) mio.
USSR	4.3	(2.0) mio.
Palestine	0.6	(0.6) mio.
European countries occupied by Germany during WWII	2.4	(1.1) mio.
Rest of the world	2.2	(2.3) mio.
	14.7	(11.0) mio.

14

G. Today, the world's Jewish population numbers 16½ million (*American Jewish Year Book* data listed in parentheses):

United States*	6.7	(5.9) mio.
USSR	3.4	(2.6) mio.
Israel	3.2	(3.2) mio.
European countries occupied by Germany during WWII	1.0	(1.0) mio.
Rest of the world	2.0	(1.8) mio.
	16.3	(14.5) mio.

* including several hundreds of thousands of gentiles in the case of the 5.9 and 14.5 million figures of the *American Jewish Year Book*.

H. The Jewish world population is likely to decrease at accelerating rates during the coming decades.

This study represents just one step in the attempt to trace the dissolution of Eastern Jewry in the course of the last fifty years. Many of the figures presented will, no doubt, be adjusted as further research discovers new and/or more reliable sources. In particular, it is to be hoped that students of this fascinating subject will follow the main thrust of this analysis which points to three distinct areas where further search should prove rewarding:

1. Soviet deportation of civilians, particularly Jews, before and during the Second World War.
2. The importance of Turkey as a transit country for refugee Jews arriving there by train (Bulgaria) or by ship (Constanza/Rumania); Turkish archives are virgin territory in this respect.
3. Jewish displaced persons camps (UNRRA) from Iran to Morocco.

PART I

THE SOVIET UNION
AND THE EASTERN JEWS

FIRST CHAPTER

Eastern Jewry

Myths die slowly, but historical myths sometimes go on to become "facts." Often it is all but impossible to unmask them for what they are, because myths have that certain ingredient generally lacking in cold facts, namely, that people *want* to believe them – often for contradictory reasons. One of the myths with a questionable influence on our understanding and analysis of historical developments concerns the fertility of Europe's Eastern Jewry.

If there is one Eastern Jewish trait which both National Socialists and Zionists agreed upon, then it was undoubtedly that particular eastern European minority's proclivity to multiply rapidly. What one side considered to be a threat, was a well of hope for the other.

Eastern Jewry, while steeped in orthodoxy and tradition, had achieved prolific natural growth rates in the last century. The reasons are close at hand: Its higher educational level enabled it to reduce death rates much sooner and faster than the surrounding native host population. At the same time, traditional values, religious beliefs and strong family bonds induced them to go on raising large families.

However, as political self-consciousness rose and industrial society enforced increased secularization, the old social fabric began to crumble – often with lightning speed. Social characteristics were overturned within a short time span. In addition, the upheavals of World War One left lasting imprints on Eastern Jewish life. The rapidity of this development went almost unnoticed by Zionists and their foes.

In this Chapter we will show that the Eastern Jewry of the 1930's had changed fundamentally since the turn of the Century and especially since World War One. Outside the Soviet Union, two-thirds of eastern Europe's Jews lived in Poland at the end of the 1920's and, therefore, we will place our emphasis on the Polish Jews in the attempt to ascertain their demographic characteristics.

According to the Anglo-American Committee on European Jewry and Palestine (Anglo-American Committee) the Jewish population in Poland numbered 3,351,000 at the beginning of World War Two. The Jewish author Gerald Reitlinger asserted though that the Polish census of December 9, 1931 discovered only 2,732,600 "racial" Jews.[1] However, a natural increase by 620,000 during the following eight years is impossible: This would have been equivalent to an annual growth rate of 2.6%, far exceeding the fertility of the native Polish and Ukrainian host population; the *Universal Jewish Encyclopedia* (Universal) denies this possibility outright and a Jewish immigration in anti-Semitic Poland was non-existent.[2]

The *Statesman's Yearbook 1944* reported that the Polish census contained two different figures for the Jewish population group: One based on "language" and the other on "religion."[3] The first corresponds exactly with Reitlinger's figure for the so-called "racial" Jews. As to religious preference the *Statesman's Yearbook* mentioned 3,113,900 Polish residents of the Mosaic faith. The resulting difference of 237,000 (3,351,000 less 3,113,900) could well represent the natural growth of a purportedly very fertile Eastern European Jewry during the period from the end of 1931 until the end of 1939.

Also, the *Universal* reported the average number of births among Polish Jews in the period from 1930 to 1935 to have been 85,000,[4] a figure which would constitute 2.8% of a population of roughly three million. If the mortality figure of about 40,000 annually as provided by the same source is correct,[5] the surplus of births over deaths between 1930 and 1935 would have averaged 45,000 per annum. Projected for the time span 1932 to 1939 the Polish-Jewish population might have increased by 360,000 to reach 3.5 million by the start of the war; this latter number is also often being mentioned in post-war literature in connection with Polish Jews.

Still, the above remarks show that the size of Poland's Jewish population at the outbreak of WWII is by no means certain; Jewish sources differ to a substantial degree from one another and often they even contradict each other. In order to remove or, at least, limit these uncertainties, it is necessary to trace the structure and development of the Jews in Poland by resorting to available primary sources; only then will it be possible to shed more light on pre-war Eastern European Jewry.

The Polish census of December 9, 1931 found 3,113,933 of the 31,915,779 inhabitants (excluding armed forces) belonging to the Jewish faith[6]and representing almost 9.8% of the total population. Compared to the non-Jewish population the Jews exhibited marked differences as to geographic distribution, urban concentration, professions, natural increase and emigration.

15% of the non-Jews, for example, lived in the western provinces (Poznan, Pomerania and Silesia), but in the case of the Jews it was only 1%. The other 85% of the non-Jews divided rather evenly between the eastern and the central provinces. Because of the large Jewish population

Table 1
Percentage Distribution
of the Jewish and the non-Jewish Population in Poland
by Provinces
as of December 9, 1931

Provinces	Jews	Others
Bialystok	6.34	5.02
Wilna	3.56	4.05
Nowogrodek	2.66	3.38
Polesia	3.66	3.53
Wolhynia	6.67	6.52
Lvov	11.00	9.67
Stanislav	4.49	4.65
Tarnopol	4.31	5.09
Eastern Poland	42.68	41.92
Warsaw-City	11.33	2.84
Warsaw-Province	7.04	8.02
Lodz	12.16	7.82
Kielce	10.18	9.09
Lublin	10.09	7.47
Cracow	5.58	7.38
Central Poland	56.37	42.62
Poznan	0.23	7.29
Silesia	0.61	4.43
Pomerania	0.11	3.74
Western Poland	0.95	15.46
Poland total	100.00	100.00

Source: *Drugi Powszechny Spis Ludności Z Dn. 9.XII 1931 R.;* Mieszkania I Gospodarstwa Domowe, Ludność, Stosunki, Zawodowe; Polska (Dane Skrócone); Głowny Urząd Statystyczny Rzeczypospolitej Polskiej, Statystyka Polski, Scria C', Zeszyt 62 (*Deuxième Recensement Général de la Population du 9 Décembre 1931;* Logements et Ménages, Population, Professions; Pologne – Données Abregées –), Warsaw, 1937.

in Warsaw – every ninth Jew lived in the capital city in 1931 – the central provinces contained far more than half of all Jews and still the eastern provinces accounted for over forty per cent of the Jewish population (*Table 1*).

Table 2
Jewish Population in Polish Provinces (in per cent) as of December 9, 1931

Provinces	Total	Cities
Bialystok	12.01	38.40
Wilna	8.68	29.17
Nowogrodek	7.84	42.55
Polesia	10.07	49.14
Wolhynia	9.96	49.12
Lvov	10.95	33.23
Stanislav	9.44	34.83
Tarnopol	8.38	34.68
Eastern Poland	9.92	36.90
Warsaw-City	30.01	30.01
Warsaw-Province	8.66	29.70
Lodz	14.38	31.24
Kielce	10.80	30.17
Lublin	12.75	43.71
Cracow	7.56	24.77
Central Poland	12.51	30.94
Poznan	0.34	0.81
Silesia	1.46	3.90
Pomerania	0.27	0.85
Western Poland	0.66	1.62
Poland total	9.76	27.26

Source: Same as Table 1.

In the central and eastern provinces the Jewish element represented "only" every eighth or tenth inhabitant, but in the cities it was an entirely different matter. There, the Jewish share was 31 and 37%, respectively (*Table 2*). Cities with a Jewish contingent of 50% and more were not at all unusual, especially in the smaller towns of eastern Poland.

Contrary to the huge percentage of Jews in Polish cities and towns there were relatively few in rural areas: In all of Poland there were about 108 Jews for every 1,000 non-Jews; in the urban areas, however, this number rose to 375 and fell to a mere 33 in the countryside (*Table 3*).

Only *one*-quarter of the non-Jewish population was urban, with the Jews it was *three*-quarters. Also, official statistics tended to overstate the portion of the "rural" Jewish population to a considerable extent. Eastern Jewry still lived in large part in mostly small, yet town-like so-called "shtetls" which constituted some kind of a local trading and manufacturing center for the surrounding peasantry. These "shtetls" were not at all comparable to "villages" (in the European sense) which is indicated by the fact that the vast majority of the Jewish population of those "shtetls" was not engaged in farming.

Table 3
Urbanization in Poland:
Jewish and non-Jewish Population
as of December 9, 1931

	Population				Jews per thousand non-Jews
	Jews	(%)	non-Jews	(%)	
Country	733,858	(23.6)	22,450,874	(77.9)	33
Cities	2,380,075	(76.4)	6,350,972	(22.1)	375
of which: Cities with a pop. of					
< 20,000	929,852	(29.9)	2,301,566	(8.0)	404
> 20,000	1,450,223	(46.6)	4,049,406	(14.1)	358
Total	3,113,933	(100)	28,801,846	(100)	108

Source: Same as Table 1.

In all of Poland only 125,123 Jews (including family members) out of 3.1 million were classified as peasants. Assuming that two-thirds of them lived in the eastern provinces, only one in five of the 400,000 "rural" Jews of eastern Poland may be counted among the peasants. For these reasons the degree of urbanization of Polish Jews should be seen to been nearer 90% in 1931. In the case of non-Jews the opposite was true: Of the 22.5 million rural non-Jewish inhabitants in Poland 19.2 million, or 85%, were engaged in agriculture.

Unfortunately, the Polish census was somewhat deficient in pro-viding data on religious affiliation in individual cities. For the eastern Polish provinces which are of primary interest in this study only 23 towns and cities could be found for which the Jewish population was specified: In two towns the Jewish percentage was 56 and 63%, in eleven towns it ranged from 40 to 49%, in seven towns it was between 31 and 36% and in three towns 27 and 28%! In other words, not one town contained fewer than 25% Jews (*Table 4*).

The insignificant representation of Jews in Polish agriculture was mentioned before. It is clear, therefore, that the role Jews played outside Polish agriculture was that much larger in relative and absolute terms. For every single Jew in industry, handicrafts, trade and the other non-agricultural professions there were only a little more than three non-Jews despite the fact that Jews constituted less than one-tenth of the total population.

Table 4
Eastern Polish Cities:
Total Population and Jews
as of December 9, 1931

Provinces	Cities	Total Population	Jewish Population	Jewish Share-%
Wilna	Wilna	195,071	55,006	28
Nowogrodek	Baranowicze	22,818	9,680	42
Bialystok	Bialystok	91,101	39,165	43
	Grodno	49,669	21,159	43
	Lomza	25,022	8,912	36
	Suwalki	21,826	5,811	27
Polesia	Brest	48,385	21,440	44
	Pinsk	31,912	20,220	63
Wolhynia	Kovel	27,677	12,842	46
	Rovno	40,612	22,737	56
	Lutsk	35,554	17,366	49
	Wlodzimierz	24,591	10,665	43
Lvov	Lvov	312,231	99,595	32
	Boryslav	41,496	12,996	31
	Drohobycz	32,261	12,931	40
	Jaroslav	22,195	6,272	28
	Przemysl	51,038	17,326	34
	Rzeszov	26,902	11,228	42
	Sambor	21,923	6,274	29
Stanislav	Kolomyja	33,788	14,332	42
	Stanislav	59,960	24,823	41
	Stryj	30,491	10,869	36
Tarnopol	Tarnopol	35,644	13,999	39
	23 Cities	1,282,167	475,648	37

(continued on next page)

Table 4 – (concluded)

Group	Cities	Total Population	Jewish Population	Jewish Share-%
50–63 %	2 Cities	72,524	42,957	59
40–49 %	11 Cities	452,706	195,631	43
30–39 %	7 Cities	517,845	169,971	33
27–29 %	3 Cities	239,092	67,089	28
27–63 %	23 Cities	1,282,167	475,648	37
	Other Cities	1,221,809	448,364	37
	All Cities	2,503,976	924,012	37
	Countryside	10,898,567	405,069	4
	Eastern Poland	13,402,543	1,329,081	10

Source: Same as Table 1, but Zeszyt 48 (Miasto Wilno);
58 (M. Lwów); 65 (Województwo Stanisławowskie);
68 (W. Lwowskie); 70 (W. Wołyńskie);
71 (W. Nowogródzkie); 78 (W. Tarnopolskie);
83 (W. Białostockie); 87 (W. Poleskie).

In this connection, it is of some interest that in the category "self-employed", i.e. merchants, artisans, doctors, lawyers, etc. the relationship of non-Jew to Jew was about one to one. Considering the small Jewish presence in the western Polish provinces – which because of their more advanced economic structure contained a considerable portion of the non-Jewish "self-employed" – the enormous Jewish influence in the secondary and tertiary sectors of the central and eastern Polish provinces becomes clearer yet. Among the Jews there were seven times as many "self-employed" as among the non-Jews; among salary earners the Jewish proportion was still 50% larger than their number would have warranted and only among blue-collar workers was there no difference between the two population segments (*Table 5*).

As one would expect, these pronounced socio-economic differences between Jews and non-Jews also affected their respective natural increase. In a population of 3.1 million the portion of the less-than-one-year-old children was only 1.7%, in numbers 52,305, but with the non-Jewish population it was 2.6%. Surprisingly, this enormous gap between Jewish and non-Jewish fertility rates actually developed only since WWI. Until the early 1920's the Jewish population averaged roughly 12% of the non-Jewish – even though a slight recessive trend from 13 to 11% was

Table 5
Professions in Poland: Jews and non-Jews
as of December 9, 1931

Economic Sector	[1] Jews	(%)	[2] non-Jews	(%)	Over- and Underrepresentation of Jews
Agriculture	125,123	(4)	19,221,825	(67)	− 94 %
Non-agricultural Sectors	2,988,810	(96)	9,580,021	(33)	+ 189 %
of which:					
Self-employed	699,244	(22)	763,617	(3)	+ 747 %
White-collar	91,970	(3)	555,274	(2)	+ 53 %
Blue-collar	277,555	(9)	2,473,344	(9)	+ 4 %
Others	54,256	(17)	420,206	(15)	+ 19 %
Not gainfully employed	1,865,785	(60)	5,367,580	(19)	+ 222 %
Total	3,113,933	(100)	28,801,846	(100)	

Source: *Drugi Powszechny Spis Ludności Z Dn. 9.XII 1931 R.* Polska: Stosunki Zawodowe – Ludność Poza Rolnictwem (Cześć II); Głowny Urząd Statystyczny Rzeczypospolitej Polskiej; Statystyka Polski, Scria C, Zeszyt 94d (*Deuxième Recensement Général de la Population du 9 Décembre 1931*, Pologne: Professions – Population hors l'Agriculture – II Partie; Office Central de Statistique de la Republique Polonaise, Statistique de la Pologne), Warsaw, 1939.

obviously in progress; after 1924, however, the tendency was steeply downhill (*Graph 1*). Finally, in 1931 there were only seven Jewish births for every 100 non-Jewish births!

But the non-Jewish population in Poland also showed a clear deceleration in its birth rate. Both the Jewish and non-Jewish population suffered great losses in the number of births during WWI and both registered a steep rise after hostilities ended. To be sure, the non-Jewish population saw no further rise in the number of births since the early 1920's, but they were kept at a relatively high level of 730,000. Not so with the Jews; after reaching a high of 74,875 in 1925 their number of births dropped consistently until it reached 52,305 in 1931 (*Graph 2*).

Thus, while the 1931 age group of the non-Jewish population was almost twice as large as the age group of the war-year 1917 and of the turn of the century – 30 to 35 years earlier – in the case of the Jews it was just barely greater in either instance. The *Universal* proved quite right when it wrote referring to the Polish Jews: "But even in Eastern Europe the birth rate was falling, and began to approach that of Western Europe"[7] – and that was already negative before WWII.

As far as is known, there are no official statistics on Polish-Jewish mortality rates before the war. If one accepts the mortality figures of the *Universal* of an average of 40,000 per year for the period 1930 to 1935 – for the Soviet Jews with a numerically similarly large population an average mortality figure of 43,000 was indicated – then the Jews should have enjoyed a surplus of births over deaths of about 12,000 in 1931 (52,305 minus 40,000), or *0.4%!*

Obviously, the huge emigration of Polish Jews prior to and following WWI influenced their natural growth rate very negatively because it is generally the younger, fertile age groups who decide to leave; the older people often have too deep roots in the country in which they were born. An excellent example of the strong ties of older people to their country of birth is provided by the very different emigration pattern of younger and older German Jews in the 1930's.

Of the roughly 500,000 Jews living in Germany in 1933 about 160,000 were 50 years or older. By August of 1939, the German-Jewish population had dropped to 272,000; included in this figure were 140,000 people aged 50 years and older. This means that the Jews of 50 years and younger had seen their numbers reduced by almost two-thirds from about 340,000 to less than 130,000, while the age group "50 years and older" had shrunk only one-eighth from 160,000 to 140,000.[8]

Now, comparable figures are not available for the Polish-Jewish population of the 1930's, but the Polish census of 1931, nevertheless, provides an indication that similar developments were under way among the Jews of Poland. The ratio of the male to female population for the age group born between 1917 and 1931 – children between zero and 14 years – averaged 102.9 to 100 for Jews and 102.5 to 100 for non-Jews. The 15-to-29-year-olds (age group 1902-1916), however, differed markedly with ratios of 85.7/100 and 93/100, respectively.[9]

It is only natural that the original numerical male predominance should change over time in favor of a slight female majority; but such a drastic reduction of the male side during peacetime must either be due to a comparably much larger emigration of young men or – as the Polish census did not include 191,473 members of the armed forces – to military service or both. If one assumes (data are unavailable) that three-quarters of these military men were less than 30 years old and that Jews constituted about 10% (in keeping with their share of the population), then we obtain additional 14,361 young Jews to be added to the 424,575 aged 15 to 29

Graph 1

Relationship of the Jewish to the non-Jewish Population in Poland by Age and Year of Birth as of December 9, 1931

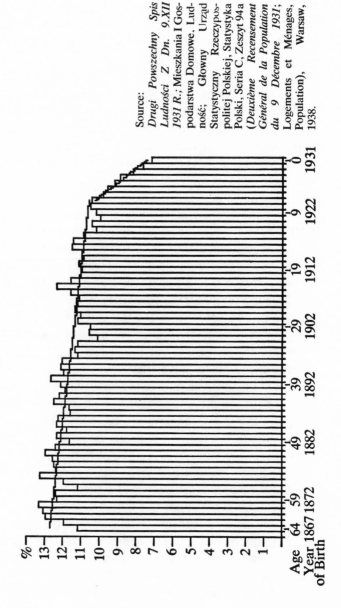

Source:
Drugi Powszechny Spis Ludności Z Dn. 9.XII 1931 R.; Mieszkania I Gospodarstwa Domowe. Ludność; Glowny Urząd Statystyczny Rzeczypospolitej Polskiej, Statystyka Polski, Seria C, Zeszyt 94a (Deuxième Recensement Général de la Population du 9 Décembre 1931; Logements et Ménages, Population), Warsaw, 1938.

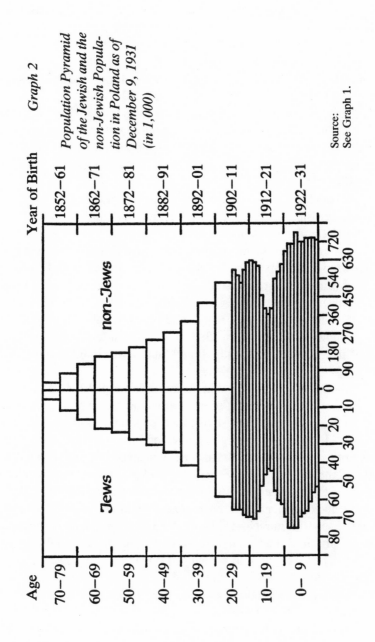

Graph 2

Population Pyramid of the Jewish and the non-Jewish Population in Poland as of December 9, 1931 (in 1,000)

Year of Birth

1852–61
1862–71
1872–81
1882–91
1892–01
1902–11
1912–21
1922–31

Age

70–79
60–69
50–59
40–49
30–39
20–29
10–19
0– 9

non-Jews

Jews

80 70 60 50 40 30 20 10 0 90 180 270 360 450 540 630 720

Source:
See Graph 1.

years. Compared with the 495,405 Jewesses of that age group, the ratio obtained is 88.6/100; the same non-Jewish age group shows an adjusted ratio of 96/100.

To be sure, the age groups of 1902 and before also show a clear female majority, but this should be expected considering the higher life expectancy of the fair sex and the losses suffered by men in WWI. The male/female ratio in the age groups "1872-1901" who were subject to military service during WWI was the same for Jews and non-Jews, namely, 88/100. It is thus very surprising to see the Jews of the age groups "1902-1916" evidence a male/female ratio of 88.6/100. In other words, there must have been very, very many young Jewish men who left Poland after WWI single without families.[10] Their approximate number may be estimated by taking the difference between male and female Jews in that age group: It is about 56,000!

It is a fact that official Polish statistics indicate only a relatively small-size Jewish emigration. But to conclude that only a small number of Jewish emigrants left Poland would be just as mistaken as to infer a small Mexican immigration in the United States after WWII on the basis of Mexican emigration statistics. Illegal border crossings cannot be traced by means of official emigration statistics.

Polish statistics list 294,139 emigrant Jews in the period 1921 to 1931.[11] Deducting the above mentioned 56,000 single young male Jews without families, there remain 238,000 who left in family groups. On the basis of five persons per family one obtains fewer than 48,000 heads of households.

The misery of the Jews in Poland following WWI unfolds in the huge number of these young, often very young men who went abroad in search of a livelihood. In Jewish historical experience this is quite without precedent. In view of the large number of Jewish families who fled the USSR in the course of the Russian Civil War, who lost their homes during WWI and the ensuing Polish-Soviet War and who practically saw no other solution to their desperate situation than to leave troubled, anti-Semitic Poland, it looks rather ridiculous to place the number of emigrant Jewish families below the number of single young Jewish males, particularly as most Eastern Jews had numerous relatives abroad, especially in North America. There is only one conclusion possible: The Polish emigration statistics are worthless.

Official Polish figures mention only 75,527 Jewish emigrants for the years 1934 to 1937.[12] How far removed these figures are from reality may be seen from the enormous Jewish immigration in Western countries and in Palestine prior to WWII, from the fact that the vast majority of extra-Soviet Eastern European Jews lived in Poland (until 1939) and from the naked truth that no country treated the Jews worse than did Poland (at least until 1938). The Poles tried to get rid of their Jews by all means at their disposal; on the other hand, the Western countries refused to accept Jewish immigrants. Therefore, it was in the Polish interest *not* to draw the world's attention to the actual extent of Jewish emigration from Poland.

Between 1934 and 1937, for example, 68,000 Jewish immigrants from Poland arrived in Palestine.[13] If Polish emigration statistics were accurate, 90% of the Polish-Jewish emigrants would have left for Palestine even though Polish Jews enjoyed the closest ties of kinship to hundreds of thousands of Jews in America. We will show in the Seventh Chapter that 400,000 Jews entered the United States between 1933 and 1943. Only a small fraction of them hailed from Germany; Jewish sources maintain anyway that until the end of 1940 just 26% of German-Jewish emigrants went to the United States, i.e. 100,000.[14]

Of course, other central and eastern European countries, too, recorded a large flow of Jewish emigration, but the largest segment of Jewish immigration in the United States must have originated in Poland. Of the 4.3 million Jews in the geographic area encompassed by Poland, the Baltic countries, Rumania, Hungary and Czechoslovakia before the war, approximately two-thirds lived in Poland. Therefore, the largest contingent of Jewish immigrants in North America between 1933 and 1943 simply must have come from that country.

At the same time, western European countries accepted un-counted tens of thousands of Jewish refugees and immigrants from Germany and eastern Europe during the 1930's. At the end of the 1920's a total of 315,000 Jews lived in France and the Benelux countries,[15] by the beginning of the war their number was put at 480,000.[16] The natural increase of this highly urbanized population with its low fertility was minimal; the growth of 165,000 was almost exclusively the result of net immigration. But since Jewish sources specify that 83% of the Jews leaving Germany were headed for North and South America, Palestine, Shanghai and England,[17] by far the largest part of these Jewish immigrants in France and the Benelux countries must have come from countries to the east and southeast of Germany, and again there is only one country in eastern Europe qualifying as the main source of Jewish emigration, namely, Poland.

In this respect, even the Institute for Contemporary History in

Munich (Institut für Zeitgeschichte) admitted:

> The wave of emigration of German Jews was only a part – and not even the largest one at that – of a general Jewish emigration from central, eastern and southeastern Europe. In the years following 1933, about 100,000 Jews left Poland every year, partly because of the increasingly anti-Semitic policies of the Polish government, but also because of the progressively worsening pauperization of the Polish Jews. Similar tendencies showed up in Latvia, Lithuania, Rumania and, to a lesser degree, in Hungary.[18]

The economic situation of Polish Jews deteriorated drastically during the 1930's. Systematic campaigns were organized to crowd them out of the economy, the boycott of Jewish stores was enforced with brutality, found to be within the law by the courts, blessed by the Catholic Church of Poland and officially sanctioned by the Central Government. Anti-Semitic incidents spread throughout Poland and resulted in many victims. Bloody persecutions took place in 1937 in Brest-Litovsk and in Czestochowa.[19]

The statement by the Institute for Contemporary History, whose pro-Zionist credentials are excellent, that the largest wave of emigration did not originate in Germany is thus quite correct. Just as correct are its findings that 100,000 Jews emigrated from Poland every year after 1933; this may contradict official Polish emigration statistics whose reliability is subject to doubt, but the tremendous Jewish immigration in Palestine, USA, South America, France, Benelux countries, England, etc. prior to WWII support the Munich Institute's testimony.

The persistent emigration, especially of young single Jewish males who would normally have raised families of their own, and the growing economic distress make it rather improbable that the reduction of the birth rate since the mid-1920's could have stopped after 1931. Everything points to an excess of deaths over births for the Jewish population in the latter part of the 1930's. Therefore, even an average growth rate of *0.2%* per annum between 1932 and 1939 seems somewhat high for the Polish-Jewish population.[20]

Placing the number of Jewish emigrants from Poland in the seven years and eight months from the beginning of 1932 until September 1939 at 500,000 – the Munich Institute for Contemporary History mentions 100,000 annually *after 1933* – the size of the Jewish population in Poland may thus be estimated at 2,664,000 at the beginning of the war. Subtracting the 31,216 Polish-Jewish soldiers reported by the Polish general staff to have been killed in the subsequent German-Polish war,[21] the final number of Polish Jews following the cessation of hostilities at the end of September 1939 may be said to have been 2,633,000. The figure of 3,351,000 as reported by the Anglo-American Committee thus is shown to be too large by 700,000!

Jews in Other Eastern European Countries

Much of what was said regarding Polish Jews applies to Jewry of the other countries in eastern Europe as well. With few exceptions its birth rate was low, even negative on a net basis, and its urban concentration was extraordinary; its average marriage age far exceeded that of the host populations and emigration, particularly among young males, was widespread. Still, there are some noteworthy differences in degree from the situation found in Poland.

The *Czechoslovakian* Jews cannot be treated as a single group; too large are the differences between Czech, Slovak and Ruthenian (Carpathian) Jews; they reflect the gap in economic development in this artificial heterogeneous country as one proceeds from west to east. There, too, young Jewish males left the impoverished eastern areas, but, instead of going outside the country, they merely migrated to the highly industrialized Bohemian and Moravian areas. Thus, whereas Ruthenian and Slovak Jewish males aged 15-29 years numbered only 81.3% and 95.1% respectively of the Jewesses of the same age group, the situation was reversed in the *Czech* areas of Bohemia and Moravia. There, Jewish males aged 15-29 exceeded the opposite sex by 23.5% as registered by the census taken in 1930.[22] This uneven migration affected the fertility of the Jews in Slovakia and Ruthenia rather adversely, yet no positive growth effects could be registered in *Bohemia* and *Moravia*.

In the latter two provinces, Jewry was declining since before WWI. In 1930, the largest age group was accounted for by those born between 1906 and 1910; this group represented almost 10% of the total, or 2% for each year. From then on a rapid decline dropped the annual average to 1.35% for the years 1911-1915 and 0.77% for 1916-1920; after WWI, a small baby boom let the group born from 1921-1925 reach 1.1% per year, only to fall again to an annual average of just over 0.8% in 1926-1930. Given the trend of those years, it is fair to state that those less than one year old in 1930 accounted for just 0.6% of the Czech Jews. This low rate would imply an excess of deaths over births somewhere between 0.5% and 1% per year.

In *Slovakia*, the Jewish demographic crisis was not yet as deep, but the trend was similar. From the 1906/1910 period to 1926/1930 the average annual strength of the mentioned age groups fell from 2% to 1.66%. Those born in 1930 probably constituted only about 1.5% of Slovakia's Jews which was just barely greater than the natural death rate.

Only in backward *Ruthenia* was the traditional Eastern Jewish family still intact, but it seems that there, too, a turning point had been reached. The age group 1926/1930 averaged almost 2.9% per year, compared to 2.8% for 1921/1925. A birth rate of 2.9%, if maintained, would have resulted in a high natural increase during the 1930's of maybe 1.5% p.a. or more. Given the considerable emigration of young males to the Czech areas, the economic crisis of the 1930's and the growing secularization of life in Ruthenia prior to WWII, it is likely that after 1930 there was a drop in the birth rate even though it probably remained fairly high by general Jewish standards of those years. In any case, when Hungary, which meanwhile had regained Ruthenia from Czechoslovakia, conducted a census in 1941 only about 109,000 (see Sixth Chapter) were found there compared to 102,542 as recorded by the Czechoslovak census of 1930; this is equivalent to a natural increase of 0.6% p.a. between 1930 and 1941. This rate would appear somewhat low for that fertile, but tiny segment of Eastern Jewry and probably reflects a continuing emigration of young males to the industrial Czech areas.

Hungary's Jews – according to the census of 1930 there were 444,567[23] – lived overwhelmingly in the larger cities. 204,371, or 46%, were concentrated in the capital city, another 130,207 lived in the Great Plain districts east of the Danube, 49,252 in the north and just 60,737 west of the Danube. Since 1920, the total Jewish population had decreased by 28,788 from 473,355.[24]

After 1927 Hungary's Jews recorded considerable excesses of deaths over births. From 1927 until 1930 the average annual decrease amounted to 467 (0.1% p.a.)[25] and reached 0.5% in 1938.[26]

Year	Births	Deaths	Balance	Natural Growth In % of the Jewish population
1930	5,533	5,917	− 384	− 0.1
1931	5,187	6,244	− 1,057	− 0.3
·	·	·	·	·
1937	·	·	− 1,574	− 0.4
1938	·	·	− 1,899	− 0.5

Obviously, the Hungarian Jews were in the midst of a serious demographic decline during the 1930's with the number of deaths probably 40% higher than that of births.

By 1941, after the acquisition of neighboring territories containing maybe 325,000 Jews, i.e. an increase by 73% over 1930, the total number of births (8,380) still was only 50% larger than in 1930, but deaths of 10,074 exceeded their 1930-level also by 73%. In 1942, the roughly 725,000 Greater Hungarian Jews counted only 8,413 births and 10,787 deaths, in relation to their total number, 1.2% and 1.5% respectively – a natural decrease of 0.3% p.a.[27]

In other words, the addition of the 325,000 Jews in the acquired territories (see Sixth Chapter) brought no significant improvement to the average rate of natural decrease despite the fact that one-third of those 325,000 "new" Hungarian Jews belonged to the relatively fertile Ruthenian Jewry. Obviously, the Jews living in the newly acquired territories of northern Transylvania, Banat and southern Slovakia had registered birth and death rates quite similar to those of the "old" Trianon-Hungary, which is to say, their natural demographic development also was gravely negative.

Thus, as a matter of record, the Jewry of the areas covered by Trianon-Hungary, the former Slovak areas, the Banat (Serbia) and northern Transylvania (Rumania) suffered large annual population decreases as a result of very low birth rates. The Ruthenian Jews whose fertility, no doubt, had lessened as well until WWII nevertheless registered positive growth rates. But they were the exception to the general Jewish demographic pattern in eastern Europe and the Balkans, and their small total number could not affect the numerical decline of Eastern Jewry before the war.

As to the growth of *Rumanian* Jewry during the 1930's the *Universal Jewish Encyclopedia* (Universal) has this to say:

> ... in 1932 it [the number of births] was 12,586 for Greater Roumania and 10,039 in 1938, whereas the death rate for the corresponding years was 9,891 and 10,250. Thus from a surplus of 2,695 in 1932 there was a deficit of 213 in 1938. The birth rate steadily declined.[28]

The surplus of births – in 1932 it averaged just 0.35% – had turned into a *deficit by 1938*; it seems that allowing for an average growth rate of 0.2% during the 1930's would be ample.

In *Latvia*, the general population's fertility rates fell long before

WWI. In 1935, the birth rate was down to 1.67% and the mortality rate of the previous 5-year-period averaged 1.38%. As a result, the net natural population increase was less than one half of one per cent and dropping further. The Jewish population – 93,479 according to the 1935 census[29] – constituted less than 5% of the total population.

Regionally, about 50% of the Latvian Jews lived in or near Riga, the capital; another 30% populated the easternmost province of Latgale. Urbanization was almost total: Almost 93% of Latvia's Jewry lived in the cities in contrast to only 34% of the non-Jewish population; but because of their relatively small number Jews made up a smaller portion of the urban populace than was usual for eastern Europe. Among the larger cities only Daugavpils and Rezekne had a Jewish share of 25%, in all the other urban centers (including Riga) Jews averaged only 11% of the population.[30]

As to natural growth, the Latvian Jews showed traits very similar to those in Poland. Until the turn of the century there was a rapid growth, followed by a levelling off until WWI. The war almost halved the number of births, but after the cessation of hostilities the birth rate jumped briefly to a level close to, but still below pre-war years. According to the census, young Jews 11 years of age numbered 1,787, thereafter a rapid decline set in. At the time of the 1935 count only 1,137 were less than one year old – a decline of at least 36% compared with 1924. Thus, the birth rate was only 1.2%.[31] As mentioned before, Latvia's total mortality rate averaged 1.4% in the early 1930's; while Jewish mortality is not known it is not likely to have departed much from the national average. This means that already in 1935 and in the years just previous the Jews failed to replace themselves. With economic conditions worsening thereafter the birth rate probably declined further, producing ever larger rates of natural decrease as the decade wore on.

This brief sketch of the demographic patterns of the various Eastern European Jewish communities outside the Soviet Union allows us to state that, on average, far from general fertility, eastern Europe's Jews had no natural increase whatever during the 1930's. We considered a total population numbering almost 4.8 million in the early 1930's – 93% of Eastern Jewry outside Russia. This population, concentrated in an area reaching from Riga to Budapest and Bukarest, was in the midst of a demographic revolution. Rapid concentration in the larger cities, the decline of Yiddish in favor of the native national languages, large-scale emigration of young single Jewish males, late marriages, the turn to the one- and two-children-family had already destroyed Jewish orthodoxy; only a few tiny remnants remained, for example in Carpathian Ruthenia –

36

too small to offset the losses suffered elsewhere and themselves subject to secularization pressures. By the end of the 1930's there was no country in eastern Europe where Jews were able to register natural growth gains. In some, mortality rates for Jews far exceeded birth rates. It is fair to state that – on average – eastern Europe's Jewry even registered a small natural decline between 1930 and 1939.

SECOND CHAPTER

The Growth of Soviet Jewry

The Division of Polish Jewry

Still unclear is the distribution of these 2,633,000 Polish Jews over the various areas incorporated into the German Reich, combined in the so-called "Government General of Poland" or occupied by the Soviet Union. According to the *Universal*, a German statistician calculated on the basis of the Polish census of December 9, 1931 the following geographic distribution of Jews among the three specified regions:[1]

Areas incorporated by Germany	632,000 (20.3 %)
Government General of Poland	1,269,000 (40.8 %)
Under German administration	1,901,000 (61.0 %)
Annexed by the Soviet Union	1,212,900 (39.0 %)
Former Polish Jews (1931)	3,113,900 (100.0 %)

The Polish census of 1931 showed that the natural development of eastern Polish Jewry did not differ from the national Jewish average, but it is unknown whether there was any change thereafter – which is improbable – and whether emigration flows during the 1930's were similar in the three areas. Thus, we have to assume that all three areas experienced roughly the same demographic development between 1932 and 1939 as far as the Jewish population is concerned.

As mentioned in the First Chapter, the number of Polish Jews declined from 3,113,900 to 2,633,000, i.e. by 15.4%, between the end of 1931 and September 1939. On the basis of this relative reduction we obtain the following Jewish population for the three areas:

Areas incorporated by Germany	534,000 (20.3 %)
Government General of Poland	1,073,000 (40.8 %)
Under German administration	1,607,000 (61.0 %)
Annexed by the Soviet Union	1,026,000 (39.0 %)
Former Polish Jews (1939)	2,633,000 (100.0 %)

As the Polish defeat began to crystallize shortly after the outbreak of the hostilities, many Polish Jews didn't bother to await the German occupation; they fled in droves to the eastern Polish cities and towns – which later were occupied and annexed by the Soviet Union in the second half of September – but smaller numbers also crossed the border into Rumania. Referring to this massive flight, the Latvian Chief Rabbi and leader of the Mizrachi Organization and of the World Jewish Congress, Mordecai Nurok, said on March 28, 1946 at a press conference in New York: "It must be emphasized that several hundred thousands of Polish and other Jews found a haven from the Nazis in the U.S.S.R."[2]

This flight away from the sphere of German influence was facilitated by the circumstance that the Soviets originally also occupied the territory between the Vistula and Bug rivers as specified in the German-Soviet agreement on the division of Polish territory; because of this, many Jewish inhabitants of the crumbling Polish state succeeded in escaping from the nearby larger cities – Warsaw, Lodz, etc. – to reach Soviet-occupied areas. One week later the Soviets withdrew from the area west of the Bug taking the entire livestock with them;[3] the Jewish refugees, along with many local Jews, accompanied the Red Army as it pulled back towards positions east of the Bug. The city of Tomaszow Lubelski may serve as an example of this systematic evasion by the Jews away from German control; according to the *Encyclopaedia Judaica* (Judaica) 75% of the city's 6,000 Jews left together with the Red Army as it withdrew to the newly established line of demarcation further east.[4]

Official German calculations show that the area between the Vistula and the Bug contained a Jewish population of 386,600 at the time of the last Polish census in 1931. If the Jewish population loss of that area in the years before the outbreak of the German-Polish war amounted to the same percentage as for the Polish Jews in general, only 330,000 Jews could have been present at the time of the Soviet occupation (after September 17, 1939). It is not known how many Jews accompanied the Soviet Army when it vacated that region after September 28, 1939, but the massed flight of Polish Jews in an easterly direction – attested to by many witnesses – and the example of Tomaszow Lubelski permit the conclusion that the vast majority of Jews living between the Vistula and the Bug must have left together with the Red Army. It is strange, therefore, that the discussions about the number of Jews who might have succeeded in escaping into Soviet-controlled territory pass over this episode almost completely, even though these more than 300,000 Jews had the best chance to evade German control.[5]

Among the Jewish refugees fleeing eastward was also the 26-year-old Menachem Begin; born in Brest-Litovsk in 1913, the latter-day Israeli Prime Minister studied at the University of Warsaw where he headed the Betar Zionist Youth Movement in Poland until 1939.[6]

In the Eichmann "Trial" in Jerusalem, the Polish Jews Zwi Patscher and Yakov Goldfine testified that the Germans drove Polish Jews marching four abreast in long columns onto the Soviet portion of occupied Poland.[7] The *Judaica* reported in a similar vein:

> With the outbreak of the war in September, the Poles began to loot stores and attack the Jews. ... the Jews were deported by the Germans [September 1939] to the area under Soviet control on the other side of the San River. ... Those who were deported to the Soviet Zone lived there in very difficult economic conditions. In the summer of 1940 many of them were deported to the Soviet interior.[8]

No one knows for certain how large the number of Jews was who either fled or were driven to the Soviet-occupied former Polish territory and who, within less than a year's time, found themselves in Siberian labor and concentration camps – if they survived the murderous trip. But we do know that the eastern Polish cities and towns which contained a large Jewish element already, suddenly had to cope with untold masses of displaced Jews. In many towns in eastern Poland the Jewish population doubled overnight. The *Judaica* refers to this mass flight again and again. Regarding Vladimir-Volynsk it writes: "... thousands of Jews from western Poland sought refuge in the city, bringing the number of Jews in the city to 25,000 [1931: 10,665 or 44% of the population]. ... In the summer of 1940 many Zionist leaders and refugees were exiled to the Soviet interior."[9] Lutsk: "Many refugees who had fled to Lutsk from Nazi-occupied western Poland were deported to the Soviet interior."[10] Pinsk: "A large number of Jewish refugees from western Poland found shelter in Pinsk, but were deported to the Soviet interior in 1940."[11] Rovno: "Many Jewish refugees from western Poland found shelter in Rovno ..."[12]

Nine years after WWII on September 22 and 23, 1954 an investigating committee of the US House of Representatives (Select Committee on Communist Aggression) conducted hearings where representatives of several Jewish organizations testified under oath on the subject of the persecution of Jews by the Soviet. One Herschel Weinrauch, formerly an associate editor of the Soviet newspaper *The Star*, declared that he was an official in the civil administration of Bialystok following the Soviet occupation in 1939. In his testimony he said the Communists made all refugee Jews from German-occupied Poland choose in the spring of 1940 between accepting Soviet citizenship or returning to German control.

Because of the barbarian treatment accorded these Jews from the western portion of divided Poland by the Soviets most of them opted *for* a return. Shortly thereafter, though, the Soviet government arrested all those who had decided to return and transported them to Siberia. In Bialystok alone, 50-60,000 Jewish refugees were arrested. All in all, the Soviets deported roughly 1,000,000 Jewish refugees from western Poland to Siberia.[13]

Another witness, Bronislaw Teichholz, chairman of the International Committee for Jewish Refugees from Concentration Camps from 1945 to 1952 confirmed Weinrauch's testimony. At that time he had been working in Lvov where about 50,000 Jewish refugees had decided to return; all of them were deported by the Soviets, in the process crowding 70 to 80 persons into railroad cars and then moving them eastward.[14]

A third witness, Adolph Held, chairman of the Jewish Labor Committee, was absent due to an incident of death in his family, but he had his testimony read to the investigating committee by the vice chairman, Jacob T. Zukerman. This witness, too, confirmed that up to 1,000,000 Jews escaped to Russia.[15] Another witness, Henry Edward Schultz, national chairman of the Anti-Defamation League of B'nai B'rith, put the number of Jewish refugees from western Poland deported on Stalin's orders to Siberian labor camps at 600,000; 450,000 of these unfortunate people have vanished without a trace.[16]

The Polish Government-in-Exile, too, declared the Soviets deported 600,000 Jewish refugees from western Poland in the spring of 1940. The Jewish statistician, J. Kulischer, asserted that Stalin "evacuated" 530,000 Jews – 500,000 from eastern Poland and 30,000 from the Baltic countries.[17] Other Jewish sources arrive at even lower figures.

Rabbi Aaron Pechenick described the Soviet mass deportation in his book *Zionism and Judaism in Soviet Russia* published in New York in 1943 as follows:

> In two days and two nights [end of June *1940*] almost one million Jews were loaded into cattle waggons under the most horrible circumstances and deported to Siberia and the Ural. ... The terrible journey lasted from four to six weeks. Having arrived at their destinations the Jews obtained only bread and water to sustain their lives after the long working days in the forests.[18]

The *Universal* reported that the Joint Distribution Committee – a large international Jewish refugee aid organization – initiated a relief program in early 1942 for 600,000 *Polish-Jewish* refugees in Asiatic Russia.[19] However, if there were 600,000 of these Jewish refugees in Soviet Asia in early 1942, many more must have been shipped off to Siberia by the Soviets, because the journey brought death and hardship to many. In connection with the inhuman transport to the east, the Joint Distribution Committee wrote in its Bulletin of June 1943: "From a fifth to a third of the number of refugees died ... whoever did not see the thousands of graves, mostly of children, cannot understand."[20] This means that the number of Jewish refugees from western Poland who were arrested by the Soviets and deported to Siberia ranged from 750,000 to 900,000! But only 600,000 survived the incredible journey and arrived at their destination.

Menachem Begin belonged to these deported unfortunates also. The Soviet secret police arrested him a short time after his arrival in Soviet-occupied eastern Poland and put him into a Siberian concentration camp. Following the outbreak of the German-Soviet war (June 22, 1941) he joined the Soviet-sponsored Polish army which left the USSR in 1942 by way of Iran. In the very same year we find the former Soviet concentration camp inmate and subsequent recipient of the Nobel Peace Prize as the commander-in-chief of the murderous IRGUN gang in Palestine.[21]

The extent of the Jewish flight before the German armies is not at all unusual. As a result of years of continuous Zionist campaigns and Polish inflammatory propaganda, the Jewish fear of the Germans knew no limits; this is probably the most likely explanation for the panic which gripped Polish Jews and non-Jews. Similar events developed in May 1940 when 1½ to 2 million panicky Belgians sought refuge in France, where they suffered severely; in mid-August 1940, there were still 1 million Belgians in France waiting to return home.[22]

Considering that up to one-fourth of this nation of just eight million fled in panic, even though the German Government can hardly be accused of hostility towards the Belgian people (but certainly towards the Jews), the extent of the Polish-Jewish flight is not very surprising. It is worth noting that in terms of time and geography, Polish Jews were much better situated to escape in an easterly direction; after all, in the German Western Campaign, Guderian's Panzer divisions had cut the escape route from Belgium to France in little more than a week.

For lack of further proof, we will accept the lower figure of 750,000

Jews as having fled from western Poland to the Soviet-occupied former Polish territory. The distribution of the Polish-Jewish population between the German and Soviet occupation zones in Poland therefore changed as follows:

Areas under German control	857,000 (32.5 %)
Areas under Soviet control	1,776,000 (67.5 %)
Former Polish Jews (end of 1939)	2,633,000 (100.0 %)

But not only the USSR, Rumania also served as an escape valve for the scared Jewish masses of Poland; this was especially true of the Rumanian provinces of Bukovina and Bessarabia. As will be discussed in the Sixth Chapter this route was used by at least 100,000 Jews. The final distribution of the Jewish population of the former Polish state thus assumes the following shape:

Areas under German control	757,000 (28.8 %)
Areas under Soviet control	1,776,000 (67.5 %)
Refugees in Rumania	100,000 (3.8 %)
Former Polish Jews (end of 1939)	2,633,000 (100.0 %)

All of these statistics have been gathered from Polish, Zionist, post-war German and American sources and they show that no more than 757,000 Jews came under German administration as German and Soviet armies occupied Poland in 1939.

How close to reality these figures are may be seen from a piece of information from the Joint Distribution Committee which stated that it had been active in German-occupied Poland without interruption, in the process reaching 630,000 persons in over 400 localities and providing them with food, medical aid, child care, clothing and other economic help.[23] Many more Jews than that simply did not exist in German-controlled former Polish territory!

But what do German sources say about the number of Polish Jews under German control? Unfortunately, the answer is: Nothing. Of course, the Germans spoke of millions of Jews in the occupied Polish territory, but their figures were not based on a census, not even on estimates. They simply used the figures of the last Polish census of 1931 and added a certain number to allow for a natural population growth. In the ghettos the Jews were accorded some kind of self-administration and the Germans never bothered to count them.

Thus, the *Krakauer Zeitung*, for instance, put the number of Jews in the Government General of Poland at 1.4 million as of the middle of 1940.[24] But a closer look shows quickly that this figure matches almost exactly that of the Polish census of 1931, inflated by 10% for the assumed population growth. The huge emigration before the war and the massive Jewish flight to Soviet-occupied territory – a fact which is admitted to by the Zionists themselves – were not taken into account.

After Soviet-occupied, former Polish Galicia was incorporated into the Government General following the outbreak of the German-Russo war, German statements suddenly referred to a Jewish population of 2 million in the enlarged Government General.[25]

The difference of 600,000 corresponds precisely to the 545,000 Jews living in the added area according to the census of 1931, augmented by 10%.[26] In this case, too, the massive Soviet evacuation of the urban population – attested to by German and Zionist sources – was not taken into consideration.

These German figures are not very surprising. For propaganda reasons the Germans were interested in magnifying the "Jewish danger" wherever possible. There are plenty of examples. In the case of Rumania, the German estimate of that country's Jewish population was 1.5 to 2 million,[27] although the Rumanian census found only three-quarters of a million and even the largest Zionist estimates never exceeded 900,000. As for France, which according to the largest Zionist estimates contained about 300,000 Jews, the Germans mentioned 1.2 million.[28] All of these German figures on the Jewish population in other European countries – France, Rumania, Government General – are instances of obvious exaggeration; in truth, the Jewish population was far less than half that size.

What happened to these 757,000 Jews? At the end of June of 1946(!) when the option for a return from the Soviet Union expired for the Jewish refugees of 1939 only 240,489 *registered* Jewish survivors were tabulated in Poland. Of the many hundreds of thousands who fled to the Soviet Union in 1939 only 157,420 took advantage of this option and returned to Poland. In other words, the primary source which released these figures – the Central Committee for Jews in Poland, a Communist organization – wants to make us believe that only 83,069 Jews of western Poland (240,489 minus 157,420) survived the Second World War under German administration.[29] But even *if* these figures were correct, they refer *only* to *registered* Jews. But how many Jews survived the war as "gentiles" in disguise and/or fled to the West between the end of the war and June 1946, never to register at all?

It is possible that hundreds of thousands of Jews used the fourteen months between the end of the war and the deadline to exercise the option to return from the Soviet Union (June 1946) in order to emigrate, flee or be evacuated from Poland; this aspect will be looked into at a later stage. But assuming that all Polish Jews survived the war under German administration, can one imagine a Communist Polish government admit to this in the face of the Soviet declaration at the so-called war crimes trials in Nuremberg that the Germans had killed just about every Polish Jew?

Still, if 757,000 Polish Jews fell under German control, but only 83,069 of them were found "officially" in June 1946, then this amounts to a difference of 674,000 missing Jews – at least, statistically.

Jewish Newcomers to the Soviet Empire

Let us summarize: 1.8 million Jews of the former Polish state found themselves overnight in the Soviet sphere of influence; of this number, one million remained for the time being as Soviet citizens in former eastern Poland and three-quarters of a million Polish-Jewish refugees, who refused to accept Soviet citizenship, were deported to Siberian labor and concentration camps in the most inhuman manner. This action alone cost the Jews up to 300,000, but at least 150,000, dead according to Zionist data!

In 1940, further large Jewish congregations were to disappear in the Soviet empire as the Baltic states and parts of Rumania were forcibly annexed. The last censuses in the Baltic countries found the following Jewish minorities:[30]

Lithuania (1923)	155,125
Estonia (1934)	4,302
Latvia (1935)	93,479
Baltic countries	252,906

As mentioned by the Munich Institute for Contemporary History, the Baltic states, too, witnessed a considerable Jewish emigration before the war. In the case of Lithuania the last census goes back to 1923 which makes it necessary to allow for the emigration in the 1920's as well. Even if one assumes a relatively much smaller flow of emigration from these three countries than was true for Poland, a net reduction of at least 10% is probably a minimum, particularly as a much longer period of time must be accounted for in the case of Lithuania. A considerable emigration and a low fertility before the war probably added up to no more than 225,000

46

Baltic Jews coming into the Soviet sphere of influence in 1940.

As will be shown in the Sixth Chapter in some detail, Bessarabia and the northern Bukovina contained 225,000 local Jews at the time of the Soviet occupation in 1940. In addition, there were about 100,000 Polish-Jewish refugees in Rumania. These refugees were spread all over northern Rumania: northern Transylvania, Bukovina and northern Bessarabia. It is not certain how many of these refugees who fled before the German armies in September 1939 lived in Bessarabia and in the northern Bukovina at the time of the Soviet annexation. Jewish sources maintain anyway that 65,000 Jews – most of them apparently of Polish origin – crossed over from Rumanian to Soviet-occupied territory at the time of the Soviet occupation of eastern and northern Rumania.[31] Furthermore, there is some evidence – see the Sixth Chapter – that 9,000 Polish refugees remained in northern Transylvania when Rumania had to cede that section to Hungary in 1940. Thus, it seems that the Soviet Union obtained not only the 225,000 native Rumanian Jews when it occupied those two Rumanian regions in 1940, but also at least another 91,000 Jewish refugees from Poland.

The territorial expansion of the Soviet Union until June of 1941 thus put 2,317,000 Jews within Stalin's empire:

Polish Jews:		
in eastern Poland and Baltic states	1,776,000	
in Rumania	91,000	1,867,000
Baltic Jews		225,000
Rumanian Jews		225,000
Jewish newcomers to the USSR in1939/1940		2,317,000

Before the month of September 1939 fewer than 20% (app. 3 million) of the roughly 16 million Jews of the world were subject to Soviet domination. *The consequence of the German-Polish war was that by 1940 one-third of world Jewry found itself within the borders of the Soviet Union.* For the non-Soviet Eastern European Jewry – which had suffered continuous losses during the 1930's due not only to persistent flows of emigration, but also to an excess of deaths over births and changes in religious preference – the Soviet "confiscation" of 2.3 million people of Jewish origin represented a blow from which it was never to recover.

The Soviet census of December 17, 1926 found 2,680,181 Jews.[32] Twelve years later the census of January 17, 1939 put the Jewish population figure at 3,020,141 – an apparent increase of 340,000 persons.[33] This change would be equivalent to an annual increase of 1%; but this interpretation of the difference between the two censuses fails to consider some important aspects.

In 1946, the American scholar and professor at Princeton University, Dr. Frank Lorimer, published a book, *The Population of the Soviet Union: History and Prospects*, under the auspices of the League of Nations; in this book he traced important differences in data collection by the Soviets in the censuses of 1926 and 1939. The census of 1926, for instance, was based on the criterion of "narodnost" (tribe, ethnic group) which corresponds more to an ethnic "tribal" affiliation than the criterion "nationalnost" (nationality) as used in the census of 1939. In any case, the result of these definitional criteria alterations was such that the changes in the numerical size of the various ethnic groups in the USSR from 1926 to 1939 bore little relationship to reality.[34]

Soviet Population Counts

Nationality	1926	1939	Changes
Russians	77,791,124	99,019,929	+21,228,805 (+27.3 %)
Ukrainians	31,194,976	28,070,404	− 3,124,572 (−10.0 %)
White Russians	4,738,923	5,267,431	+ 528,508 (+11.2 %)
Jews[35]	2,680,181	3,020,141	+ 339,960 (+12.7 %)
Germans	1,246,540	1,423,534	+ 176,994 (+14.2 %)
Others	29,376,171	33,665,747	+ 4,289,576 (+14.6 %)
Total	147,027,915	170,467,186	+23,439,271 (+15.9 %)

This juxtaposition of the two censuses seems to reveal three developments:

a) The Russians, with barely 53% of the total population in 1926, nevertheless, furnished 90% of the population increase of the Soviet Union between 1926 and 1939!

b) The rural Ukrainians decreased by 10%!

c) The urban Jews increased at a rate which exceeded that of the children-blessed White Russians and almost equalled that of the rural German population in the USSR!

A comparison of the Jewish population figures for the USSR in 1926 and 1939 thus is bound to lead to the wrong conclusions as to the fertility of this minority. In order to ascertain the natural fertility of each of the ethnic groups, Prof. Lorimer investigated the so-called "Child-Woman Ratios," i.e. the number of children aged 0-4 years per 1,000 women aged 20-44 years. For the year 1926 he found the following ratios:[36]

Needed for permanent population replacement	500
European Russia	844
Russians	832
Ukrainians	871
White Russians	966
Jews	509 (!)
Germans	933

These fertility figures contrast sharply with the purported changes of individual ethnic groups.

Even supposing the enforced collectivization at the end of the 1920's and beginning 1930's caused much greater losses among the Ukrainians than among the other peoples of the Soviet Union, the result of the census of 1939 can only be explained by the changed definitional criteria. The fertility of the Russians was below the European part of the Soviet Union and – much more important for our analysis – the Soviet Jews had barely enough children to replace themselves. Prof. Lorimer noted: "The lowest fertility is indicated by the Jews, a predominantly urban and highly literate group. ... It is apparent that the Jewish population was barely replacing itself ..."[37] This was true in 1926 already!

It is impossible that the Jewish fertility improved markedly during the following twelve years, because in those years the Soviets initiated a huge program of forced industrialization with an accompanying scarcity of homes and apartments in the cities. In addition, the Jews continued to migrate northward to Leningrad, Moscow and other Russian cities. The pronounced tendency toward mixed marriages between Jews and the native population of the Russian cities certainly added to a still lower fertility of the Jews until 1939.

This is not to deny that there were 3 million Jews in the Soviet Union in 1939. Considering the aspirations of the Jews to assimilate, it is quite probable that the census of 1939 still left several thousands of them uncounted. However, Prof. Lorimer's investigations showed that the Jewish population figure for 1926 was understated to the tune of several hundreds of thousands. The conclusion thus must be that the Jewish population of pre-war USSR was already stagnating and an excess of deaths over births cannot be excluded altogether.

Of the 2.7 million Jews as published by the Soviet census of 1926, 1,981,487 lived in the Ukraine and in White Russia.[38] In 1939 only 1,907,951 Jews were counted in those regions.[39] The foregoing illustrations prove, however, that the Soviet census of 1926 had underestimated the Jewish population by perhaps 300,000, or 11%. If this underestimate was distributed rather evenly throughout the Soviet Union, it is possible that the Ukraine and White Russia really had 2.2 million Jews in 1926 instead of the published 1.98 million. Compared to 1939 this represents a reduction of about 300,000 or 25,000 per year.

The north and the east of the Soviet territory, which up until WWI contained only very few Jews, thus must have been populated by the beginning of 1939 by over 1.1 million Jews the majority of whom lived in Moscow and in Leningrad. The unbelievable migration of Jews from the west and the south is best demonstrated by these two large cities:[40]

Year	Jewish Population in Leningrad	Moscow
1920	25,453	28,000
1923	52,373	86,000
1926	84,505	131,000
1940	200,000	400,000 (450,000)[41]

Obviously, between the two world wars one-third of the Soviet Jews had left the once traditional area of settlement in the west and south of the Soviet Union and moved to the less anti-Semitic north and east.

The *Universal*, too, took account of this enormous migration from the Ukraine and White Russia to the north and east (incl. Siberia) in its calculation of the Jewish population distribution within the Soviet Union; the *Universal* calculated that in 1939 alone the Ukraine and White Russia lost 33,000 (net) of their Jewish population to the east and north.[42] The basis on which the *Universal* made the estimate is not known – official figures are not available – and, to be conservative, one should not assume that the migration movement accelerated. Therefore, if we limit ourselves to the assumption that the trend existing before 1939 continued until the middle of 1941, this would amount to a net migration loss for both "republics" totalling 63,000 Jews. The Jewish population of those Soviet areas, i.e. the north and the east, which were never occupied by German forces thus could have increased by 63,000 as a result of an internal migration from the south and the west.

According to Zionist sources, on January 17, 1939 2,092,951 Jews lived in those areas which were later occupied by the Germans during

WWII.[43] These areas included primarily the Ukraine and White Russia.

In the "free" territories, i.e. those regions which never saw German occupation during the war, there were 927,190 Jews at the time of the last census. If one adjusts both parts of the USSR, the "free" and the occupied, by the changes incurred until June 1941 – primarily arising from an internal migration of 63,000 from the south to the north because the excess of births over deaths, if it existed at all, probably was minimal indeed – then the distribution of the 3.02 million "old" Soviet Jews must have looked something like this:

"Free" Soviet territory	990,000
Soviet territory occupied by German forces in the course of the war	2,030,000
"Old" Soviet Jews in June 1941	3,020,000

Adding it all up, there were 5,337,000 Jews in Stalin's sphere of influence at the beginning of the war:

Jews "acquired" in 1939/1940	2,317,000
"Old" Soviet Jews	3,020,000
Jews in the Soviet Union in 1941	5,337,000

These figures match just about the numbers as provided by the *Universal*, according to which the Soviet Union contained 5.5 million Jews as of June 22, 1941 after having acquired roughly 2.2 million through the annexation of neighboring areas to the west.[44] The *American Jewish Year Book* (Year Book) even believes this figure of 5.5 million may be a "conservative estimate."[45]

Now, if reputable Zionist sources put the number of Jews living in the Soviet Union at the outbreak of the war at 5.5 million – obviously, this figure includes those who didn't survive the inhuman deportation of 1940 – then they are in effect providing a rough indication of the number of Polish Jews who fell into German hands. In the course of its territorial expansion the Soviet Union acquired the Jewish population of the Baltic states – at most 225,000 – and of eastern Rumania estimated at 225,000. If one adds the "old" Soviet Jews of 3.02 million and subtracts the total from the 5.5 million, the remaining figure should correspond with the number of those Jews whom the USSR acquired from Poland; it is about 2 million. This figure exceeds the one arrived at in this analysis by far more than 100,000 and shows the relative conservatism with which our computations were made.

51

Since Poland had no more than 2¾ million Jews at the outbreak of WWII, it is impossible that more than three quarters of a million Polish Jews could have fallen under German control.

Summarizing the events until the spring of 1941, one obtains the following table:

Poland (August 1939)		2,664,000
Soviet Union (1939)		3,020,000
Baltic states (1940)		225,000
Bessarabia and northern Bukovina (1940)		225,000
Total		6,134,000
deduct:		
Polish-Jewish soldiers killed in action	31,000	
Polish-Jewish refugees in N. Transylvania	9,000	
Polish-Jews under German administration	757,000	797,000
Jews under Soviet domination in (1939/1940)		5,337,000
deduct:		
Jewish losses during the deportation to Siberia in the spring of 1940		150,000
Jews living in the USSR in 1940 max.		5.187.000
deduct:		
Polish-Jewish refugees in Siberia	600,000	
"Old" Soviet Jews in the "free" parts of the Soviet Union	990,000	
Jews in the area of the Soviet Union which always remained outside the limits of German military expansion (1940)		1,590,000
Jews living in the subsequently German-occupied parts of the Soviet Union (spring 1941)		3,597,000

THIRD CHAPTER

Scorched Earth

Soviet Military Build-up

After Hitler's refusal to accede to further Soviet demands for territorial concessions in Europe, the Soviet Union changed over to a war economy in the summer of 1940; on June 26, 1940 the obligatory eight-hour-workday and the seven-day workweek was decreed in this connection.[1] Other decrees made it a criminal offense if workers arrived more than twenty minutes late for work, punishable by up to six months forced labor. No one was allowed to change jobs except with the written permission of the director in charge; in contrast, the commissariats were empowered to send any worker anywhere in the Soviet Union if they so desired. The Soviet press, the radio, the teachers, the travelling public speakers as well as party, union and youth organization functionaries lectured the population in innumerable meetings that a "Capitalist" attack allegedly planned for a long time was liable to be forthcoming at any time.

The American engineer John Scott, who had been working in the USSR until 1942, described the Soviet preparation for war as follows:

> The Russian defense budget doubled almost every year. Huge reserves of war materials, machines, fuels, food and other supplies were stored. The Red Army grew from about two million in 1938 to 6.5 million men in the spring of 1940.[2]

Already in early 1940, the USSR had gathered 150 divisions in the western military districts, 100 of which were stationed in the former eastern Polish territories, confronting only 6 (six!) German divisions.[3]

At the end of March 1941, another 500,000 reservists were called up and placed in the military districts bordering the German frontier; they were followed by a further 300,000 specialists from the reserve units. With these measures the Red Army grew a total of 800,000 men just before the outbreak of the war. Subsequently, General Zhukov confirmed the mobilization of 170 divisions and 2 brigades in the districts close to the border.[4]

The Swedish air attache in Moscow estimated that by mid-1941 60% of the Red Army had been positioned in the western Soviet Union, concentrating particularly heavily in areas near the Rumanian border. Obviously, Stalin was aiming at the Rumanian oil fields whose possession would have given him a strangle hold on the German war machine. The Rumanian espionage learned of Stalin's remarks to the effect that the Soviet Government would still have to make great sacrifices in order to gain time, because the coming war could be postponed but it could not be averted.[5] The Yugoslavian ambassador in Moscow warned Stalin early in 1941 of the German "Barbarossa" Plans; in his reply Stalin speculated on the possible date of the German attack and said: "Let them come. We will be ready for them!"[6]

In April, the Soviet infantry was equipped for military action.[7] German intelligence discovered that the Russians had been building airports and ammunition depots in feverish haste throughout the entire spring. Polish agents reported Russian troop movements from the Far East to the western border and the formation and movement of new armies which could only serve aggressive purposes. The Soviets instructed their commissars that they should prepare for a long and cruel war with Germany.[8] Scientists and party functionaries sent to the Baltic countries from Moscow spoke openly of the Soviet Union's intention to enter the war: The Soviet Union is prepared "to come to the assistance of the European nations suppressed by Capitalism just as it had come to the assistance of the Baltic nations;" the start of the war, they said, depended only on the Soviet Union, but first, all of the preparatory work must be finished.[9] Also, the amply staffed and equipped air support organization established near the border in the center of the frontier with Germany was of a clearly offensive character, because for defensive purposes new airports packed with planes make no sense near the border.[10]

After April 7, even the German embassy in Moscow was able to observe the steady call-up of reservists and raw recruits. On April 8, the Russians started to evacuate the families of the members of their trade delegation in Berlin. In Kiev, trainloads of military hardware could be seen moving toward the former Polish border. On April 9, the German military attache in Bukarest reported that Marshall Timoshenko, regarded by many as the only really capable Soviet general, had called a council of war in Kiev and ordered an alert for all units along the western border.[11]

The extent of the Soviet military preparations was such that General Halder, the German Chief of the General Staff, feared that –

according to his diary entries of April 6 and 7 – the Soviet attack could be expected at any time.[12] General Halder, a member of the "Resistance", wrote after the war: "... [it] was his [Hitler's] unshakable and not unfounded conviction that Russia was preparing to attack Germany. We know today from excellent sources that he was right."[13]

At the political level, too, Stalin was taking calculated steps to solidify his position vis-a-vis Germany. A high point of Soviet hostility toward Germany was reached on March 27, 1941, when Soviet agents in the Serbian army overthrew the pro-German government in neighboring Yugoslavia just two days after Yugoslavia joined the Axis.[14] On April 5, 1941 already Stalin hastily signed a treaty of friendship with the new anti-German regime; the following day the German air force attacked Belgrade.[15] Still more ominous from the German point of view was the treaty of neutrality signed by Japan and the Soviet Union on April 13; with this, Moscow was now free to devote all of its attention to the European theater as the immediately accelerating pace of troop movements from the Far East to the European parts of the country showed.

Hitler and his advisors now had no further doubts about Stalin's martial plans. Halder was sure that if one would have shown the Soviet military build-up to a neutral military expert he would have had to admit that it was of an aggressive design. Throughout the month of March the Soviet troop movements near the border were so intense and the supply transports from Moscow toward Smolensk and Minsk assumed such proportions that Halder feared a Soviet attack on Germany could be imminent. At the time, he said that this danger could last until April 20, 1941 because the Soviets were expected to have far superior forces until then.[16]

But then, the Soviets knew very well that the Germans had no illusions about the Soviet intentions and were preparing hastily to attain first-strike capability. Already on April 10, high alert was ordered for the entire Red Army.[17] General Klokov of the Politburo announced on April 16 to a select group of officers that the war could erupt "at any moment" and that the Red Army should not be "caught off guard."[18]

On April 23, new reports of gigantic Soviet reinforcements in the Bukovina and Bessarabia arrived from Bukarest; the following day the German military attache in Bukarest reported from Bukarest that ships loaded with Red Army men arrived in Odessa and were being transported from there by train to the Bug and Dniester rivers and that the Soviets were evacuating the *civilian population* along their side of the Pruth river.[19]German intelligence had reported since *February 1940* already that the Soviets were systematically deporting the Polish, Jewish and Ukrainian population from the western Ukraine. The people to be deported were given only a little time to prepare and were allowed to take just a few bags along.[19a] The accuracy of these reports was verified after the recapture of the former Rumanian areas by the combined German and Rumanian armies. The census conducted by Rumania in the regained territories on August 16, 1941 registered a total population loss of about 20%. The urban population in particular had suffered from the Soviet measures; its share of the total population had shrunk to 10% (before the war it was about 20%). Kishinev, for example, lost 62% of its inhabitants and Chernovitsy approximately 42%.[20]

In May 1941, several armies were moved from the interior to the western USSR:[21]

– The 22. Army from the Ural to the Velikie Luki area north of Vitebsk;
– the 21. Army from the Volga to the Gomel area;
– the 19. Army from northern Caucasus to the Shepetovka area midway between Kiev and the German-Soviet line of demarcation;
– the 16. Army from Transbaikalia (near Manchuria) to the Belaya Tserkov area (southwest of Kiev);
– the 25. Rifle Corps to the western Dvina.

On May 5, Stalin delivered speeches to officers of the Frunse Military Academy. Among the listeners were Molotov, Mikoyan, Voroshilov, Kalinin and Beria; also present were two generals and a major who later happened to fall into German hands and independently reiterated the contents of that speech with a high degree of unanimity. Both Ribbentrop and Göring claimed in 1943 and after the war, respectively, that details of this speech had been forwarded to Hitler by agents almost immediately. The gist of Stalin's speech was:

> He referred to the need to prepare for the coming war with Germany and promised that within two months the Soviet Union would possess some of the best and fastest aircraft in the world. The war plan, he said, is completed, the airfields have been built and the frontline aircraft are there already. Everything has been done to clear out the rear areas, all the *foreign elements have been removed*. Within the next two months the USSR can begin to battle Germany. The pact with Germany was just a trick. A
> . carefully developed, vast partisan movement built up throughout Europe since the war began in 1939 would paralyze the supplies of the German Army. The era of forcible expansion for the Soviet Union has begun.[22]

On May 10, the German Air Force reported the concentration of 4,000 Soviet aircraft on the airfields near the border and the stationing of another 1,000 in rear areas as detected through radio reconnaissance.[23]

General Vlassov, taken prisoner in 1942, confirmed later that the Soviets intended to attack in late summer of 1941.[24] Jakob Dschugaschwili, Stalin's son who fell into German hands in July 1941 as an artillery lieutenant in an armored division, told his German interrogators "that they were preparing to attack when, suddenly, they....were smashed to pieces."[25]

No doubt, the German preventive action of June 22, 1941 hit the Soviet military build-up before the Red steamroller started to move. Six weeks earlier, on May 12 and 15, the Soviet spy Sorge had reported the imminent attack by 150 German divisions, disclosing the exact date of June 22, 1941 and the German operative plans to Moscow.[26]

The very first days of the German invasion furnished ample proof that the Soviet Army had indeed been prepared for an attack on central Europe. Even in those frontier pockets extending far to the west around Lvov and Bialystok – which were quite exposed to German encirclement and for this reason were useless for defensive purposes – the German troops encountered massive Soviet assault forces. As a result, the head-on clash with the Soviet army and air force occurred just as soon as the Germans crossed the border.

But since the Soviet high command was limited to just 150-200 air strips adjacent to the German border because of the unfavorable terrain (large parts in the center portion of the German-Soviet border were swampy), the available strips were particularly crowded with planes ready to execute the planned attacks on German positions. Thus, the very first military operations of the German fighter and reconnaissance squadrons encountered numerous airfields of which several were packed with up to 100 Soviet planes. The German air force cut into this massive concentration of several thousand Soviet planes which were ready for the onslaught on Germany. Just between June 22 and 28, 1941 4,107 Soviet planes were destroyed, about 3,000 on the ground.[27] Similar losses were suffered by the Red Army in the Bialystok area. Between June 22 and July 1, it lost 5,774 tanks, 2,330 artillery pieces and 160,000 prisoners, not counting the fallen Red Army men.[28]

In his speech of February 25, 1956 at the 20th Party Congress in Moscow, N.S. Khrushchev called Stalin's claim of a German surprise attack a lie and noted that the Soviet leadership knew from many excellent sources (for instance, Churchill; the British ambassador to the USSR, Cripps; the Soviet embassy in London and other Soviet military and diplomatic channels, as well as the Soviet deputy military attache in Berlin, Chlopov) that the German attack was imminent.[29]

Also, Stalin's preparations to wage war against Europe were made from a strategic-economic point of view long before Hitler appeared in the political arena as the leader of a resurrected Germany. In contrast to Stalin, Nikolaj Bucharin who was liquidated in 1938 and other old Bolsheviki favored the development of light industry; they felt that total industrialization could only be pursued once consumer goods were made available to the population. Stalin won the dispute and silenced the others: The Soviet Union thereupon embarked on the most gigantic industrialization program the world had ever seen.

The foundations for this giant undertaking were laid in the first Five-Year-Plan (1928-1932) which called for the establishment of completely new industrial sectors and bases. The core of the Plan was the development of heavy industry in the Urals and in Siberia.

The German army had penetrated the Ukraine in 1918 and a repetition could not be excluded entirely; therefore, in Stalin's opinion the Soviet Union needed a heavy industry located out of reach of possible enemies. In February 1931 Stalin said: "Russia must overtake the most advanced capitalist countries with respect to industrial and military capacity within ten years [i.e. until 1941] or else those countries are going to destroy us." He emphasized that these new industries would be located in the Urals and in Siberia thousands of kilometers from the nearest border and outside the reach of enemy planes.

In order to attain this goal, thousands of foreign experts were engaged who, while working for the Soviet Union or foreign companies, had to be paid in gold. The American John Scott wrote that in Magnitogorsk alone there were three to four hundred German and American specialists. Relative to general Soviet living conditions, these foreigners enjoyed almost unbelievable luxuries while millions of men and women died of hunger, froze to death or succumbed to inhuman work requirements and living conditions.[30]

Thus, the naivete of many Western historians is best demonstrated by their stubborn adherence to the thesis that Stalin, who from the very start concentrated the Soviet Union's forced industrialization in the Urals for strategic reasons only and who was very well informed of German military preventive plans, had been surprised by Germany's attack. The opposite is true. Even before the outbreak of hostilities the Soviet Union was hurriedly moving people and industrial installations out of the western provinces and districts. John Scott reports that

> *before* war broke out important installations for the production of electrical materials had been moved from White Russia and the area around Leningrad to western Siberia [and] at least one armaments factory, formerly located near Leningrad, was *transferred to Magnitogorsk together with the entire machinery and all of the personnel.* ... Except for the largest blast furnaces, steel making and chemical installations everything else was transported by rail rather easily to other regions and without significant damages.[31]

According to Prof. Lorimer the Soviet plans for transporting *people* and machines to the interior were immediately put into action at the start of the hostilities.[32] Prof. Boris Semjonowitsch Telpuchowski from the Institute for Marxism-Leninism at the Central Committee of the Communist Party in Moscow confirmed that this eventuality had been taken into account in the plans to switch the railroad traffic immediately to serve military needs. In the first few months one million railroad cars loaded with industrial equipment, materials and *people* left the endangered areas near the frontline.[33]

The Germans estimated the Soviet stock of passenger and freight cars at the beginning of the war at 36,000 and 850,000, respectively. At the end of 1941, 40% of the Soviet railroad network was in German hands; still the Soviets managed to take the bulk of the rolling stock along with them: At the end of 1941 German troops had captured only 1,100 passenger and 43,300 freight cars[34] – almost half of these during the first four weeks. In other words, the Russians were not at all surprised by the German attack; they seem to have expected it.

Assuming that up to 50%, i.e. more than 400,000 railroad cars, had their home stations in the areas occupied during the war by German forces, the Soviets obviously were able to evacuate about 90% of that rolling stock before the Germans could lay their hands on them. Of course, all of these lorries were shipped further east fully loaded. If one adds to these the number of cars arriving from the east carrying military personnel and weaponry, ready to transport people, materials and machines on their return trip, then one can understand how the Soviets managed to evacuate huge masses of people in such a short time; the fact that the areas close to the German border were neither very highly industrialized nor greatly urbanized permitted the use of a correspondingly greater number of cars for the removal of the relatively small urban population. John Scott had this to add:

> The Russian railroad tracks running in an east-west direction are crowded with trains bringing supplies and reserves to the front. Going east, the freight trains are loaded with machines and workers. Even though I know of no numbers I am convinced that a large part of the industrial machinery, which was located previously in the areas temporarily occupied by Germany, did not fall into German hands, but is in full operation in Stalin's Ural fortress fifteen hundred or two thousand kilometers east of the frontline of spring of 1943.

The Ural area was capable of producing every type of material required for the production of tanks, heavy trucks, artillery and airplanes. Until the outbreak of the war, two things still were in short supply in that region: Machines and labor. "Both," Scott continued, "have been transferred there recently in large numbers."[35]

Prof. Lorimer confirmed also that the Soviets set out immediately after the German attack to activate their plans for the dismantling of factories and resurrecting them in the interior; in addition, he says, a large part of the agricultural machinery and a lot of livestock was removed. Even Khrushchev admitted that the Soviets succeeded in increasing military production during the war in the eastern sections of the country and to re-install the removed means of production from the western industrial territories.[36]

The re-use of the machines transported from western regions was facilitated by the circumstance that the Soviet leadership had put up factory shells in the Urals and Siberia long before the war started, ensuring that sufficient electric energy was available. John Scott, an eyewitness to these happenings, wrote:

> Railroad and factory construction in the Urals, Central Asia and Siberia was speeded up [until the spring of 1941]. ... Here, new factory buildings rose which were not to be found on any blueprints. Nobody knew what they were to be used for. At the same time, great efforts were undertaken in order to enlarge the output of power stations even though there was enough power for the local industry, at least in Magnitogorsk.

This, Scott emphasized, occurred only in the Urals region.[37]

The Soviets had covered the entire Ural industrial region with a fine railroad system and a far-flung network of power lines together with the appropriate power stations. In 1934, the electric power plants in the Ural area produced 2 billion kWh already, in 1940 it was twice as much;[38] until the outbreak of hostilities and during the war electric power production was increased further. Possibly, these figures are more meaningful to the reader once he realizes that the entire occupied Soviet territory, administered by the Germans under the name of "occupied eastern territories," with its huge heavy industry produced no more than 10 billion kWh of electrical power *before* the war. As we know from Wilhelm Niederreiter, the Germans were able to produce just 1 billion kWh in this wide area in 1943 despite their utilization of large numbers of German personnel and considerable amounts of German equipment.[39] Comparisons not only show the extent of the Soviet orgy of destruction, but also the gigantic potential for the production of armaments built up by the Soviets east of the Volga before the war. Telpuchowski describes the Russian measures as follows:

> The evacuation of industrial enterprises proceeded along a uniform economic plan of mobilization. The plan specified the places of destination where the enterprises were to be transported and the successive turns in which the removal was to take place. The interconnections between the individual factories and plants and their dependence on one another was also taken into account. ... Hundreds of industrial enterprises were transplanted to the eastern territories. 455 enterprises were moved to the Urals which served as the arsenal of the Soviet Army. In just three months of the year 1941 more than 1,360 industrial complexes were transplanted. The movable equipment of thousands of collective and state farms was transported to the interior. Thanks to the heroic work of the blue- and white-collar workers the evacuated enterprises rose in a very short time at their new locations. It should be noted that as a result of the evacuation of the enterprises, the enemy did not succeed in using the industrial stock of the occupied regions for his own purposes as he did in western Europe. Because of the successful removal and re-activation of the enterprises the main stock of industrial equipment was saved. All of this made it possible that the production of tanks, planes, cannons and other arms could even be increased a few months later. ... The evacuated enterprises rose in an unbelievably short time at their new localities. The workers and cadres ... worked under the open sky, quite often in rain and snow. ... Work continued throughout the day. The workday often lasted from 12 to 14 hours

and even more. ... The assembly of the larger plants and factories was finished in three to four weeks and within 3 to 4 months production attained pre-war levels. On average, one-and-one-half to two months were needed to reactivate the evacuated plants. ... The falling trend of production was stopped already in December of 1941.[40]

The accessible remains of the secret documents of the German Economy Staff East (Wirtschaftsstab Ost)[41] show clearly that the Soviets succeeded indeed in evacuating a large part of their means of production within the framework of a detailed plan of removal or, at least, to make them unusable for the Germans. In this connection, the secret No. 3 Fourteen-Day-Report of the German Economy Staff East dated August 30, 1941 has this to say:

The *Russian* and *Jewish* upper classes withdrew together with the Red Army. The leading Ukrainians have been partially deported and, if they held leading positions in administration and industry, they were also forced to move east of the Dnieper. Numerous tractor and other specialists on the countryside met the same fate. In June, many young men were called up and put in garrisons in the interior of the USSR. ... Because of this development there is a tremendous scarcity of people capable of assuming responsible positions in administration, industry and agriculture in the Ukraine...

Extensive economic losses have been sustained because of the systematic clearing and destruction operations of the Red Army before withdrawal. These damages have increased progressively from west to east. In the cities, the damage caused in this way affects factories and stores and, in part, also the living quarters and their contents; in the countryside, especially the stock of machinery, livestock, grain dumps and the gasoline supplies of the collective and state farms have suffered.

The clearing action begins usually about 8-10 days before the withdrawal of the Red Army. The critical machines of the enterprises, especially motors, have been removed, carefully packaged and loaded to be shipped to the east of the USSR. Destination addresses found in the Ukraine as a rule point to the Ural industrial area, specifically the region encompassed by Sverdlovsk - Molotov (Perm) - Ufa - Chkalov (Orenburg) - Magnitogorsk. It seems that in that area arrangements have already been made for the re-use of the machines removed from the Ukraine. ... The destruction usually sets in 24 hours before the Soviet troops withdraw. These actions are prepared carefully and include the burning of smaller factories, the blasting of important machine complexes and apparently also the handing over of supplies to the population to loot (contents of the stores in the cities, grain supplies in rural areas). It is quite obvious that the military resistance met in several places (e.g. the giant power station Dnepro-Ges and the aluminum-complex in Zaporoshye as well as the iron-works in Dnepropetrovsk) had one purpose only, namely, to destroy the remaining important industrial works.[42]

Similarly, the Mid-Month-Report dated December 8, 1941 explained that

the destruction of the city of Kharkov began on October 21, 1941 according to accounts of the population. The destruction was carried out with extreme brutality. In many cases, the inhabitants had their houses burned to the ground before they could vacate them. Without doubt, only the rapid occupation by German troops prevented them [the Soviets] from carrying out their plans to burn down the entire city. ... Totally destroyed are especially the water works, a bread factory, a large laundry, and by far the largest portion of factory installations. ... Local inhabitants reported that the systematic clearing of the most important industrial works started in August already and assumed a vast scale. *Specialists and their families* were forcibly evacuated. Apparently, Kharkov's industry has been re-assembled in a rough-and-ready manner above all in Chelyabinsk (western Siberia). The inhabitants say that they received letters from there according to which the deportees face a *desperate situation*, *lack of living quarters* and *hunger*. Observations in other places, too, reinforce the impression that the disassembly and removal of machinery follows a detailed clearing plan with the objective of moving important bottleneck equipment to areas not endangered as much in order to restart the production of war materials in substitute factories. Thus, the Soviets not only disassembled and removed machinery, but also smaller equipment and tools.[43]

Even before the war, the lot of the people exiled to the new industrial regions in the Urals and western Siberia was sad indeed. As elsewhere in the USSR, shoes and clothing were practically unavailable in 1939 already and in 1940 even bread was rationed. Hospitals consisted of barracks, were without running water, brutally hot in the summer, ice-cold in the winter, rarely clean and always overcrowded. In 1938 still, only 25% of the population of Magnitogorsk was fortunate enough to live in houses, whereas 50% were crowded into barracks and other "temporarily constructed houses" and 25% had to be satisfied with so-called "semlianki" (Tatar huts, etc.).[44] Into this region, deficient in even the most basic civilian infrastructure, the Soviets deported shortly before and after the outbreak of hostilities untold millions of Russians, Jews, Ukrainians and other nationalities of the western Soviet Union.

The hopeless situation of the deportees in Siberia is also evident in the words of the Soviet court historian Telpuchowski who said, referring to the *evacuation* of *millions* of *civilians*,

> the accommodation of the *masses going into the millions*, who had been evacuated from the areas occupied or threatened by the enemy, posed a serious problem in the hinterland ... which lacked the most elementary lodging facilities; they had to live in tents and sod huts. Food was scarce.[45]

Obviously, there are no large differences between Telpuchowski's description of the Soviet measures and the secret reports of the German Economy Staff East with regard to the desperate situation in the Soviet areas of retreat – with the one exception that Telpuchowski did not think it worth mentioning the application of the inhuman Soviet "scorched earth" policy even towards the infrastructure and supplies critically needed by the civilian population that remained behind.

Soviet Mass Deportations

The Soviet rulers believed that hostilities would break out at the German-Soviet line of demarcation regardless. An evacuation of the "threatened" and "foreign" civilian population near the border was thus entirely possible before June 22, 1941 and was carried out, too, as we learned from Stalin's speech. When the German naval attache left Moscow on May 19, 1941 – five weeks before the beginning of the war – taking the train through Soviet-occupied former eastern Poland in the direction of Berlin, he met locked prison trains escorted by blue-uniformed GPU troops deporting "undesirables" from eastern Poland.[46]

The extent of the Soviet deportation program is subject to the most contradictory speculations. Contrary to Edward C. Carter, president of the Russian War Relief, who mentioned 37 millions in September 1942,[47] the *Year Book* maintains that the German advance was so rapid that the Soviet railroad system was incapable of effecting evacuation to any noteworthy degree.[48] The Soviets, anyway, have never actually published figures on the magnitude of this human tragedy.

The task to obtain a somewhat reliable picture is complicated by the fact that there are no exact figures available for the total Soviet population at the beginning of the war in 1941; the census of January 1939 was outdated soon after because of the Soviet annexation of huge regions on the western border in 1939 and 1940. Of course, the German administration carried out more or less detailed counts of the population present, but a comparison with pre-war figures is difficult because the borders of the various German administrative districts in the occupied territories were rarely comparable to the administrative and political pre-war borders. The Reichs-Commissariat (RK) Ostland contained the Baltic countries and parts of former eastern Poland and of the Soviet-Republic of White Russia; the RK Ukraine included parts of eastern Poland in the west (until Brest-Litovsk) but not Galicia; on the other hand, Rumania not only regained its former provinces of Bessarabia and northern Bukovina, but also annexed a part of the former Soviet-Republic Ukraine, calling it "Transdniestria"; towards the east, large parts of the former Socialist Soviet Republic (SSR) Ukraine was subject to German military and not civilian rule. For these reasons, it is necessary to scrutinize the pre-war population of the Soviet Union very closely.

The census of January 17, 1939 found a total population of 170.5 million.[49] Since the last count on December 17, 1926 the population of the USSR had grown by 15.9% which corresponds to an annual rate of 1.2%. The natural growth rate, though, must have been much higher because the enforced collectivization of agriculture in the early 1930's cost the lives of millions of people, especially in the Ukraine. Exact figures, of course, will never be available on the mass starvation of the early 1930's, but a comparison of the census of 1926 (before the forced collectivization) and of 1939 should provide some indications.

Soviet Censuses of 1926 and 1939
(in millions)[50]

| Year | Age (Year) | | Census of | | Changes | |
	1926	1939	17.12.26	17.1.39	Millions	Per Cent
1927–1938	–	0–11	–.–	47.82	+47.82	(–.–)
1919–1926	0– 7	12–19	31.94	28.46	– 3.48	(–10.9)
1909–1918	8–17	20–29	32.91[51]	30.64	– 2.27	(– 6.9)
1899–1908	18–27	30–39	27.47[51]	25.33	– 2.14	(– 7.8)
< 1899	> 27	> 39	54.71	37.27	–17.44	(–31.9)
Total			147.03	169.52[52]		

A comparison of the two censuses shows that between 1926 and 1939 there was an unbelievably large reduction of those born in the years 1919-1926 – the group which at the time of the Great Hunger in the early

1930's was still of childhood age. Between 1926 and 1939 (peacetime!) this population group shrunk 11%, or 3.5 million, from 31.9 to 28.5 million. The age groups 1899-1918 numbered 60.4 million in 1926 but only 56 million in 1939 – a reduction of 4.4 million or 7.3%! In short, of the 92.3 million Soviet inhabitants who were *less* than 28 years old in 1926, only 84.4 million, or 91.4%, had survived until 1939!

Even if one postulates a reduction by 2% as a consequence of a normal mortality for these young age groups in the period 1926-1939,[53] there are still 6.6% whose disappearance must have been caused by the starvation policy; applied to the 92.3 million this amounts to 6 million people. Applied to the 150 million Soviet citizens at the end of the 1920's, we obtain 10 million people who starved to death – and in this connection we haven't even considered the much higher, hunger-induced infant mortality of those children born after December 17, 1926 but before and during the Great Hunger.

Without the more than ten million victims of the great starvation of the 1930's, the census of January 17, 1939 would have found far more than 180 million people. Compared to the 147 million Soviet citizens of 1926 that would have corresponded to a natural increase of over 22%; since emigration and immigration were almost impossible, this is equivalent to an annual rate of natural growth of 1.8%! Applying this growth rate to the 2½ years from January 1939 to June 1941, the actual Soviet population (excl. the inhabitants of the newly acquired western territories) would have increased from 170.5 million (January 1939) to 178 million (June 1941).

After the incorporation of the Ukrainian and White Russian regions of former eastern Poland and the annexation of Bessarabia and the northern Bukovina, the Soviet population rose by another seventeen million.[54] In addition, there was the occupation and annexation of the Baltic countries in 1940 with a population of six million.[55] Finally, many Polish citizens from western Poland – Jews in particular – fled in the first half of September 1939 to the eastern parts which were occupied by the Soviet Union after September 17, 1939.

As a result, the population living in the Soviet Union on June 22, 1941 must have reached at least 202 million. Thus, the findings of the American scholar Prof. Lorimer that the total population of Soviet Russia was about 200 million in those days matches just about our own calculations.[56]

Besides these newly acquired Soviet territories with a population of roughly 23 million (excl. refugees), the German Wehrmacht succeeded in occupying the following "old" Soviet areas, wholly or in part:

"Old" Soviet Areas under German Occupation[57]

Region	1,000 sq. km	Population (in 1,000) as of January17, 1939 Total	Cities
White Russian SSR	126.8	5,568	1,373
Ukrainian SSR	445.3	30,960	11,196
Crimea ASSR	26.0	1.127	586
Rostov Oblast	100.7	2,894	1,263
Orel Oblast	64.4	3,482	693
Kursk Oblast	55.7	3,197	286
Voronesh Oblast	76.7	3,551	658
Kalinin Oblast	106.4	3,211	703
Smolensk Oblast	72.2	2,691	448
Krasnodar Kray	81.5	3,173	765
Ordzhonikidze Kray	101.5	1,949	394
Kabardino-Balkar ASSR	12.3	359	85
North Osetin ASSR	6.2	329	155
	1,275.7	62,491	18,605

In addition, large portions of the Stalingrad, Tula, Moscow and Leningrad districts (oblast) had been conquered, but the capital cities of these oblasts always remained outside German control. Without the urban population of Tula, Moscow, Leningrad and Stalingrad the population of these areas amounted to 11.6 million as of January 17, 1939. If the German forces occupied only a section containing just one fifth of their total population another 2.5 million must be added; therefore, it seems the "old" Soviet regions which were occupied by German troops in the course of the war were populated by 65 million people as of January 17, 1939.

Considering, furthermore, a natural increase of about 3 million until mid-1941, the population of all Soviet territory occupied by the Axis armies – including the newly acquired regions to the west in 1939/1940 – must have numbered 91 million at the time German-Soviet hostilities began. This figure comes rather close to Lorimer's own of 85 million;[58] but Prof. Lorimer obviously didn't allow for a natural population increase in the 2½ years between the last census and the outbreak of the war.

Telpuchowski wrote, "40% of the population of our country [lived] in the area occupied by the enemy until November 1941."[59] This means that official Soviet sources put the pre-war population of the territories occupied by the Germans until November 1941 at about 81 million (i.e. 40% of 202 million). If one adds the additional territory conquered in

1942, it seems that our calculations of 91 million people are almost too low.

German investigations during the war provide a similar picture. In the areas under German control on November 1, 1942 the pre-war population was calculated at 83.81 million.[60] It should be noted that in the meantime there had been some losses of territory due to military reverses by the Germans, so that these figures were already reduced by several millions. If a natural increase until mid-1941 is taken into account, it would seem that 91 million is to be regarded as the absolute minimum pre-war population of all the Soviet territories conquered by the German armies.

According to Prof. Lorimer, 31% of the population of occupied "old" Soviet regions was urban before the war;[61] a similar situation existed in Estonia and in Latvia. However, in Lithuania the urban population was smaller and it was still smaller in the areas taken from Poland and Rumania.[62] All in all, one may say that the total urban pre-war population of the occupied Soviet Union must have been at least 25 million.

Regarding the time and the number of the evacuated civilian population Prof. Lorimer wrote:

> Another wartime movement, begun on a relatively small scale at an early stage and augmented just *before* and after the German attack, was the selective evacuation of such persons as former army officers, government officials and executives, and, later, workers of various kinds from areas annexed by the U.S.S.R. to the interior of the Soviet Union. ... Kulischer estimates the total number of civilians evacuated from the annexed areas at 1,500,000 to 2,000,000 persons. ... Finally, we come to the most important population movement in the U.S.S.R. during the war – apart from the mobilization of military personnel, which we shall not attempt to estimate – namely, the planned, selective evacuation from the path of the invader. When the Germans crossed the frontiers, plans were immediately put into effect for the rapid removal of *people* and equipment. In fact, *large-scale evacuation of persons from the annexed areas bordering on the German zone* seems to have been initiated *at least several days before June 22, 1941.* Most of this evacuation was by railway. Whole factories were dismantled and set up in the interior; a large part of the farm machinery and much of the livestock were removed. There is no precise official information about the number of persons evacuated, and widely divergent estimates have been made by competent authorities. ...
>
> In general, the *population of Ukrainian cities in 1942* seems to have been *half as large or less than it was in 1939.* ... The depletion

of urban population by evacuation may have been less marked in the most western districts of the annexed areas than in the Ukraine as a whole, but scattered Soviet references indicate far greater depletion of population in some other cities, such as Smolensk and Kalinin. German discussions of agricultural problems in the occupied area give added evidence of the large-scale removal or destruction of farm equipment, but indicate the shortage of agricultural labor was not serious except in certain districts. ... This evidence furnishes some reason for believing the thesis of the Chief of the War Economy Department in the German Economic Administration in the East [Assistant Secretary Dr. Rachner] that the evacuation from the area occupied in 1941 was equal to about half of the urban population, with refugee movements to rural districts about offsetting the evacuation of the rural population. This German authority estimated on this basis that the number of evacuated from occupied to free Soviet territory in 1941 was about 12.5 million persons.

Two estimates by independent authorities, based on an analysis of the railway carrying capacity, result in divergent figures for evacuation from areas occupied prior to 1942. Habicht estimates 15 million as a maximum and Vassiliev places the total number of evacuees as from 7.5 to 10 million. ... Kulischer estimates the grand total of evacuees from both the annexed and original Soviet territories at 12 million persons, excluding only military personnel mobilized before the German invasion. This is a very possible figure. ...

In general, these displaced people were located in the area of the Central Industrial Region which had been marked by most rapid expansion during the preceding decade. ... It would appear that large numbers were located in regions near the Turkestan-Siberian Railway, and that Tashkent was an important distributing point for refugees and evacuees. A great many were assigned to various established and relocated industries in the Central Volga Region, the Urals, western and central Siberia, Kasakhstan, Central Asia, and the Far North. The industrial output of the Ural region is reported to have increased threefold during the war.[63]

Referring to these Soviet measures, the Zionist author Reitlinger wrote:

... it became the Russian policy to remove the working population so that the towns should not benefit the enemy. ... Not to consent to be evacuated was regarded as a hostile act, often visited with dire consequences later.[64]

And the Jewish Chief of the Soviet Information Bureau, S.A. Lesovsky, announced the official version of the Soviet Government with these gory words:

> In fact, the Germans never did occupy any territory with a population of 75,000,000. Well aware of the wolfish proclivities of the Nazi plunderers, ravishers and murderers, the *mass of the Soviet population departed beforehand for the Eastern districts* of the Soviet Union.[65]

The fourteen large Ukrainian cities listed by Prof. Lorimer were evacuated by 53% on average. However, Prof. Lorimer did not take into consideration that these cities must have had a much larger population in mid-1941 than in early 1939. At the start of the First Five-Year-Plan (1928) blue- and white-collar workers represented just 17% of the Soviet population according to Molotov's remarks at the 18th Party Congress in 1939, but eleven years later, in 1939, their percentage was 50%.[66]This revolutionary industrialization policy of the Five-Year-Plans not only had an enormous effect on the societal composition of the masses, but on the growth of the cities as well. The 174 cities with 50,000 or more inhabitants in January 1939 contained a total population of 34.1 million (1939) compared to only 16.2 million in 1926; this is equivalent to a rate of increase of 6.5% annually during this 12-year-period.

But the 14 Ukrainian cities as listed by Prof. Lorimer registered "only" a per annum growth rate of 5.5% since 1926.[67] There is no reason to assume that the expansion of Soviet cities slowed between 1939 and 1941 while preparations were made for the coming war with Germany; the opposite is true, as the feverish war preparations of the Soviets made a still more rapid industrialization necessary. The assumption is not far-fetched that the cities listed by Lorimer – Kiev, Odessa, Dnepropetrovsk, Zaporoshye, Mariupol, Krivoi Rog, Nikolaev, Dneprodzerzhinsk, Poltava, Kirovograd, Kherson, Shitomir, Vinnitsa and Melitopol – evidenced large rates of growth after January 1939 also.

Assuming a rate of increase somewhat less than the average of the past twelve years, let us say 10% for the 2½ years from January 1939 to June 1941, those fourteen Ukrainian cities must have had a total population of over 4 million when the Germans crossed the border. Following the occupation of these cities, the Germans found only 1.69 million inhabitants; thus, the Soviets succeeded in evacuating almost 60% of their urban population. Applied to the entire urban population of more than 25 million, this would mean that only ten million inhabitants remained in the cities when the Germans arrived; the other 15 million had been removed by the Soviets before the Germans reached the cities.

Reitlinger, too, noted categorically in his book *The Final Solution:* "In most captured towns *less than half the population* stayed."[68] Dr. Rachner commented in the *Reichsarbeitsblatt:*

> ... in general, one can assume that the countryside in the occupied areas has suffered no loss of its population. Granted that the occupied regions contained a total population of 75 million before the start of hostilities, about 50 million of these were living in rural areas. If one assumes this population to be still present and needed – one should note that agricultural work had to change over in part to more manual labor because of the loss of machinery – then a figure of 25 million is left for the cities of the occupied areas. Investigations show, though, that only one half of the [urban] population was left *at most*; this is equivalent to 12½ million."[69]

One should not forget that Dr. Rachner's remarks were made in early 1942 when German population counts had only started. To what extent political considerations colored his statements is uncertain. The Soviets in any case were busy exploiting the success of their policy of evacuation, destruction and sabotage propagandistically in every way. The Japanese Government was so impressed by the Soviet propaganda that the Japanese ambassador in Berlin, Oshima, notified the German Government to this effect with the accompanying request to supply him with data on the raw material and production situation in the agricultural and industrial areas of the Ukraine and White Russia, as well as the size of the population under German administration, especially in the Ukraine; he wanted to forward this information on to Tokyo to counter Soviet reports.[70] One should certainly assume, therefore, that Dr. Rachner's evacuation figure of 12½ million people evacuated by the Soviets probably tended to be somewhat too rosy.

In any case, Inspector Krüger of the Chief Group Economy, Statistical Department, in the Economy Staff East noted on February 17, 1943 in a secret report that the population of the so-called "occupied eastern territories" contained a population of 70 million before the war and that only 50 million had been found.[71] The "occupied eastern territories" mentioned by Krüger included only the Reichs-Commissariats Ostland and Ukraine, which were under civilian administration, and the military-ruled areas east of them. They did not include the population of the district of Bialystok, Galicia which was incorporated in the Government General of Poland, the provinces of northern Bukovina and Bessarabia regained by the Rumanians and the so-called "Transdniestrian" part of the former SSR Ukraine. The total population of these excluded former Soviet territories, which were administered neither by the Economy Staff East nor by the German military, probably contained at least 13 million people before the war. However, if one can assume that these areas, too, because of their nearness to the German border and their relatively small urban population lost only 15% of their population, which was the percentage missing in the RK Ostland, then the Soviets could have evacuated 2 million of these 13 million people.[71a]

Finally, adding a natural increase of perhaps 4 million likely to have occurred in the period between January 1939 and June 1941, it seems that the area which was in German hands as of February 17, 1943 must have contained 87 million people before the war, the whereabouts of only 61 million of whom, however, could be traced; 26 million, or almost 30%, had disappeared!

Other German sources, too, point to a similar figure. The *Deutsche Zeitung im Ostland*, for instance, reported in 1943 that the losses of the Soviet Union in terms of soldiers and resident population in the lost territories must be put at *at least* 70 million.[72] Deducting the many millions of Soviet prisoners in German custody and fallen Red Army soldiers, the remaining figure for the Soviet population in German-occupied territory was about 60-65 million.

Indications are that Dr. Rachner's figures on the number of the deported Soviet population were too small and that Stalin's propaganda of having denied the Germans a large portion of the human and industrial stock in the occupied areas – and, from the point of view of martial requirements, the most important part at that – matched reality more closely than the Germans might have wished.

These figures are supported by an analysis of the Chief of Supply of the 200th Rifle Division of the 5th Army on the "Perspectives on the Supply Situation of the USSR in the Winter Campaign 1942/1943."[73] The study notes that 65 million people lived under Axis administration in all of the regions taken from the Soviets (as of autumn 1942). The author of the anlysis assumed, however, that 100 million people had populated that area before the war and thus arrived at an evacuation figure of 35 million – probably erroneous. If, as explained, that region actually contained only 91 million, this estimate, too, would arrive at 26 million evacuated.

On the other hand, it is rather interesting that this German figure of 35 million is almost a duplicate of the 37-million-number of the American Edward C. Carter. Carter's number, however, apparently includes not only the evacuees from the German-occupied territories, but also the civilians evacuated from endangered cities near the frontline – i.e. Leningrad, Moscow, etc. – which were never conquered by the German armies. As vice chairman of the American Institute of Pacific Relations and president of the Russian War Relief, Carter was indeed well placed to size up the entire extent of Soviet evacuation actions. The Russians knew why they decorated this gentlemen with the Order of the Red Banner of Labor.[74] In any case, Carter's figure is an indication that our computations of over 25 million evacuees from the German-occupied areas are about correct. Already in mid-November 1941 – less than five months after the German-Russo war began – Andrew Grajdanzev mentioned an evacuation and refugee figure of 10 to 20 million in the *Far Eastern Survey* published by the Institute of Pacific Relations; in this number the men called to arms from the occupied areas hadn't even been included.[75]

In his distorted description of the German administration of the "occupied eastern territories", the Jewish author Alexander Dallin, too, specifies the size of the population under German control at 65 million.[76] But the "most official" Allied statistic on the number of the people remaining behind in German-occupied Soviet territory came from Wendell Willkie, the presidential candidate of the Republican Party in the United States. In September 1942 Willkie visited the Kremlin where he was briefed on the military and economic situation of the battered Soviet empire. On September 26, Stalin hosted a dinner for Willkie; other Soviet notables present at the dinner were Molotov (Foreign Affairs), Mikoyan (Foreign Trade), Beria (Secret Police), Marshall Voroshilov, Admiral Kuznetozov and Information Director Alexander Scherbakaff.[77] On that occasion Willkie detailed the requests and information provided to him by the Soviet leadership stating that at least 60 million Soviet citizens were now living in the Soviet areas occupied by the Germans.[77a] The release of this figure by Stalin to Willkie represents an official, though indirect, Soviet admission of the magnitude of their evacuations – up to 30 million people. It is not possible to pin down the evacuees to the exact million, but concluding the subject one may state that the people evacuated and deported to the Urals and Siberia – including the mobilized men – must have numbered more than 25 million; of these, over 15 million came from the cities in the occupied Soviet areas.

These evacuation and deportation measures of the Soviet rulers must be seen in the context of the Soviet policy to wage war. Everything which could aid the German enemy in any way had to be destroyed or at least removed. This strategy affected not only the countryside, the factories, the infrastructure, etc. but also, or rather, especially people; after all, if the Germans could have laid their hands on trained specialists ready to be integrated into their war machine this had to be prevented by means of evacuation, deportation or mass murder. The leading and industrial sections of the population, of course, were given "preferential" treatment in this evacuation program. The extent of this horrendous action so far has not been given the attention in the literature which it deserves.

Vacated Cities

Soon after the occupation of the various Soviet cities, the German authorities began to initiate detailed counts of the remaining population. Obviously, the German occupiers had to obtain some information on the available stock of the working population. In this connection, Dr. Rachner wrote,

> the labor service offices ... were instructed again and again to obtain exact data on the local population based on the methods used in Germany. ... It should be noted that in most places not only the unemployed have been recorded but also those employed in the factories and in the public offices, classified by professional groups and types.[78]

In addition, the Soviet policy of systematic destruction of food supplies caused a stinging crisis in feeding the local population; just to carry out an effective program of rationing it was necessary to obtain an exact count of the population. Understandably, these population censuses were handed to the press only intermittently and the war documents in German archives today are so incomplete that, as far as we know, there are only very few cities for which evacuation figures are available.

The Soviet cities listed on *Table 6* have been grouped regionally – former Baltic, eastern Polish, Rumanian and "old" Soviet – in the rough order of their occupation. Quite noticeably, the Baltic cities' evacuation rate of "only" 26% is very much lower than those of the "old" Soviet and former Polish cities. Furthermore, the table furnishes no evidence that the cities conquered later in time registered a higher deportation loss than those cities occupied in the very first days of the war.

It is not clear to what extent these listed cities are representative for all occupied urban centers; nevertheless, they constitute almost one fourth of the urban population present in the German-occupied areas at the beginning of the war. The average evacuation rate of 50% is almost

Table 6
Soviet Deportation of the Urban Population in World War Two

Cities*	Jewish Population	Total Population before and after Deportation		Deported and/or Evacuated Population**	(%)
		before	after		
Former Baltic Cities:					
Taurage[a]	?	13,000	7,900	5,100	39
Kaunas ('34)	27,200[e]	150,000[b]	117,000[b]	33,000	22
Daugavpils ('35)[d]	11,106[e]	49,700[d]	24,227[d]	25,473	51
Lepaya ('35)[d]	7,379[e]	62,800[d]	45,982[d]	16,818	27
Riga ('35)[d]	43,672[e]	423,600[d]	301,391[d]	122,209	29
Ventspils ('35)[d]	1,246[e]	17,200[d]	13,226[d]	3,974	23
Jelgava ('35)[d]	2,039[e]	37,500[d]	28,908[d]	8,592	23
Rezekne ('35)[d]	3,342[e]	14,500[d]	7,994[d]	6,506	45
Other Latvian Towns:					
8 (5–9,000 inhabitants)[d]	?	63,100[e]	49,318[e]	13,782	22
19 (2–5,000 inhabitants)[d]	?	74,300[e]	55,743[e]	18,557	25
20 (1–2,000 inhabitants)[d]	?	32,800[e]	23,980[e]	8,820	27
Kallaste (Lake Peipus)	?	?	?	?	33[f]
Paernu	?	22,600[g]	18,815[g]	3,785	17
Toerva	?	?	?	?	27[f]
Tartu	?	58,400[g]	48,194[g]	10,206	17
Vijandi	?	12,900[g]	10,679[g]	2,221	17
Joegeva	?	?	?	?	26[f]
Narwa	?	25,300[g]	19,615[g]	5,685	22
Tallin ('34)	2,203[e]	164,296	134,705[g]	29,591[g]	18
"Baltic" Cities app.	100,000	1,250,000	930,000	320,000	26

(continued on next page)

Table 6 – (continued)

Former Eastern Polish Cities:					
Brest-Litovsk ('31)[h]	21,440[i]	58,100[i]	33,563[i]	24,537	42
Vladimir Volynsk ('31)[h]	10,665[i]	29,500[i]	8,628[i]	20,872	71
Kovel ('31)[h]	12,842[i]	33,200[i]	16,233[i]	16,967	51
Baranowicze ('31)[h]	9,680[i]	27,400[i]	2,740[i]	24,660	90[k]
Lutsk ('31)[h]	17,366[i]	42,700[i]	16,495[i]	26,205	61
Rovno ('31)[h]	22,737[i]	48,700[i]	17,531[i]	31,169	64
Sdolbunov	?	10,200[i]	7,650[i]	2,550	25
Pinsk ('31)[h]	20,220[i]	38,300[i]	12,029[i]	26,271	69
"Eastern Polish" Cities	120,000	288,000	115,000	173,000	60
Former East Rumanian Cities:					
Chernovitsy ('41)	50,000[c]	135,900[kk]	78,825[kk]	57,075	42
Kishinev ('41)	70,000[c]	137,900[kk]	52,962[kk]	84,938	62
"Eastern Rumanian" Cities	120,000	274,000	132,000	142,000	52

(continued on next page)

Table 6 – (concluded)

Former "Old" Soviet Cities:					
Minsk ('41)[m]	90,000[c]	262,600[m]	100,000[e]	162,600	61
Novograd-Volynsk[p]	?	?	?	?	90[j]
Shitomir ('39)[m]	50,000[d]	104,600[m]	42,000[j]	62,600	60
Proskurov ('26)[r]	13,408[e]	48,000[s]	12,510[j]	35,490	74
Kamenets-Podolsk ('26)[r]	12,774[e]	64,000[s]	15,044[j]	48,956	76
Vinnitsa ('26)[m]	21,812[e]	102,200[m]	42,500[j]	59,700	58
Smolensk ('26)[m]	12,887[e]	172,300[m]	20,000[j]	152,300	88
Kirovograd ('26)[m]	18,358[e]	110,400[m]	63,403[j]	46,997	43
Odessa ('39)[m]	180,000[e]	664,600[m]	300,000[j]	364,600	55
Nikolaev ('39)[m]	30,000[e]	183,800[m]	84,213[j]	99,587	54
Krivoi Rog ('26)[m]	5,730[e]	217,400[m]	125,000[j]	92,400	43
Kherson ('39)[m]	30,000[e]	106,900[m]	59,210[j]	47,690	45
Dneprodzerzhinsk[m]	?	162,600[m]	75,000[j]	87,600	54
Dnepropetrovsk ('39)[m]	100,000[e]	550,700[m]	280,000[j]	270,700	49
Zaporoshye[m]	?	318,100[m]	120,000[j]	198,100	62
Mozhaisk[u]	?	18,000	5,000	13,000	72
Melitopol ('39)[m]	11,000[e]	83,300[m]	65,054[j]	18,246	22
Chernigov ('26)[m]	10,607[e]	74,100[m]	30,000[r]	44,100	60
Poltava ('39)[m]	35,000[e]	143,300[m]	74,821[j]	68,479	48
Kiev ('39)[m]	175,000[e]	930,900[m]	304,570[j]	626,330	67
Mariupol ('26)[m]	7,332[e]	244,700[m]	178,358[t]	66,342	27
Taganrog ('26)[m]	2,673[e]	207,700[m]	120,000[w]	87,700	42
"Old" Soviet Cities app.	860,000	4,792,000	2,120,000	2,672,000	56
Soviet Cities app.	1,200,000[x]	6,604,000	3,297,000	3,307,000	50

(For sources and notes see following pages)

Sources and Notes:

*) The annual figures listed right after the city name refer to the Jewish population only.

**) The deported and evacuated inhabitants of the Soviet cities were determined either on the basis of the difference between the number of inhabitants before and after the deportation or, if only the percentage of the deported and the figures for the pre-war population were available, by multiplying the latter two figures.

a) *Kauener Zeitung*, Kovno/Lithuania, "Wiederaufbau in Kelmen und Tauroggen," No. 31, 11/15/1941, p. 3.

b) According to the *Kauener Zeitung*, "Die Stadt Kauen vor neuen Aufgaben," No. 76, 3/31/1943, p. 5, the city's population was 150,000 in 1939. In issue No. 87, 4/13/1943, p. 3, the population under German control within the same urban area was given as 117,000.

c) *Encyclopaedia Judaica*, Jerusalem, 1972 (diverse volumes); for Kovno, see *Kauener Zeitung*, "Jerusalem im Osten," No. 15, 8/19/1941, p. 3. Further: Publikationsstelle Berlin-Dahlem. *Bevölkerungsstatistik Lettlands* (Joh. Papritz and Wolfgang Kohte, Ed.), Berlin, 1942, p. 10/11, 28/29, 32/33, 38/39, 42/43, 46/47; for Melitopol: Hilberg, Raul. *The Destruction of the European Jews*, New York, 1973, p. 192; for Poltava, Kherson and Nikolaev: Reitlinger, Gerald. *The Final Solution*, New York, 1961, pp. 237 and 241.

d) *Zahl der Einwohner Lettlands für das Jahr 1941 (Stand 1.8.1941)*, Lettl. Statistisches Amt (Bundesarchiv R 92, Vorl. 1427). For the individual cities the following population figures were obtained for 1935 and 1941, respectively: Riga (385,063/301,391), Lepaya (57,098/45,982), Daugavpils (45,160/24,227), Jelgava (34,099/28,908), Ventspils (15,671/13,226), Rezekne (13,139/7,994). The "normal" increase since 1935 amounted to at least 10%.

e) *ibid.*; eight of the listed towns of 5-9,000 inhabitants contained a population totalling 57,336 and 49,318, respectively (1935 and 1941), 19 of 2-5,000 inhabitants each possessed a total population of 67,517 and 55,743, respectively, and 20 townlets of 1-2,000 inhabitants each had a total population of 29,789 and 23,980, respectively.

f) *Deutsche Ukraine-Zeitung*, Lutsk/Wolhynia, No. 7, 1/30/1942.

ff) *Deutsche Zeitung im Ostland*, Riga/Latvia, "Estlands Aderlass," No. 107, 11/19/1941, p. 5.

g) Parming, Tönu. "Population Changes in Estonia, 1935 - 1970," *Population Studies*, London, Vol. 26, No. 1, March 1972, p. 68.

gg) *Deutsche Zeitung im Ostland*, "Der Blutverlust des estnischen Volkes," No. 213, 8/6/1943, p. 5.

h) The last available census figures for Polish cities exist for 1931; from these it is possible to infer that the natural increase in Poland must have been around 1.5% annually. During the economic difficulties of the 1930's the rate of growth decelerated but the pace of urbanization continued unabatedly. The average growth of the Polish cities during the 1930's was, nevertheless, set at only 20% in order to remain on the cautious side.

i) The population figures of the Polish census for the listed cities may be taken from *Table 4*.

j) *Zentralblatt des Reichskommissars für die Ukraine*, Rovno, No. 2/2, January 9, 1943, p. 8-20.

k) Institute of Jewish Affairs. *Hitler's Ten-Year War on the Jews*, New York, 1943, p. 186.

kk) Publikationsstelle Wien. *Die Bevölkerungszählung in Rumänien 1941* (Geheim), Vienna, 1943, p. 70-73: On August 16,1941 – *before* the Rumanian deportations of parts of the Jewish population to Trandniestria – a census was conducted in the regained provinces of northern Bukovina and Bessarabia: In Chernovitsy only 78,825 inhabitants (1930: 112,427) were found and in Kishinev just 52,962 (1930: 114,896); the population of these cities must have increased by at least 20% between 1930 and 1941.

l)   *Deutsche Ukraine-Zeitung*, 3/8/1942.

m)   As mentioned in the text already, between 1926 and 1939 the Soviet cities experienced a population growth of 6.5% per annum (in the Ukraine 5.5%). For the listed "old" Soviet cities the figures were raised 10% above that of January 1939; considering the preparations for war against Germany and and the continuing industrialization efforts this must be viewed as a minimum.

n)   Lorimer, Frank. *The Population of the Soviet Union: History and Prospects*, Geneva: League of Nations, 1946, p. 250-253. Prof. Lorimer lists the following population figures for 1939: Kiev (846,293), Odessa (604,223), Dnepropetrovsk (500,662), Zaporoshye (289,188), Minsk (238,772), Mariupol (222,427), Krivoi Rog (197,621), Taganrog (188,808), Nikolaev (167,108), Smolensk (156,677), Dneprodzerzhinsk (147,829), Poltava (130,305), Kirovograd (100,331), Kherson (97,186), Shitomir (95,090), Vinnitsa (92,868), Melitopol (75,735), Chernigov (67,356).

o)   Reitlinger, *Final Solution*, p. 223; *Kauener Zeitung*, "Die Stadt Minsk im Aufbau," No. 298, 12/19/1942, p. 5, mentions the same figure.

p)   The pre-war population of Novograd Volynsk is unknown, but must have been between 20,000 and 30,000. Regarding the number of the evacuated, there are contradictory reports; German investigations (for source see footnote j above) found 12,000 inhabitants, but the Zionist Institute of Jewish Affairs (*Hitler's Ten-Year War*, p. 186), maintains that 90% of the population had withdrawn with the Red Army.

q)   Institute of Jewish Affairs, *Hitler's Ten-Year War*, p. 196.

r)   Census figures for 1939 are not available in the case of Proskurov and Kamenets-Podolsk; the last obtainable were for 1926. Even though the urban population in the Soviet Union more than doubled between 1926 and 1941 we assumed only an increase of 50%.

s)   According to the *Encyclopaedia Judaica* (Vol. 13, p. 1195) 13,408 Jews lived in Proskurov in 1926, constituting 42% of the population; this means that the total population of the city in 1926 must have been 32,000. In Kamenets-Podolsk were 12,774 – 29.9% of the population; thus, this city's total population must have amounted to 42,700.

t)   Institute of Jewish Affairs, *Hitler's Ten-Year War*, p. 185; *Kauener Zeitung*, "Odessa - Laune einer Zarin," No. 182, 8/6/1942, p. 3, mentions the same figure for Odessa.

u)   *The New York Times*, 1/27/1942.

v)   *Deutsche Ukraine-Zeitung*, No. 57, 3/29/1942.

w)   –, No. 175, 8/14/1942.

x)   This figure probably is too low by one-quarter of a million because
(1) for some cities no Jewish population is known at all, and
(2) in the case of several "old" Soviet cities only the population figures for 1926 could be obtained; not only did the Soviet census of 1926 understate the Jewish population, since 1926 the huge industrialization program had been set in motion, in the course of which many rural Jews migrated to the cities.

79

certainly too low. *Table 6* shows that the Slavic cities suffered much more extensive deportations; unfortunately, rates were available for only one-fifth of the urban inhabitants of the Slavic cities which made up the lion's share, while in the case of Baltic cities – whose urban population amounted to just six per cent of the pre-war population of all Soviet cities occupied by Germany during the war – data for more than half the urban population was available. In short, the Baltic cities are overrepresented in *Table 6*; but inasmuch as they registered relatively low evacuation losses, the average evacuation rate for the entire Soviet urban population turns out to be too low.

The weighted average – evacuation rates of Baltic and Slavic cities multiplied by their share of the pre-war population – is nearer 55%:

	Baltic Cities	Eastern Polish Cities	Eastern Ruman. Cities	"Old" Soviet Cities	All Soviet Cities
Rate of evacuation as shown in *Tabelle 6*:	26 %	60 %	52 %	56 %	50 %
Weight: Share of the Baltic, eastern Polish an "old" Soviet urban population in per cent of the entire urban population of the regions later occupied by Germany	6 %	11 %	3 %	83 %	100 %
Probable evacuation rate of the entire pre-war urban population of the occupied Soviet territories	1,6 %	6,6 %	1,6 %	45 % =	55 %

In order to show the varying degrees of evacuation more clearly, these 48 cities were divided into three groups – according to the severity of population loss – and entered on *Chart 1*. As expected, the Baltic cities are to be found in the group with the lowest evacuation rates, while the Slavic cities – with few exceptions – showed high evacuation rates throughout. It even appears that the western Soviet cities suffered greater percentage losses than those further east!

The element of surprise which is cited regularly today as one reason for the swift German advance, cannot be substantiated from the evacuation and deportation rates. Surprising is rather that the Soviet cities near the German frontier, occupied in part by German troops during the very first days of the war, had up to two-thirds of their population removed by the Soviets.

Certainly, the high rates of evacuation for the White Russian and western Ukrainian cities prove two points:

a) Prof. Lorimer's findings, that the Soviets had begun to evacuate the civilian urban population near the frontier some time *before* war erupted, are correct and

b) the assertion that the fast German advance delivered the largest part of local urban population into German hands is simply wrong!

These numbers show quite clearly that the clearing actions of the Soviets were extremely successful. Even though millions were evacuated by force, the Soviet measures were facilitated by the circumstance that a large number of the evacuees moved willingly, at least without much opposition. This is especially true of Ukrainian communists in leading positions and probably even more so of the non-Ukrainians who controlled the peasant Ukrainian population in this Soviet Republic in the name of Moscow – the Russians and the Jews.

Ukrainians were in the minority in their own cities; only 47.4% of all city people in the SSR Ukraine were Ukrainians and the remaining 52.6% were largely accounted for by Russians (25%) and Jews (23%). Both of these latter two nationalities occupied most of the important positions in industry, party and administration; in the eyes of the Ukrainians they represented the long and heavy hand of Moscow. The entire grotesque situation is depicted in the professional structure of the Ukraine's pre-war population:[79]

Education and Professions	Ukrainians	Russians	Jews
1) Among 1,000 inhabitants were in			
– primary colleges	8%	13%	24%
– secondary colleges	10%	24%	60%
2) Public officials and employees:			
– enterprise management	34%	20%	41%
– "arts"	27%	31%	36%
– doctors and medical aides	38% (mainly orderlies	23%	32% (mainly doctors)
3) Industrial blue- and white-collar workers	40%	22%	32%
4) Construction	38%	51%	?
5) Mining	31%	58%	?
6) Servants	60%	28%	5%

Naturally, the much larger income disparities in the Soviet Union enlarged the gap between the masses of the Ukrainian population on the one side and the Russians and especially the Jews on the other. John Scott, for example, mentions the following earnings patterns for 1933:[80]

Untrained laborer	100 roubles monthly	
Qualified worker	300 "	"
Engineer (without experience)	400–500 "	"
Engineer (practical experience)	600–800 "	"
Administrators, directors, etc.	800–3000 "	"

Whatever changes in income may have occurred until 1941, it is certain that there was no equalization of the drastic income disparities in the interim period.

The Ukrainians not only constituted a minority in their own cities, they were the real proletarians, while Russians and Jews occupied the socially and economically more lucrative positions. The idea that the subjugated Ukrainian population might not behave very friendly towards the Russian and Jewish upper classes after liberation from the Soviet yoke, certainly must have crossed the mind of many of these "foreigners." Under the circumstances an evacuation must have appeared as the lesser evil to large sections of both minorities in the Ukraine. In White Russia, the situation was not very different.

For the Soviet government this proved to be a favorable starting position from which to evacuate the urban population. The politically more reliable non-Ukrainian population groups accounted for more than 50% of the urban inhabitants. Secondly, the two large minorities – Russians and Jews – occupied mostly leading and specialist positions in industry and administration, whereas Ukrainians were to be found largely in the lower ranks. Thirdly, the two population groups which were most valuable under the circumstances on account of their better training, experience and attitudes, i.e. the Russians and the Jews, showed a considerably greater willingness to go on the uncertain journey to the east.

The fact that the evacuated population included a relatively large share of women and children must be explained by the phenomenon of the eminent role of women in the economic life in Communist societies; no doubt, even a dictatorship would find it difficult to separate these working mothers from their children. Also, considerations of maintaining morale in the case of these minorities certainly called for the evacuation of the closest relatives as well.

Quite obviously, the Soviet evacuation measures were very well organized in anticipation of the coming German-Soviet conflict. If, as happened in Melitopol and Mariupol both of which fell into German hands in the autumn of 1941, a relatively large part of the population remained behind this was simply the exception to the rule. German war reports mention that both cities were taken by surprise action – apparently catching the Soviets off guard – and that for this reason the destruction inflicted by the Soviets was relatively minimal. Another indication of the Soviet expectation of the German attack is the Soviet success of taking with them almost the entire rolling stock of their railways: 40% of the railroad network was in German hands, but they captured only 5% of the rolling equipment.

Finally, reports of the German administration of the conquered territories provide a glimpse of the singlemindedness with which the Communists carried out their evacuation program. We mentioned before that non-Ukrainian population groups dominated Ukrainian cities. German publications show though that this picture changed drastically in the course of these evacuations. Many cities, i.e. Vinnitsa, Dnepropetrovsk, Kirovograd, Chernigov, Kherson, etc., all of a sudden had a Ukrainian majority which in some cases attained 80% and more.[81] In other words, the Soviets geared their evacuation actions to very particular population segments, namely, public officials, party functionaries, specialized industrial blue- and white-collar workers, artisans and the so-called intelligentsia. But since the Ukrainians had been regarded to be politically unreliable, educational and other training facilities were made available to them within narrow limits. As a consequence, the Ukrainian – unless he was active in agriculture – usually performed the less demanding jobs. In short, in their understandable attempt to save that part of the population which was most valuable for their own war effort and, vice versa, to prevent the Germans from making use of their skills, the Soviets evacuated above all the Russians and the Jews.

Therefore, the obviously much higher evacuation ratios for the Slavic regions as compared to the Baltic countries are not the result of longer periods of preparation before the war. Decisive was whether or not the cities contained large minorities which, at the same time, were dominant in the management of enterprises and in public administration. These criteria were met by the Ukrainian and the White Russian, but generally not by the Baltic cities. It is no coincidence that the Latvian cities of Daugavpils and Rezekne registered large evacuation ratios. In this exceptional case, the native Latvian population was in the minority in both cities while the Russian and Jewish inhabitants together accounted for 40% to 50% before the war; in contrast, the remaining urban population of Latvia was largely of Latvian origin, with the Russian and Jewish elements averaging about 17%.[82]

Chart 1 shows the eastern frontlines as of July 1, July 11 and August 20, 1941. It also shows which Soviet cities were occupied (or encircled) by Axis troops within the first ten days, during the second ten-day period and the following 40-day period, and after the sixtieth fighting day. The evacuation ratios for the cities were taken from *Table 6*.

Comparing these four time periods with the *average* evacuation ratios of the Baltic and Slavic cities, one obtains a remarkable development (*Table 7*). In general, Ukrainian and White Russian cities occupied during the first ten fighting days and containing large Jewish populations had been more thoroughly evacuated by the Soviets than the Slavic cities to the east which were occupied as late as September and October!

Also, the fact that the evacuation ratios of the Baltic and Slavic cities did not increase as time elapsed but actually decreased, allows the following conclusions to be drawn:

a) The Soviets did indeed begin to evacuate the frontier towns before the start of the hostilities. This action was facilitated by the circumstance that the western Soviet regions were not very highly industrialized and that the urban population was accordingly relatively small.

b) As the German military successes continued, the industrial areas were drawn into the fighting arena; consequently, it became more and more difficult to withdraw not only the retreating Red Army but also the growing volume of machinery and the millions of the civilian population; as a result, the evacuation ratios for the cities began to decrease as the war progressed.

Table 7
Soviet Evacuation of Baltic and Slavic Cities
by Periods of Time

Period of German Occupation	Evacuation in Per Cent	
	Baltic Cities	Slavic Cities
1st–10th day of war (6.22.–7.1.1941)	29 %	60 %
11th–20th day of war (7.2.–7.11.1941)	25 %	59 %
21st–60th day of war (7.12.–8.20.1941)	21 %	55 %
After the 60th day of war (after 8.20.1941)	–	54 %
	26 %	57 %

Source: *Chart 1* and *Table 6*.

The size of the cities was of no major consequence for the evacuation program. Large cities with a population of a quarter of a million and small towns with fewer than 50,000 inhabitants were treated alike; all of them averaged evacuation ratios of around 50%.

Number of Cities	City Size (in 1,000)	Pre-war Population	Evacuated Inhabitants Persons	Per Cent
6	> 250	3,150,500	1,744,539	55 %
21	50–250	2,744,696	1,238,862	45 %
64	< 50	658,900	299,679	45 %

(Note: The low evacuation rate of the smaller towns is due to the relatively large number of small Baltic cities in this group).

There are no indications whatever that the distance from the German frontier or the size of the city had any direct connection with the extent of the evacuation. The Soviets concentrated their evacuation efforts above all on the White Russian and the Ukrainian cities with their large, dominant minorities – the Russians and the Jews.

Depopulated Ukraine

The German authorities embarked on a rather extensive program of registering the population that remained behind. Unfortunately, the largest part of these statistics is not obtainable. But even the sorry remains provide enough clues to permit a size-up of the Soviet evacuation effort. Regretfully, precise pre-war figures which would allow an exact determination of the extent of the evacuation are not available either.

The local population living under German administration in the RK Ukraine numbered 16.91 million as of January 1, 1943. The total number of inhabitants – classified by general districts, areas and counties – was published in the *Zentralblatt des Reichskommissars für die Ukraine*.[83]

General District	Area in sq.km	Inhabitants
1. Wolhynia-Podolia	80,508	4,211,916
2. Shitomir	64,800	2,916,890
3. Kiev	71,790	4,455,927
4. Nikolaev	46,880	1,920,253
5. Dnepropetrovsk	52,398	2,743,041
6. Crimea (Tauria)	22,900	661,981
RK Ukraine	339,276	16,910,008

German estimates of the pre-war population pertain either only to January 1939 or else they just mention rough ranges within which the probable pre-war population size was estimated to have been. The *Jahrbuch für Weltpolitik 1943*, for example, cites the figure of 21.5 million without mentioning the year to which it applies;[84] the context, however, makes it apparent that the above figure refers to the year 1939 as far as "old" Soviet areas are concerned and to the year 1931 for the former eastern Polish areas located in the RK Ukraine. If one adds the population increase likely to have occurred between those dates and mid-1941 – perhaps 1.2 million – the pre-war population of the RK Ukraine must have numbered *more* than 22.5 million; however, the Germans found less than 17 million. One-quarter of the population had disappeared.

The secret documents of the German Economy Staff East put the number of the pre-war population in a range between 20 and 25 million; this, of course, could not be used as a basis for calculating the evacuation ratio.[85]

Luckily, the Soviet census of 1959 provided some comparable statistics for the year 1939.[86] These indicate that those Ukrainian oblasts which remained outside the RK Ukraine under German military rule contained 10.98 million people in early 1939, 51% of whom lived in the cities. The oblasts later administered by the RK Ukraine were populated by 18.25 million inhabitants of whom only 27% were urban. The Rumanian-administered oblast Odessa contained 2.07 million people in 1939 (0.78 million in the cities). This means the area encompassed later by the RK Ukraine included only 60% of the 31 million inhabitants of the "old" SSR Ukraine; in the case of the urban population it was even less, namely, 43%! The industrial part of the "old" SSR Ukraine obviously remained outside the RK Ukraine. Inasmuch as the Soviet evacuation efforts were concentrated on the urban population, it is to be expected that the share of evacuees in the RK Ukraine should have been below the general average of around 30%.

Of the 16.91 million people of the RK Ukraine several millions lived in the former Polish provinces Polesia and Wolhynia as well as the former Soviet SSR White Russia. Fortunately, the German statistics on the RK Ukraine were detailed enough that it was possible to determine the population within those areas: In former Polish Polesia and Wolhynia there were 2.78 million and in the part of the former Soviet SSR White Russia 0.48 million. Deducting both numbers from the 16.91 million of the total RK Ukraine, we obtain 13.65 million people in the "old" Soviet areas of the German-occupied RK Ukraine. Before the war, this area had a population of 18.25 million;[87] obviously, one-quarter of the total population had disappeared.

Before the war, the greater portion of the Ukrainian urban population, however, was concentrated in the eastern Ukraine which remained under German military rule. Inasmuch as the Soviets concentrated their evacuation efforts on the cities and the share of the urban population was over 50% in the eastern Ukraine, it is certain that the portion of the population evacuated there was comparably larger than in the western Ukraine. Quite probably, almost every third inhabitant of the Ukraine had been deported or evacuated by the Soviets before the Germans occupied that region.

The degree of urbanization in the Soviet Union increased from west to east and Soviet evacuation measures concentrated above all on the urban population important to the armaments industry. Thus, as the German-Soviet battlefront moved eastward an ever larger share of the population had been removed by the Soviets, despite the fact that the urban evacuation ratio tended to decrease at the same time. As a result, while westernmost areas lost "only" one-sixth of their total population, the western "old" Ukraine suffered a loss of one-fourth and the highly industrialized Donets basin and eastern Ukraine may even have registered a population decline of up to 40%.

Chart 1

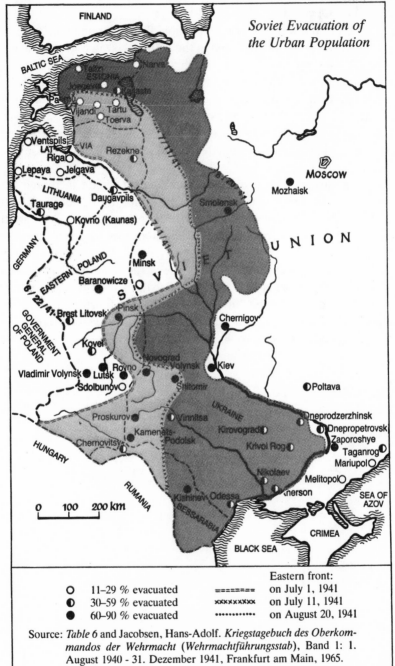

Soviet Evacuation of the Urban Population

FINLAND

BALTIC SEA

ESTONIA
Narva

Jõgeva
Rakvere

Parnu
Viljandi
Tartu
Toerva

Ventspils
LAT.
Riga
VIA
Rezekne

Lepaya
Jelgava

LITHUANIA
Taurage
Daugavpils

Kovno (Kaunas)

Smolensk

MOSCOW
Mozhaisk

GERMANY

EASTERN POLAND
Minsk

6/22/41
Baranowicze

S O V I E T   U N I O N

GOVERNMENT GENERAL OF POLAND

Brest Litovsk
Pinsk

Chernigov

Kovel

Kiev

Vladimir Volynsk
Lutsk
Rovno
Novograd Volynsk
Shitomir

Sdolbunov
Poltava

Proskurov
Vinnitsa
Dneprodzerzhinsk

Kamenets-Podolsk
Kirovograd
Dnepropetrovsk

Chernovitsy
Krivoi Rog
Zaporoshye

HUNGARY
Taganrog

Mariupol

Nikolaev
Melitopol

Kishinev
Odessa
Kherson

BESSARABIA

SEA OF AZOV

RUMANIA

0   100   200 km

CRIMEA

BLACK SEA

		Eastern front:
○	11–29 % evacuated	======== on July 1, 1941
◐	30–59 % evacuated	xxxxxxxx on July 11, 1941
●	60–90 % evacuated	••••••••••• on August 20, 1941

Source: *Table 6* and Jacobsen, Hans-Adolf. *Kriegstagebuch des Oberkommandos der Wehrmacht* (*Wehrmachtführungsstab*), Band 1: 1. August 1940 - 31. Dezember 1941, Frankfurt am Main, 1965.

Chart 2

Jewish Population in Pre-War Soviet Cities (in per cent)

○	00–15 % of the urban population	
◐	16–30 % of the urban population	
●	31–53 % of the urban population	

Eastern front:
======== on July 1, 1941
xxxxxxxxx on July 11, 1941
············ on August 20, 1941

Source: *Table 6* and *Chart 1*.

FOURTH CHAPTER

The Jewish Fate in the Soviet Union: 1941-1945

Soviet Jews in the German Sphere of Influence

The Jewish population was accorded a very special attention within the framework of the Soviet clearing measures. The Zionist Institute of Jewish Affairs (Institute) wrote for instance:

> In numerous cities and towns, particularly in the Ukraine and White Russia, Jews were among the first to be evacuated.[1]

The reason for this preferential treatment was seen by the Institute to be connected with the high percentage of Jews in the Soviet administration, among the office and blue-collar workers and the intelligentsia; it added:

> For this reason, despite the Army's urgent need for transportation, thousands of trains were provided for evacuation. Thus, not only were hundreds of thousands of human lives saved, but military highways were quickly cleared of millions of refugees.

The Institute emphasized that there was no shortage of time to remove the civilian population, especially in the larger cities such as Kiev, Odessa, Smolensk, etc.:

> ... there was time enough to evacuate the civilian population.[2]

The technical prerequisites had been met and the same means of transportation which brought the masses of the Red Army to the western front, were used on their return trip for the evacuation and the deportation of the civilian population. Also, one must assume that the Soviets, following their own example of the spring of 1940 when they deported the Polish-Jewish refugees from eastern Poland to Siberia, were not overly concerned with the comfort of the population scheduled to be removed.

Shitomir, which contained 50,000 Jews before the war, was presented by the Institute as an example of the relatively high percentage of Jews evacuated. Of these, 44,000 (88%) left with the Soviet troops; considering that 53,000 of the 95,000 inhabitants (minimum) of Shitomir had been evacuated, the Jewish share amounted to four-fifths of all evacuees![3]

Minsk, too, confirms Zionist reports of a preferential treatment accorded the Jews by the Soviets in the evacuation program. After the occupation of Minsk within the first few days of the war, General Halder found no more than 100,000 of the former population of 240,000 (1939); the rest had fled, been evacuated or deported.[4] Kube, the German Reich Commissar for White Russia, stated that all but a few thousand of the Jews of Minsk had gone with the Red Army.[5] Before the war, there were approximately 90,000 Jews in Minsk.[6] Assuming that the words "few thousand" referred to a figure of 5,000, we obtain the following picture: About 60% of all evacuees (85,000 of 140,000) were Jews even though they constituted only 38% of the population; the Jewish population was removed almost in its entirety, in the case of the non-Jewish population it was just over one-third.

A Soviet Union specialist, Joshua Rothenberg of the Brandeis University, put it bluntly:

> Much of the Jewish population of the conquered territories escaped annihilation by fleeing *before* the invading armies arrived.[7]

The *Judaica* says that most of the 7,000 Jews of Lepaya (a few miles from the German border) escaped *before* German troops occupied the city six days after hostilities began. In Lithuania, too, which was liberated from the Soviet yoke within a week, a considerable number of Jews escaped to the interior of the Soviet Union even while the German invasion was in progress.[8]

Baranowicze, a town with a very large Jewish population, was populated by just 10% of its former population even though occupation by German troops occurred within days after they crossed the border.[9] Of Vitebsk's 100,000 Jews only 22,000 remained behind according to a report by the Soviet Jewish author David Bergelson of the Jewish Anti-Fascist Committee in the Moscow newspaper *Eynikeyt* dated 9/5/1942.[10] Reitlinger, who estimated the number of Jews in Soviet White Russia (borders of 1941) at 861,000, said the Germans found no more than 172,000 of them.[11]

Kishinev in Bessarabia was occupied by the Axis on July 17, 1941. The Rumanian count of August 16, 1941, however found only 201 Jews of the former 70,000 living there before the war.[12] The non-Jewish population apparently suffered a loss of roughly 15,000 because of deportations; this is equivalent to a rate of "only" 20-25%. Of the approximately 200,000 Bessarabian Jews the Soviets had removed all but 6,882; fewer than 5% could be traced by the census.[13]

The situation was very similar in the Ukrainian town of Novograd Volynsk which also was located very close to the border and contained a very large Jewish population; only 10% of the town's inhabitants remained behind when the Germans occupied it three days after war broke out. As for Kiev, the Institute said:

> In Kiev, practically the entire Jewish youth left the city together with the Soviet Army. Only elderly people remained behind.[14]

The Zionist sources are unanimous that the evacuation or deportation of the Baltic Jews and the native population was started some time *before* the war began. The Institute dates the initiation of mass arrests and deportations in Lithuania at *ten days before* hostilities started.[15] The *Judaica* declared that

> the phase *before* the German attack on Lithuania was marked by deportations to Siberia. ... In mid-June 1941, *one week before* the German-Soviet war, many people, including Jews, were hastily deported as politically unreliable ...[16]

And the *Year Book* complained:

> The evacuation of Baltic Jews was not started until *a week before* the actual invasion.[17]

German investigations after the conquest of the Baltic countries confirm these reports. It was found that the Soviets had initiated sudden arrests, deportations and murders in the night from June 13 to 14, 1941; these atrocities continued until the liberation of these countries by the German army.[18]

Thus, if in a larger town like Dnepropetrovsk only 20,000 of the former 100,000 Jews remained behind[19] – German reports however mention less than 1,000[20] – then this is not very surprising in view of the Soviet preparations for a mass removal in case of war and the available time interval until German troops reached the larger cities. Melitopol and Mariupol, two large cities on the Sea of Azov where only a quarter of the total population was missing because German troops had taken these cities in a surprise action, are just the exception to the rule; still, in the first city only 18% of the Jewish population was present and in the second it had disappeared completely.[21]

However, it is truly remarkable that the towns which were located far to the west and which contained often very large Jewish populations had been almost completely denuded of their Jewish inhabitants by the time the German troops took control of them. This was only possible because – as Zionist sources confirm – the evacuation program had been put into action long *before* the war began and because the Soviet clearing measures even allowed for a removal of the population as the German invasion was in progress.

The large degree of urbanization and concentration of the Jewish population certainly aided this effort. In the "old" Ukraine 39% of the Jews lived in just four cities – Kiev, Odessa, Kharkov and Dnepropetrovsk none of which were occupied or cut off until 7½ weeks after June 22, 1941.[22] In total, 85.5% of the Ukrainian Jews lived in the cities in 1939; in White Russia it was 87.8%.

This advantage was reinforced by the circumstance that the population group upon which the Soviets put the greatest emphasis in their evacuation efforts consisted of government officials, party functionaries, specialists and office workers; in this group the Jewish share was far in excess of their numerical size.[23]

No wonder that David Bergelson was able to declare at the end of 1942 (!) that 80% of the Jews in the conquered areas had been evacuated. He continued in the Moscow newspaper *Eynikeyt* of December 5, 1942 – 1½ years after the war started:

> *The evacuation saved a decisive majority of Jews* of the Ukraine, White Russia, Lithuania, and Latvia. According to information coming from Vitebsk, Riga and other large centers which have been captured by the Fascists, there were few Jews there when the Germans arrived. ... This means that a majority of the Jews of these cities was evacuated in time by the Soviet government.[24]

The Soviet poet Itzik Feffer declared formally in New York during the war that the Red Army "saved a few million Jews!" On March 15, 1943(!), *Eynikeyt* reported D. Zaslavsky telling a plenary session of the Soviet-sponsored Jewish Anti-Fascist Committee: "The Red Army saved the Jewish people at the most critical hour of its history."[25]

Also, the fact that in many cities for which Jewish evacuation ratios were ascertained – e.g. Baranowicze, Lepaya, Novograd Volynsk,

Minsk, Kishinev – much more than 80% of the Jewish population was gone even though these cities were occupied by German forces within days after hostilities began, points toward an almost total evacuation by the Soviet authorities.

In this connection, we should refer back to the findings in the Third Chapter which show that the evacuation ratios of the Baltic cities were far below those of the Slavic cities. It is truly astonishing how close the relationship is between the evacuation ratios of the urban population and the relative size of the Jewish population in those cities. On *Chart 2* we recorded the Jewish population share of individual Soviet cities – to the extent available. Quite obviously, in the center area of the war theater where the evacuation ratios were very high (see *Chart 1*), the Jewish share of the urban population also was very large.

The Evacuation of Wolhynia

The General District Wolhynia-Podolia in the RK Ukraine encompassed not only the "old" Soviet areas in Podolia, but also the former Polish province of Wolhynia and the largest part of former Polesia. The northern sections of Polesia had been incorporated in the RK Ostland. Thus, the only area for which we can obtain relatively exact population figures for the periods *before* and *after* the German occupation is Wolhynia.

The territory of the former Polish province of Wolhynia included in the General District of Wolhynia-Podolia covered the areas of Dubno, Gorochov, Kostopol, Kovel, Lutsk, Kremianets, Lubomil, Rovno, Sarny and Vladimir Volynsk;[26] in this region the Polish census of 1931 registered a total population of 2,085,574, including 207,792 Jews.[27]

For years the birth rate of the non-Jewish population was around 2.7% or even slightly more, while that of the Jewish population was only 1.8% in 1931 – a drop by 33% since the early 1920's. Applying a mortality rate of 1.2% the surplus of births over deaths must have registered 1.5% in the case of the non-Jewish and 0.6% in the case of the Jewish population. It may be assumed that this positive growth rate was reduced in the course of the economic crisis of the 1930's, especially as far as the Jews are concerned. For the period after 1932 one should, therefore, apply natural population changes of 1.4% and 0.5%, respectively.

In the First Chapter we referred already to the enormous emigration of young male Jews in the inter-war period. For the years 1932-1939, we also calculated a Jewish emigration loss of 15%. To be sure, there is no reliable information as to whether or not this emigration was as high among the eastern Polish Jews, but the even more unfavorable male/female ratio of 86/100 (after adjusting for men in military service) of the age group "15 to 29 years" in Wolhynia indicates that emigration among the eastern Polish Jews was possibly even higher than that of all Polish Jews, certainly not lower.

Table 8 provides details on Wolhynia's total population as recorded by the Polish census of 1931 as well as adjustments for population growth and Jewish emigration thereafter. Furthermore, both population groups have been classified by age in order to show that age group separately which later became subject to Soviet military draft calls. On this basis, one should have expected to find 2,374,663 inhabitants in Wolhynia in 1942 under "normal" circumstances, including 186,585 Jews and 585,134 males (Jewish and non-Jewish) of the years of birth 1897-1926.

The German count, however, found only 1,984,406 inhabitants as of January 1, 1943;[28] more than 16%, or 390,257 were missing. But since this figure included those former Red Army men who had been released from prisoner-of-war camps in the meantime, the actual number of missing people right after the occupation must have been somewhat larger yet. The question is which nationalities and which age groups accounted for the bulk of these 390,257 missing persons.

If it were true that the Soviets were unable to evacuate the civilian population because of the rapid German advance, all or most of the 390,257 missing should be allocated to the young men of the years 1897-1926 subject to the Soviet draft. In this case, of the 585,134 in this age group only about 200,000 remained behind; the majority would have gone with the retreating Soviets. Applied to all male age groups, the Soviets would have taken one-third of the entire male population with them and the male share of the population would have fallen from 49% to 39%.

This interpretation contradicts the fact that even though German reports tell of huge losses among the male population of the occupied territories, no deportation of this magnitude among the economically most active population part has ever been mentioned. Fortunately, German population counts in the Baltic countries which, like eastern Poland, were incorporated into the Soviet empire just prior to the war gave separate figures for the two sexes; the statistics indicate that thousands of families were deported by the Soviets before the Germans arrived, but that the majority of the evacuees were male. And still, the male share of the total Baltic population had shrunk to only just over 46%[29] even though

Table 8
Development of the Wolhynian Population: 1931 until the German Occupation

Year of Birth	Total Population			Non-Jews		Jews	
	Total	Male	Female	Male	Female	Male	Female
A) According to Polish Census of December 9, 1931:							
Years 1897–1926	1,217,412	595,630	621,782	539,427	559,007	56,203	62,775
Other Years	868,162	425,418	442,744	382,515	396,833	42,903	45,911
Total	2,085,574	1,021,048	1,064,526	921,942	955,840	99,106	108,686
B) Population after correction for the number of births over deaths for the period 1931 to 1942 (1.4% and 0.5% p.a. for the non-Jewish and Jewish natural rate of increase):							
Years 1897–1926	1,217,412	595,630	621,782	539,427	559,007	56,203	62,775
Other Years	1,190,176	586,425	603,751	537,663	551,981	48,762	51,770
Total	2,407,588	1,182,055	1,225,533	1,077,090	1,110,988	104,965	114,545
C) Population after correction for Jewish emigration of 15% for the period 1932 to 1939 (two-thirds of the immigrants were applied to the years 1897-1926 and one-third to the other years):							
Years 1897–1926	1,195,461	585,134	610,327	539,427	559,007	45,707	51,320
Other Years	1,179,202	581,177	598,025	537,663	551,981	43,514	46,044
Total	2,374,663	1,166,311	1,208,352	1,077,090	1,110,988	89,221	97,364

Source: *Drugi Powszechny Spis Ludności Z Dn. 9.XII 1931 R.*: Mieszkania I Gospodarstwa Domowe. Ludność. Stosunki Zawodowe; Województwo Wołyńskie; Główny Urząd Statystyczny Rzeczypospolitej Polskiej. Statystyka Polski. Seria C. Zeszyt 70 (*Deuxième Recensement Général de la Population du 9 Décembre 1931*: Logements et Ménages. Population. Profession. Warsaw 1938.

large parts of the Baltic countries, especially Estonia, were conquered as late as eight weeks after the occupation of Wolhynia.

The Soviets deported especially the urban minorities – by family – which belonged to the pillars of an industrial society; in Wolhynia, this was true particularly of the Jews. The enormous evacuation ratios of the former eastern Polish cities – e.g. Brest Litovsk, Vladimir Volynsk, Kovel, Baranowicze, Lutsk, Rovno, Sdolbunov and Pinsk all of which registered rates of between 25 and 90% (see *Table 6*) and may have averaged 50% if we allow for an increase in the urban population since 1931 – prove that the roughly 400,000 missing persons in Wolhynia were *not* to be found predominantly among the male age groups subject to the Soviet draft.

Everything seems to indicate that the above mentioned evacuation ratios for the eastern Polish cities were quite typical. If we assume that the urban population of this region had increased by 50,000 since 1931 and if we add the population of the Jewish "shtetls" as well, we obtain a total urban population of roughly 400,000 for the former Polish province for mid-1941; of these, 200,000 were deported by the Soviets.

The sex composition of Wolhynia's population probably was similar to what we found in the Baltic countries after the German occupation; there, the male/female ratio was 46/54. Consequently, Wolhynia's remaining population before and after the German occupation looks as follows:

	Total (%)	Male (%)	Female (%)
Before occupation	2,374,663 (100)	1,166,311 (49)	1,208,352 (51)
After occupation	1,984,406 (100)	912,827 (46)	1,071,579 (54)
Missing persons	390,257 (100)	253,484 (65)	136,773 (35)

Now, the question is, how these missing persons should be divided between the Jews and the non-Jews. Between 1931 and WWII, urbanization proceeded in eastern Poland as almost everywhere else and then there was the emigration of large numbers of Jews. Thus, the Jewish population constituted roughly 50% of the Wolhynian urban population in 1931, but just before WWII this was hardly the case; by then, their share must have been less than that. On the other hand, it is a fact that the Jews were much more affected by the Soviet evacuation program than other population segments.

The large number of women among the missing persons (35%) points to the evacuation of tens of thousands of families. The population group in this category probably consisted of artisans, doctors, specialists, the intelligentsia, office workers, etc. among all of whom the Jews may have had an absolute majority. Also, the willingness to be evacuated probably was much greater among the Jewish families than among the Polish and Ukrainian.

In view of the almost grotesque relationship between evacuated Jews and non-Jews in Soviet cities – e.g. Minsk, Shitomir, Lepaya, Dnepropetrovsk – and the political unreliability of the Polish and Ukrainian population segments in Wolhynia, it would indeed have been very surprising if less than 60% of the evacuated female civilians would have belonged to the Jewish group, particularly as almost half the urban population was Jewish. Applying a matching male share corresponding to the composition of the pre-war Jewish and non-Jewish populations and, finally, subtracting the evacuated family members (as calculated) from the total number of missing persons, one obtains 125,243 young men subject to the draft; these males probably were drafted directly from the countryside into the Red Army. In tableform it looks as follows:

Total population *before* the German occupation	of which: Missing (%) persons	Male	Female	Population group
2,374,663	390,257 (16)	253,484	136,773	(Missing females: 60% Jewish, 40% non-Jewish)
186,585	157,265 (84)	75,201	82,064	Jewish civilians
2,188,078	232,992 (11)	53,040	54,709	non-Jew. civil.
		125,243		Men subject to draft

(The computed figure of 125.243 "drafted" individuals, of course, is much too low since some of the male "civilians" certainly were also drafted into the Red Army).

Thus, it seems that more than 80% of Wolhynia's Jewish population was removed by the Soviets. Considering that the vast majority of the Jewish population of many Soviet cities conquered by German troops during the first ten days of the war had been removed by the Soviets, the computed ratio of 84% evacuated Jews in Wolhynia is quite realistic. To be sure, compared to the "old" Soviet cities which registered Jewish evacuation ratios of over 80% (*Table 9*), the Soviet evacuation of the Jewish population of these Wolhynian cities close to the German frontier is quite impressive, but not surprising (see *Chart 1*).

Before the war, 2.03 million Jews lived in the "old" Soviet areas occupied by the Axis troops (Second Chapter). More than half of them were concentrated in the cities listed on *Table 9* and fewer than one-fifth fell into German hands. Reitlinger put it like this:

> Not only did the bulk of the three million Jews of pre-war Soviet Russia escape into the interior but also a very large proportion of the 1,800,000 Jews of the annexed territories. ... in the historic towns of the pre-industrial Russian Ukraine, Winnitsa, Zhitomir, Berdichev, Uman, Nikolaev, and Kherson only a quarter or a fifth of the Jews stayed on and this was equally true of the enormous Jewish agglomerations to the East, the towns along the Dnieper, Kiev, Kharkov, and Dniepropetrowsk. Further East still in the Donetz and Kuban basins and North of the Caucasus only a small percentage of the Jews awaited the Germans.[37]

The picture unfolding here is one where Wolhynia fits perfectly into the overall clearing and evacuation program of the Soviet leadership. No matter whether we turn to the Baltic countries, former eastern Poland, White Russia or the Ukraine, the bulk of the Jewish population of all of these Soviet areas had been removed either *before* hostilities started or withdrew together with the retreating Red Army to the east on a more or less voluntary basis. Reitlinger's admission certainly is not subject to suspicion and matches the evacuation ratios for the Jewish population of the "old" Soviet cities as listed on *Table 9*.

The fact that the main area of settlement of the urbanized Soviet Jews was still concentrated in the western Soviet Union at the beginning of the war, did not hinder the Soviet efforts to remove the Jewish population to the east. Quite the opposite is the case; because urbanization was much lower in the west than in the east and the bulk of industry was to be found in the eastern Ukraine, the Soviets were in a position to devote a greater proportion of their efforts to the evacuation of the urban population of the western territories than was possible in the industrial east.

Table 9
Soviet Evacuation of the Jewish Population of "Old" Soviet Cities

Cities	Jewish Population		Evacuation in percent
	before Evacuation	after Evacuation	
Minsk[5][6]	90,000	5,000 (est.)	94 %
Shitomir[3]	50,000	6,000	88 %
Novograd-Volynsk[14]	?	?	90 %
Vitebsk[10]	100,000	22,000	78 %
Dnepropetrovsk[19]	100,000	20,000	80 %
Nikolaev[30]	30,000	5,000	83 %
Kherson[30]	30,000	5,000	83 %
Poltava[31]	35,000	1,500	96 %
Odessa	180,000 [32]	30–60,000 [33]	67–83 %
Melitopol[21]	11,000	2,000	82 %
Kharkov	130,000 [a]	20,000 [31]	85 %
Kirovograd	18,400 [b]	6,000 [36]	min. 67 %
Chernigov	10,600 [b]	300 [21]	97 %
Mariupol	7,300 [b]	none [21]	100 %
Taganrog	2,700 [b]	none [21]	100 %
Vinnitsa	21,800 [b]	}	
Kiev	175,000 [34]		
Uman	25,300 [b]	50–62,000 [35]	75–80 %
Berdichev	28,400		
	1,045,500	173–215,000	79–83 % [c]

(For notes and sources see next page)

Sources and Notes (Table 9)

(a) Reitlinger[31] said the last Jewish census figures for Kharkov pertain to 1926 (81,139); until 1939, Kharkov's total population more than doubled to 833,400 but it is unlikely that the city's Jewish population doubled, too. On the other hand, the *Judaica*[21] notes that Kharkov, Kiev, Odessa and Dnepropetrovsk contained 39% of the Ukraine's Jewish population in 1939. This means that 585,000 of the 1.5 million Ukrainian Jews were accounted for by these four cities; the Jewish population of the last three towns added up to 455,000. Consequently, 130,000 remain for Kharkov.

(b) For these cities no more recent population data for Soviet Jews are available. The listed Jewish population figures pertain to the year 1926 and in the case of Taganrog, Mariupol, Vinnitsa, Chernigov and Kirovograd they have been taken from *Table 6*; for Uman and Berdichev Hilberg's[38] Jewish population figures refer to 1920 and 1923, respectively. It is all but certain that the Jewish population of these cities was considerably higher in the year 1939 than in 1920, 1923 or in the census year 1926, because the census of 1926 tended to underestimate the Jewish population and because many Jews had moved from the smaller country towns into the larger cities in the course of the enforced Soviet industrialization program.

(c) The stated evacuation rate of 79-83% is almost certainly too low for the following reasons: (i) for some cities the higher 1939-population figures were not available and the utilized 1926-figures are known to be too low; (ii) Reitlinger[39] writes in the case of Odessa that two-thirds of that city's Jews had been removed by train. Odessa was encircled on August 13, 1941 by the Rumanians and taken on October 16. In the meantime, the Soviets evacuated tens of thousands of Red Army men and civilians, 86,000 soldiers and 15,000 civilians just in the period from October 1 to 10. The number of civilians evacuated in August and September is not known to the author, nor is the percentage of Jews among them. In view of the obvious preference for the Jews in the evacuation of other cities their share must have been large. For these reasons one should assume that the number of Jews who fell into Rumanian hands must have been less than 50,000.

Reitlinger's data are rather informative when attempting to pin down the number of those Jews who remained behind to face German occupation. Providing many examples including evacuation ratios he wrote that the "bulk" of the Jews of pre-war Russia escaped. Since one-third of the Jews found in the Soviet census of 1939 lived outside those areas later to be conquered by Germany, only a small number of the remaining Jews – in absolute and relative terms – of the pre-war Soviet Union can possibly have fallen into German hands. In addition, "a very large proportion," as he puts it, of the 1,800,000 Jews of the annexed areas escaped German control. The conclusion thus is compelling that Reitlinger himself believes the number of Jews who remained behind to be less than a million. Actually, this puts Reitlinger in direct opposition to the usual post-war literature on Soviet Jews.

In early 1941, 3,597,000 Jews lived in the Soviet areas occupied by Axis troops in the course of WWII (see Second Chapter). If only 80% of this number were evacuated during the war, this would be equivalent to 2,877,000. Subtracted from the 3.6 million, one obtains a mere 720,000 as the number of Soviet Jews remaining under German administration. In this connection, a report by the Canadian-Jewish journalist Arthur Raymond Davies, who spent the war years in the Soviet Union as a correspondent and published his impressions and experiences after the war in New York, is rather interesting. Besides his words of praise for the valor of the Jewish Red Army men and partisans, he mentioned a plenary session of the Jewish Anti-Fascist Committee in the autumn of 1944 (!), on the occasion of which its secretary Shachne Epstein reported the evacuation of 3.5 million Jews from the territories occupied by Germany.[40] Epstein's figure of 3.5 million evacuees – which apparently also included the three-quarters of a million Jewish refugees from Poland deported to Siberia in the spring of 1940 – matches our own computations on the number of Jews removed by the Soviets until 1941 and 1942 very well.

We should also remind ourselves that most of these 720,000 Jews in German-occupied Soviet territory belonged to the older age groups, because the Soviets had little interest in the evacuation of additional eaters and also, as one witness before the investigating committe of the US House of Representatives put it, because "the older people who knew the Germans from World War I, they thought that the Germans are not so bad and that they can live better with Germans than the Soviets."[41] The natural mortality rate of a population group consisting mainly of older people, of course, is far higher than for a normal age structure. This should not be forgotten when considering those events, particularly because in this case births were practically non-existent.

Certainly, a large number of these roughly 700,000 remaining Soviet Jews did not survive the war. The age structure itself must have effected a considerable negative natural change. The extremely hard, often fanatical battles between German and Soviet troops happened to take place to a large extent in and around the cities; since almost 90% of the Jews were city dwellers, it is quite probable that the remaining older Jews suffered proportionately greater civilian losses. In addition, there were many pogroms against the Jews initiated by the *local* populations in the Baltic countries, White Russia and in the Ukraine after the Soviet troops pulled back; only the decisive action taken by German and allied troops put a stop to these murderous activities.[42] Shootings of Jewish hostages in retaliation for the murder of German soldiers by the partisans,[43] among whom the Jews were very active according to their own accounts – Soviet statistics mention more than 500,000 German soldiers murdered by partisans[44] – were not at all unusual.

To what extent the taking of hostages among the Jewish population was practiced in the sense of a systematic annihilation program is not our subject. All one needs to do, is to check the pertinent literature of the post-war period in order to appreciate the extraordinary role Jews played during the war as partisans against the German Wehrmacht. Even Dr. M.W. Kempner[45] does not question the taking of hostages as "in accordance with international law." He writes: "Hostages are taken in periods of occupation, in order to keep the population of the occupied territories from committing crimes *against* the occupation forces."[46] Lastly, hunger, cold, epidemics and lacking medical attention among the mainly elderly remaining Jews probably caused many losses.

The Zionist Gregor Aronson mentioned that the Soviet Jew Lev K. Zinger reported in his book *Dos Oifgekumene Folk* (Moscow, 1949) that tens of thousands of Jews could be found in early 1946 in the various smaller and larger towns of the Ukraine, White Russia, Moldavia, Latvia and Lithuania; he cited the following cities:[47]

Kharkov	30,000
Dnepropetrovsk	50,000
Odessa	80,000
Mohilew-Podolsk	3,000
Novograd Volynsk	3,000
Malin	1,000
Czernowitz	70,000

Reitlinger who based his figures on the Moscow newspaper *Eynikeyt* mentioned the same figures for Odessa and Dnepropetrovsk and added

Kiev	100,000
Vinnitsa	14,000
Shitomir	6,000

He remarked, furthermore, "these figures were recorded at a time when the homeward trek from the deep interior had only begun."[48] It is also interesting that Shitomir's population size of 1946 equalled exactly that of the Jews who remained behind to face German occupation in 1941.[49]

In other words, these listed cities which contained a total of about 360,000 Jews in the former German-occupied parts of the Soviet Union represent largely the Jews who survived the war *and* the German occupation. Also, a homeward trek must be understood to mean that these people had been evacuated previously; here, too, Reitlinger contradicts the current literature according to which the rapid German advance prevented the Jews to escape in appreciable numbers.

Nobody knows the number of Jews who survived in the western parts of the Soviet Union at the time the Red Army proceeded to re-occupy that territory. But this extract of only ten cities with a population of 360,000 Jews (early 1946 !) as well as the fact that other Soviet republics – e.g. Moldavia, Lithuania and Latvia which Zinger mentioned by name without providing figures – also were inhabited by thousands of survivors, show that the vast majority of the three-quarters of a million Soviet Jews under German administration survived the war.

The extent of the losses suffered by the Soviet Jews who remained under German control is debatable. It seems that because of their age structure – elderly people predominated – the natural excess of deaths must have reached at least 3% per year;[50] in three occupation years, this adds up to a reduction of 65,000. This means that the Jewish population under German control – the figure of 720,000 probably is too high – was reduced to 655,000. Other losses could have occurred on account of the general negative environment as described above and because of the Jewish participation in partisan activities in violation of international law; all of this makes a further reduction by roughly 10%, or 65,000, to about 590,000 possible. Thus, it would seem that if 360,000 Jews were found in just ten cities in former German-occupied territories in early 1946 and many other thousands survived in other, not specified Soviet cities, our figure of 590,000 surviving Jews after the German retreat seems realistic.

Fate was much worse for the Jews living under Soviet domination during the war. Among the the 750,000 Polish-Jewish refugees, 150-250,000 died from hardships on the way to the east and the north. Those who arrived in Asia were put in labor and concentration camps; as mentioned already, among these unfortunates was also Menachem Begin, the subsequent Jewish IRGUN-terrorist in Palestine and recent recipient of the Nobel Peace Prize.

Even the *Universal* which was quite sympathetic to the Soviet cause in 1943 spoke of "Siberia, where they underwent great hardships."[51] The Joint Distribution Committee which aided the Jewish victims in Siberia and the Russian North during the war with food and medicine was a little more outspoken. In its Bulletin of June 1943 it informed us that the survivors of the deportations had to put up with further privation: "The [Soviet] government gives each refugee from a half to one pound of bread each day. ... Food can only be bought with things. Money has lost its value."[52]

Apart from the monotony of this kind of food supply those tortured people received less than a third of the calories needed for survival – a fatal deficiency in the inhumane environment of Siberian labor and concentration camps. The Jewish author Reitlinger commented:

In Southern Siberia, the death-rate was very high for ... Jews ...[53]

The small number of 157,500 Polish-Jewish refugees returning from Siberia to Poland in 1945/1946 gives us an idea of the terrible fate Jewish deportees from Poland met in Siberia. *600*,000 have *disappeared*. Even if one includes those few who unimaginably preferred to remain in the Soviet Union, the total of the Jewish victims of Soviet labor camps hardly would be affected. The argument that the Soviets forced most of them to stay there after the war does not hold up. The 157,500 returnees left Poland soon after their arrival from Russia to move on to the West. They would have known if a considerable number of their compatriots had been kept in Soviet Russia against their will. But there are no indications of this to be found in post-war literature. Everything seems to point to the horrible fact that *600*,000 Polish-Jewish refugees died in and on the way to Siberia.[54]

Another 2.9 million were evacuated to Siberia shortly before and after the start of the German-Soviet war. The fate of these people is unknown, but the sacrifice of the Jewish refugees from Poland is not a good omen. Certainly, in 1940 foreigners were deported after having refused the citizenship of the workers' and peasants' paradise, proving in this way that they were truly enemies of the glorious Soviet Union, whereas in 1941 the USSR's own citizens were moved to "safety." On the other hand, in 1941 the circumstances were such in many places that the Soviets had to introduce hasty measures; after all, their primary goal was to deny these trained people to the Germans and, in the second place, to save as many good workers for their own war effort. The transport of millions of people in a few weeks across a distant and rather primitive railroad network simply must have been costly in terms of human lives. These people, too, faced a life of hardship and misery in Siberia.

How badly those evacuated and deported Soviet citizens fared in Siberia in 1941/1945 may be gleaned from the words of the Soviet court historian Telpuchowski:

> The provision of accommodations for the *millions* evacuated from the enemy-occupied territories to the areas of the hinterland posed a serious problem. [In re-constructing the transplanted factories the evacuated people] worked under the open sky, quite often in rain and snow. The most elementary lodging facilities were lacking; they had to live in tents and sod huts. Food was scarce. Work continued throughout the day. The workday often lasted from 12 to 14 hours and more.[55]

No comments.

Referring to the mass deportation measures initiated in Lithuania one week *before* June 22, 1941, the *Judaica* says that the deported people were interned in forced labor camps and set to work in coal mines, wood cutting, and other heavy labor.[56] Without question, death must have reaped a terrible harvest under those conditions. After the liberation from the Soviet yoke, the shocked Baltic population told of unimaginable occurrences during the deportation and evacuation measures initiated on June 13/14, 1941. Thousands upon thousands of people simply were shot to death. If persons the Soviets were looking for could not be found, another family member or person living in the same house was taken in their place. The arrested people were crowded into cattle wagons in batches of 50 to 60, the men were separated from their wives, the children torn from their mothers. Doors and ventilation openings were nailed shut; there were no benches. The locked-up people were left to themselves, without food or drink. Many died on the way east. In a car left behind at the Oger railroad station, 60 suffocated children were found. These people were treated worse than cattle.[57]

Some deportees managed to return to Estonia, Latvia and Lithuania; they told of terrible conditions in Soviet territory. People, they said, were being forced to work in the icy cold of the north and east with no other clothes and shoes than those they wore when they were arrested. Medical attention was lacking completely and the persistent undernourishment caused people to die in huge numbers.[58]

It is all but impossible to place a figure on the total number of Jewish victims in Siberia and the Urals. One should keep in mind that the evidence given by Western Zionist sources on the extent of Jewish losses in Siberia hardly can be called objective. The Soviets would never assume moral or financial responsibility. The temptation to keep that number as low as possible is obvious; after all, defeated Germany presented an easy scapegoat to be blamed for all of the Jews who were missing, killed in action or murdered by the Soviets.

The Hungarian Minister in Moscow, Prof. Szekfu, provided a vivid description of the shape in which the Jewish deportees and evacuees returned from Siberia; he said to Dr. Zoltan Klar from the Council of the Budapest Jewish Community:

> ... these people arrived from Siberia in Moscow in a desperate situatiom, sick and enfeebled, starved and bedraggled, in rags, without clothes or any other possessions.[59]

If the condition of the Jews in Siberia was this terrible in 1946, what might the situation have looked like during the war? Obviously, putting the number of Jewish dead in Siberia at 700,000 probably is not enough to allow for all the victims of the barbarian Soviet policy.

But the war itself also created huge gaps in the Jewish population. From 1939 to 1942 200,000 Jews fell in all Allied armies.[60] Deducting the Polish-Jewish soldiers killed in action and the unknown number of killed Jews in the British, French and American forces – in the US Army 550,000 Jews are said to have served during WWII – then it is quite possible that the Red Army suffered 100-150,000 Jewish soldiers killed in action during the first 1½ costly years of war against Germany. In any case, the *Judaica* maintained as late as 1971 that the Soviet-Jewish losses among the soldiers killed "in action" amounted to 200,000.[61]

The "loss" of 157,500 returned Polish-Jewish refugees after the war was compensated by the Soviets by chalking up "gains" among other European Jews. As will be shown in the Sixth Chapter, 65,500 Hungarian

Jews disappeared in the Soviet Union. In addition, the Soviets annexed Ruthenia in 1945 with a Jewish population of probably less than 100,000.

Adding it all up, one obtains the following picture: Of the 5.3 million Jews under Soviet domination in 1939/1940 at least 700,000 lost their lives during the deportation to the east or in the Siberian "accommodations", labor and concentration camps. 200,000 were killed in combat while serving in Red Army and partisan units and a further 130,000 may have died because of the fighting in the cities, pogroms of the *native* population, hunger, epidemics, lack of medical attention, over-aging and, last but not least, because of German retributions against Jewish hostages in retaliation for Germans murdered by partisans. All of these developments may well have caused a loss of over one million. For this reason, one should not expect that more than 4.3 million Jews survived the war in the Soviet Union – a loss of 20% compared to early 1940. In tableform the development looks like this:

Under Soviet domination – 1939/1940		5,337,000
deduct:		
War and deportation losses		
– Jewish Red Army men killed in combat	200,000	
– Deportation and concentration camp losses in Siberia	700,000	
	900,000	
Losses in the German-Soviet theater of war	130,000	
Total losses		1,030,000
Remaining		4,307,000
Other changes:		
Hungarian Jews retained in the USSR[62]	65,500	
Annexation of Ruthenia[62]	86,000	
	151,500	
Jewish refugees returned from the USSR	157,500	6,000
Jewish population in the USSR at the end of WWII (max.)		4,301,000

FIFTH CHAPTER

The Jews in the Post-War Soviet Union

The Survivors

Post-war literature usually puts the number of surviving Jews in the Soviet Union at about two million or even fewer. The *Year Book* arrived at 2,032,500[1] and other Zionist sources mentioned figures as low as 1,500,000. They simply deny the established historical fact that the Soviets succeeded in evacuating the bulk of the Jewish population before and after the German "surprise" attack. If 600,000 Jews served in the Red Army[2] then this must probably be explained by the Soviet evacuation of the male Jews of military age.

Age-specific data on the Jews living before the war in areas never occupied by Germany are not available as far as we know; for this reason, the age structure of the Polish Jews of 1931 was used. On this basis, males aged 16-45 years composed 22.7% of the total Soviet-Jewish population.[3] Before the war, 1.6 million Jews lived in those parts of the Soviet Union never occupied by Germany.[4] 22.7% of 1.6 million amounts to 360,000 male Jews aged 16-45 years in 1941 in the "free" Soviet territories.

It is not likely that all Jews of military age were drafted into the armed forces. Deferments on account of the necessity to leave specialists in industry and administration, physical impairments, etc. hardly permitted more than 70%, i.e. 250,000, to be inducted. This means that 350,000 must have come from the occupied areas. Assuming the same deferment ratio for them, the Soviets must have evacuated 500,000 Jewish males of military age from the occupied territories.

On the basis of these calculations we arrived at 2.1 million. Deducting from it the 200,000 Jews killed in combat and adding the supposedly very few Jews who survived German occupation, one obtains about 2 million or even fewer surviving Soviet Jews. The contradiction of so many Jews serving and dying in the Red Army, even though most Jews supposedly fell into German hands, can only be resolved in this way.

111

But there is a catch to it. All in all, 860,000 male Jews of military age were available to the Soviets; most of them were drafted and 200,000 never returned. At the end of the war, only 660,000 male Jews of this age group remained. Now, if the Soviets restricted themselves to evacuating just half a million male Jews of military age and left the bulk of the elderly, women and children behind to face German annihilation, the surviving 660,000 male Jews would have faced only about 400,000 Jewesses of the same age group – a ratio of 66 to 40! However, such an "upside-down" sex ratio never has been reported in post-war literature – which is very strange.

The opposite proved to be true. The Soviet census of 1959 recorded a sex distribution for the Jews as is "normal" for a population that suffered huge losses of men in two world wars; similar developments occurred in other countries affected by these terrible wars. Specifically, the male/female ratio for Soviet Jews in 1959 was 45.4% (i.e. 1,030,629) to 54.6% (i.e. 1,237,185).[5] Ten years later the Soviet census of 1970 began to show the first slight indication of a normalization of the sex structure among the Jews: It was 45.9% to 54.1%.[6]

On the basis of the age distribution of the Jews in the RSFSR[7] 705,290 Jews of the recorded 2,267,814 Jews in the Soviet Union (1959) belonged to the age group "0-28 years" which at the end of WWII hadn't either been born yet or was too young for military service; its sex structure should have been more or less balanced. The male/female composition among those 29 years and older thus was 677,984 and 884,540, respectively:

Age group	Male	Female	Total
All age groups	1,030,629	1,237,185	2,267,814
0—28 years old	352,645	352,645	705,290
29 years and older	677,984	884,540	1,562,524

For the age groups over 28 years this corresponds to a male/female ratio of 43.4/56.6 which is far better than the overall Soviet ratio (1959) of 38.4/61.6 for those aged 30 years and more.[8]

In any case, the age groups which participated actively in *both* world wars showed a gap of 200,000 in favor of the fair sex. Several tens of thousands of this difference, no doubt, must be attributed to the lower life. expectancy of men; further tens of thousands are accounted for by World War *One*. The *Second* World War cannot be responsible for very many more than 100,000 men killed in action.

As mentioned above, Zionist sources put the number of Jews who died in the Soviet armed forces at at least 200,000. It is obvious that the Soviet census of 1959 did not register the Jewish population in its entirety; otherwise we would have found more than 100,000 or maybe even 125.000 male casualties of WWII.

The following facts crystallize:

1. More than half a million male Jews served in the Red Army during WWII.

2. It would have been impossible to draft 600,000 soldiers from a population of only two million; therefore, the largest part of the Soviet-Jewish population must have been evacuated by the Soviets to areas outside the German sphere of influence.

3. The contention that the Soviets removed only the male population of military age, leaving the elderly, women and children behind to be annihilated, is untenable; if so, the number of male Jews would have had to be far larger after the war than that of the Jewesses despite the many men killed in action. This, however, is not the case as is shown by the census of 1959 which – 14 years after the war – still evidenced a sex ratio of 43% to 57% in favor of the female sex for the age groups subject to military duty in the Second World War.

The Soviet census of 1959 thus can serve as proof that the mass evacuation of the Jewish population by the Soviets did indeed take place in 1941. At the same time it provides information on the relative size of losses incurred by Jews in the Red Army.

How reliable is the Soviet census? The stigma of manipulation attaches to all Soviet statistics. But even leaving this argument aside, the greatest disadvantage must be seen in the manner in which the census was conducted. It was left up to each individual to register for statistical purposes under any nationality desired. In this way, the Soviets provided an opportunity not only for the assimilated Jews but also for those who still maintained ties to Judaism, not to appear to the outside world as Jews; in view of the anti-Semitic attitudes of large sections of the Slavic and Baltic populations, many Jews tried to evade recognition by having themselves recorded as Russians, etc.[9]

Fortunately, other means exist for verification. During the 1970's a growing number of Jews left the Soviet Union for Israel. Contrary to the immigrants of the first post-war years – mainly from Europe – whose male/female ratio among those aged 50-64 years averaged 49/51,[10] the elderly Jewish immigrants from the USSR in the years 1976-1979 recorded a male share of only 37-40%:[11]

1976	40 %
1977	37 %
1978	38 %
1979	37 %

In other words, the Jews arriving in Israel from the Soviet Union showed a sex ratio roughly in line with that indicated by the Soviet census of 1959.

We can summarize as follows: The Soviet census of 1959 is reasonably correct as far as the sex and probably also the age distribution of the Soviet Jews is concerned, but it vastly understates the total number of Soviet Jews.

The figures published before 1959 in post-war literature of about two million surviving Jews in the Soviet Union are *by no means* based on *official* Soviet statistics. The way this number was "created" originally is described by the *Year Book:*

> Statistics concerning the Russian Jews were meager and not always reliable even before the war. ... Pieced together from a wide variety of *unofficial* Soviet data and other sources, available information is necessarily fragmentary and often *hypothetical.* There is *no* adequate basis for presenting a complete picture of present-day Soviet Jewry or assessing the far-reaching changes caused by the war and the period of post-war reconstruction. ...
> In 1939-40 the eastern part of Poland, Bessarabia and Bukovina, and the Baltic states were incorporated into the USSR. ... the total number of Jews within the bounderies of the Soviet Union before the outbreak of the Russo-German war in June 1941 can therefore be taken as about 5,500,000, including about 350,000 war-refugee Polish Jews. Corliss Lamont (*The Peoples of the Soviet Union*, Harcourt, Brace & Co., New York, 1946) estimates the number of Soviet Jews at this period as 5,300,000, exclusive of non-Soviet refugees.
> But these figures by themselves contribute little to an estimate of present Jewish population of the Soviet Union. For this we *would* have to know not only the number who lost their lives as a result of Nazi atrocities, but the birth rate of the Soviet Jews, the number of Jewish soldiers who fell during the war, mortality among the deported and evacuated to Central Asia and Siberia, and the scope of postwar repatriation to Poland and Rumania. *Only* on the last of these points, however, do we have accurate information. Of about 350,000 Jews from Eastern and Central Poland who sought refuge in the Soviet zone in 1939-40, the vast majority were deported by the Soviet authorities to Siberia, Central Asia, etc. (a substantial number to concentration camps). It must be emphasized that these people went as compulsory

114

exiles, not as refugees. A few thousand left the USSR with the Polish army evacuated to Iran in 1942, approximately 150,000 returned to Poland in 1946, and only a few thousand elected to stay in the USSR. The remainder – about 200,000 – probably died there.

The most conspicuous *discrepancies* concern the *estimated* number of victims of the German mass-murders. These *estimates* range between 1,500,000 (Corliss Lamont, *op. cit.*) and 3,000,000 (Jacob Lestschinsky). Only an insignificant percentage of Jews (perhaps only 1 per cent) who remained in the territories overrun by the Germans managed to escape alive. The number of Jews evacuated from these territories prior to the German occupation is, therefore, exceedingly important, but this cannot be accurately determined. It *seems* certain that the optimistic estimates published outside the Soviet Union both during the war and at its close were exaggerated. The German occupation of the Baltic states, the Ukraine, and White Russia – all areas with large, concentrated Jewish settlements – proceeded very quickly and the Soviet transportation system was unable to carry out the evacuation speedily enough, nor on a sufficiently large scale. Many evacuation transports were overtaken by the swift German offensive.

Kulischer, in his study *The Displacement of Population in Europe* (International Labor Office, Montreal, 1943), *estimates* that 1,100,000 Jews from the pre-1939 territory of the Soviet Union, 30,000 from the Baltic States and 500,000 from Western Bielorussia and Western Ukraine, were evacuated into unoccupied Soviet territories. In this latter figure he includes those forcibly deported in 1939-1940. Others consider these figures excessive.

These *discrepancies* naturally lead to *different estimates* as to the number of *Jews living* in Russia. Even Dr. Frank Lorimer of Princeton, an outstanding authority, in his work, *The Population of the Soviet Union: History and Prospects* (Geneva, League of Nations, 1946), does not venture such an estimate.

Unofficial Soviet publications mention 2,500,000 as the present [1947] Jewish population of the USSR. This figure, which is also Kulischer's estimate, (*Rescue*, July-August 1946), appears to be exaggerated. ...

These unofficial estimates are severely criticized by the Jewish economist Jacob Lestschinsky. According to his analysis, the total number of Jews within the present Soviet bounderies does not exceed 1,500,000 (*The New Leader*, March 8, 1947, New York). He claims to have calculated, on the basis of unofficial Soviet information, that the maximum number of Jews living in the 60 major settlements of European Russia is 800,000. To the smaller settlements of the European part of the USSR, Lestschinsky ascribes a figure of less than 100,000 Jews; to the Asiatic parts, 500-600,000 Jews. Thus he arrives at his total of 1,500,000 Jews in the Soviet Union.

This figure, when compared to the 5,500,000 Jews on Soviet soil before the outbreak of the war in 1941, shows a difference of 4,000,000. To explain these missing 4,000,000 Jews, Lestschinsky estimates that about 200,000 Jewish Red Army men lost their lives in the fighting, and about 500,000 Jews died in Siberia and Central Asia (principally from among the deported and evacuated). It would thus follow that the Germans massacred more than 3,000,000 Soviet Jews. Lestschinsky's figures are also, obviously, hypothetical.

The Research Department of the American Jewish Joint Distribution Committee in New York *estimates* the present number of Soviet Jews as 1,800,000. This includes the Asiatic provinces, but is exclusive of the Baltic states [Lithuania, Latvia, Estonia] where there are reported to be 32,500 Jews. (The pre-war Jewish population of these countries was 255,000.)

The *estimates* of the JDC *appear* to be closest to the facts; however, until the publication of official, reliable statistics, the actual present Jewish population of the USSR cannot be definitely determined.[12]

In the following year's issue the *Year Book* wrote again:

... neither the Russian-Jewish organizations nor the general USSR statistics contain information on this very important subject. Our *estimates*, based on a careful study of Russian and Jewish material concerning persons evacuated to the unoccupied part of the country ...[13]

Here is the confirmation of a leading Zionist publication that the information on Soviet Jewry is fragmentary at best, that the number of Jews supposedly killed by the Nazis is totally unknown and that the guesswork about the number of Jewish survivors in the Soviet Union has led to great differences of opinion and figures of a purely speculative character. It is even admitted that the number of only two million or fewer surviving Jews rests on two *hypotheses:* First, the Germans allegedly killed most of the Jews who remained behind in German-occupied territory. Secondly, it is *assumed* that only a small part of the Jewish population managed to escape. The "estimates" for the number of the deported supposedly have been arrived at by a "careful study" of Russian and Jewish material on the number of people evacuated to the unoccupied territories. The lack of diligence applied becomes obvious when one observes that the enormous evacuation carried out by the Soviets in 1941 is simply denied. That's how history is fabricated.

The number of two million surviving Jews in the Soviet Union is seen to be without foundation as the "creators" of that figure freely admit. Still, they had to wait until 1959 for an official confirmation of this hypothetic figure when the Soviets conducted a census in 1959; the published figure of 2,267,814 was not all that different from Zionist "estimates." To be sure, it was known that the Soviet method of taking a census leads perforce to too low a Jewish population figure, but, said the *Year Book*, there is nothing one can do but accept it. It continued: "The question of the number of Jews in the Soviet Union was to a large extent answered by the publication of the January 1959 census of Soviet population."[14]

However, the following census of January 1970 recorded only a Jewish population of 2,151,300 – 117,000 fewer than eleven years before.[15] The Soviet demographer A.M. Maksimow commented, in the USSR there is going on "a process of fusion of nations which, under the conditions of a socialist society, has the character of friendship ..."

Shaken by this process of friendship the Zionists noticed that the Soviets were engaged in having the Jews disappear statistically in a slow but steady manner. The *Year Book* objected: "... a 'hidden' Jew, or an assimilated Jew, remains a Jew and should be counted as such," and "it is questionable whether one should accept improbable figures supplied by a not overly friendly source."[16] An excellent question. In any case, the *Year Book* is again of the opinion that under the circumstances it is impossible to specify at present the exact number of Soviet Jews.

To be sure, the press carried reports prior to 1970 already that probably there are more Jews in the USSR than "estimated" until then; but ever since about that year reports are regularly being published which draw an entirely different picture of the numerical size of post-war Soviet Jewry. Among the most prominent was the *Year Book* which admitted that well-informed Russian Jews in the USSR and Soviet emigrants continue to assert that there are up to 4,000,000 Jews in the Soviet Union.[17] Similar figures were mentioned by the *New York Times* on January 22, 1975.[18]

Prof. Shapiro who is in charge of the Jewish world demographic statistics published by the *Year Book* wrote:

> The estimate of the emigrants is also important since *all* of them (with whom I spoke) suggest a more or less similar figure, which they say is current among the Jews in Russia.[19]

The *Judaica*, too, behind which there are Zionist personalities of the stature of an Arthur J. Goldberg and Dr. Nahum Goldmann, speaks of 3 to 4 million Jews in the Soviet Union at the beginning of the 1970's.[20]

Prof. Michael Zand, who is teaching at the Hebrew University in Jerusalem today and who left the Soviet Union after a great many difficulties some years ago, said, according to a report by the Israeli newspaper *Beth Shalom*, that there are still 4.5 million Jews in the USSR as far as he knows. In his opinion, the official statistics of the Soviet Union reflect merely those Jews who are willing to acknowledge their Jewish nationality.[21]

We should note at this point that a Soviet census does not represent the official Soviet version on the question of the actual number of the Jewish population. In that society the purpose of a census is not at all to determine the numerical size of a particular people in an ethnic sense. It was possible, for instance, that due to a change in the definition of nationality between 1926 and 1939 the share of the Russians increased from 52.9% of the total population to 58.1% despite the fact that the fertility of the Russians was not only below the national, but also below the Ukrainian and the White Russian averages. Following the territorial expansion in the years 1939/1940, the Soviet Union acquired another 25 million Ukrainians, White Russians, peoples from the Baltic countries, Rumanians (but only very few Russians); one should have expected, therefore, that the Russian share would have dropped back to about 51% before the outbreak of the German-Soviet war. Since then the Russian surplus of births over deaths was below the average and still the census of 1959 recorded the Russian share to be 54.6% of the Soviet population.[22]

It is evident that the "Russians" as shown in the Soviet census include millions of people of White Russian, Ukrainian, Jewish and other origin. Small wonder that other *official* publications – e.g. *Jews in the Soviet Union*, Moscow, 1967, p. 45, by Solomon Rabinovich – speak of 3 million Jews in the USSR.[23]

Unfortunately, Western Zionist circles still have not come around to accepting "for the record" a higher estimate of the Soviet Jewish population. Nor is this very surprising because the overdue correction would, of course, invite inconvenient questions.

Nevertheless, one can observe a slow, almost unnoticeable turn of attitude if one is willing to scratch below the surface. The *Judaica*, for example, published under the guidance and cooperation of prominent Jewish and Israeli personalities,[24] cites the Jewish population figure in the usual manner as published in Soviet statistics for 1970, but then arrives at the significant conclusion that hundreds of thousands of Soviet Jews were not recorded as Jews during the Soviet census; it continued, "for more correct estimates, see articles on individual cities."[25]

Well, we did; and we found fifteen Soviet cities for which Jewish population figures were published in the Soviet census of 1959 and for which the *Judaica* listed corresponding Zionist estimates as well. The comparison is depicted in *Table 10*.

According to the Soviet census of 1959, these fifteen cities included 906,479 Jewish inhabitants, or 40% of all "official" 2.27 million Soviet Jews. The estimates of the *Judaica* arrive at 1,493,000 Jews for the same fifteen cities – 65% more than recorded officially. In other words, among ten Soviet Jews only six acknowledged their Jewish nationality at the time the census was taken. Now, there is no reason why the Jews living in other Soviet cities behaved very differently; the logical conclusion is that leading Zionist circles put the number of Soviet Jews in 1970 at 3¾ million (i.e. 165% of 2.27 million).

Table 10
Jewish Population
in 15 Post-War Soviet Cities

City	Soviet Census of 1959	Estimates of the J u d a i c a for 1970	Difference
Moscow	239,246	500,000	260,754
Leningrad	162,344	200,000	37,656
Kiev	154,000	200,000	46,000
Odessa	102,200	180,000	77,800
Kishinev	42,934	60,000	17,066
Minsk	38,842	55,000	16,158
Riga	30,267	38,000	7,733
Baku	26,263	80,000	53,737
Rostov	21,500	30,000	8,500
Donetsk (Stalino)	21,000	40,000	19,000
Gorki	17,827	30,000	12,173
Nikolaev	15,800	20,000	4,200
Shitomir	14,800	25,000	10,200
Dnepropetrovsk	13,256	25,000	11,744
Proskurov	6,200	10,000	3,800
15 Cities	906,479	1,493,000	586,521
	(100 %)	(165 %)	(65 %)

Source: *Encyclopaedia Judaica*, Jerusalem, 1972 (div. volumes)

Considering that cautious estimates for the Soviet-Jewish population are still in the Zionist interest, one may presume that leading and knowledgeable world Zionist personalities themselves believe that the real size of the Jewish population in the Soviet Union is as high as 4 (four) million! One example of the restraint with which these estimates for Soviet cities listed on *Table 10* have been arrived at, is offered by another unsuspicious Zionist source, the *American Jewish Year Book:* It put the Jewish population of Leningrad, for instance, as high as 325,000 in 1963 already; this is 60% more than admitted to by the *Judaica* and 100% more than the number found by the Soviet census of 1959.[26]

The complete lack of credibility for the official Soviet statistics on the *number* of Soviet Jews can also be demonstrated by the example of Moscow. In 1940, this Russian city contained at least 400,000 Jews,[27] but in 1959 only 239,000 were reported by the census. This is strange. The Germans never occupied Moscow and the attractiveness of this hub of Soviet life with its incomparable career possibilities more likely than not increased during these decades. A reduction of the Jewish minority by 40% (!) between 1940 and 1959 is completely out of the question. To the contrary, reinforced by a migration to this city from other sections of the country, Moscow's Jewish population should have been expected to increase and even the *Judaica's* estimate of 500,000 Jews in 1970 appears conservative.

According to the calculations of this study, the USSR was inhabited by 4.3 million Jews at the end of World War Two. Is there a logical explanation for a possible reduction of this number to 4 million or less during the 25 years between 1945 and 1970? There are many indications that the Soviet Jews suffered indeed a drastic numerical decline during the *post-war period*. The huge war losses among men and the enormous children mortality rate in the course of the Soviet evacuations in the years 1940/1941 were mentioned already. These developments were compounded by the high degree of urbanization (96%) of Soviet Jews.[28]

Another factor – probably the most important today – for a negative growth balance is the trend toward assimilation through mixed marriages; this development set in long before WWII and grew in strength after the war. As a rule, the children born to these couples are lost to the Jewish nationality.[29] In 1926 already, 26% of all Jewish males living outside the Ukraine and White Russia married gentile women; in the latter two provinces the percentage was only 4.6 and 2.0%.[30]

The shift of the Jewish population center from the traditionally anti-Semitic regions (Ukraine and White Russia) to the north and east persisted ever since the Revolution and was further reinforced by the mass deportations of 1940/1941. The *Year Book* complained:

According to a reliable source, intermarriages involving Jews in Moscow and in Leningrad had reached about 50 per cent in the early 1960s. The same source indicated that in the new cities of Siberia – many with a young academic population – the rate remained extremely high.[31]

Of course, mixed marriages do not change the nationality of either partner. But if the children from these marriages are lost to the ethnic minority the effects on the natural growth of this ethnic group are the same as if those marrying outside their group remain childless.

If, as the *Judaica* maintains, 20% of the Soviet Jews of the post-war period lived in Leningrad and Moscow[32] where every second member of the Jewish community married outside his nationality, the effect is the same as if 10% of all young Jews of marriageable age remain without children. Zionist literature claims, however, those two cities are not unique in this respect. In the 1920's the percentage of mixed marriages involving Jews was less than 5% in the traditionally anti-Semitic regions of the Soviet Union. Assuming that the native population of these non-Russian areas continues to exhibit those attitudes even today, although possibly in a milder form, the share of mixed marriages among the Jews living there – about 45% of all Soviet Jews – might have risen to, let us say, ten per cent.

Conceding, furthermore, that the Jews living outside the traditional settlements in the south and west, but excluding Moscow and Leningrad, did not experience the enormous mixed marriage rate of the two metropolitan areas, one can use a rate of 30% as a starting point; in this case, the incidence of mixed marriages among the Soviet Jews might appear as follows:

Region	Percentage of Jews in the USSR	Percentage of mixed marriages	"Childless" Jewish mixed marriages partners
Moscow and Leningrad	20 %	50 %	10,0 %
Other areas in the north and the east	35 %	30 %	10,5 %
Ukraine, White Russia, Moldavia and Baltic area	45 %	10 %	4,5 %
			25,0 %

Following this hypothetic example, every fourth Jew in the Soviet Union remains "without children" – at least as far as the growth of his nationality is concerned – because he is marrying outside his ethnic group and because the children born to these mixed couples are lost to the Jewish minority as a rule. Now, the purpose of this exercise was not at all to pinpoint the exact percentage of "childless" Jews (as defined); it does not matter at all whether the average percentage of mixed marriages among Soviet Jews is closer to 20 or 30% or even higher. The fact is that mixed marriages are extremely common among the Jews of the USSR. Inasmuch as the highly urbanized Soviet Jews had a preference for the small family in the 1920's already (as shown by Prof. Lorimer) and total births in those days barely managed to cover natural mortality, one has to presume that the enormously strong trend toward mixed marriages in the post-war period must have resulted in large annual excesses of deaths over births.

The Israeli demographer and professor U.O. Schmelz of the Hebrew University in Jerusalem reported that only 7% of the Jews in the Russian Soviet Federated Socialist Republic (RSFSR) belonged to the age group "0 to 10 years" and 26.5% were sixty years and older – a very high "aging" indeed. For the sake of comparison: the Federal Republic of Germany which does not have a "young" population had percentages of 13.5 and 19.7%, respectively, in 1977. The extent of "aging" of the Soviet Jews and their lower birth rate is shown in the table below:[33]

Jews in the Russian Federated Republic (RSFSR)
Distribution by Age – 1970

Age Group	Share (%)	Average Share per Year
0–10 years	6.9	0.63
11–15 years	4.3	0.86
16–19 years	3.9	0.98
20–29 years	10.9	1.09
30–39 years	15.1	1.51
40–49 years	16.1	1.61
50–59 years	16.3	1.63
60 years and older	26,5	?
Total	100.0	

Considering that the men in the age groups from 40 to 59 years had suffered huge losses during the war, their share would have been even larger without this external effect. It is fairly obvious that the decline of births is not a post-war phenomenon but that it started decades before the war. In the Sixties, finally, the birth rate seems to have fallen to 6 per

1,000 Jewish persons; but in order just to maintain their population size the share of the youngest age groups would have had to be more than twice as large!

The very large proportion of the older age groups indicates also a rather high natural mortality rate. Prof. Schmelz wrote that the natural *decrease* of the Soviet-Jewish population amounted to 1 (one) per cent per year between 1959 and 1970! The above age distribution shows furthermore that a population decline must have been recorded in the Fifties already. And there are no signs whatever that this situation has improved during the past ten years. Even if there had been a surplus of births over deaths right after the war this must have been of a very short duration due to the catastrophic losses of men in the war and the difficult post-war conditions; this is definitely indicated by the relative size of the age group "20 to 29 years."

The size of the average excess of births over deaths in the post-war period cannot be determined with the data available. Prof. Schmelz argues that the Jewish population of the other Soviet republics registered essentially the same age distribution as the RSFSR. All we know is that since 1945 the Jewish population must have suffered substantial negative average growth rates. Whether this deficit averaged a rate below or above −0.5% is impossible to determine given the paucity of Soviet statistics.

As mentioned above, the number of Soviet Jews at the end of WWII must have been 4.3 million at most. Applying various *average* negative growth rates for the period since 1945 and accounting for the roughly 250,000 Jewish emigrants between 1970 and 1980[34] – before 1970 emigration was negligible – we obtain the following alternative developments:

Average decrease per annum since 1945	Jewish Population in the Soviet Union	
	1970	1980
a) – 0.3 %	3.98 million	3.61 million
b) – 0.4 %	3.88 million	3.48 million
c) – 0.5 %	3.77 million	3.35 million
d) – 0.6 %	3.69 million	3,23 million

Obviously, it is not just a possibility but there is a high degree of probability that the Soviet-Jewish population fell by more than 10% below 4.3 million by 1970. This figure is completely in accord with statements by Soviet Jews on the size of their ethnic group in Russia; Prof. Shapiro from the *Year Book* confirmed this in writing.

Even the *Judaica*, whose estimates of the Jewish inhabitants of individual Soviet cities point to a total population of just under 4 million, concludes that this number of present-day Jews in the USSR is *not* the result of a positive natural growth; it wrote:

> Moreover, there are fragmentary indications and a general likelihood that the growth of the Jewish group in the U.S.S.R. since the War has been small, *if there has been any at all* (because of aging, enhanced by war losses; low fertility; intermarriage; assimilation pressure by the majority population; etc.)[35]

This is putting it very cautiously. The *Judaica* could have said as well that at the end of WWII there were at least as many Jews in the Soviet Union as there are today, probably even more – over 4 million!

In this connection we received an interesting admission from Dr. Nahum Goldmann, the one-time chairman of the World Jewish Congress. He declared without qualifications that the Jewish population group in the USSR numbered about three to three-and-one-half million people in 1980;[36] this figure corresponds to a population size which might have been expected considering the emigration of a quarter million Soviet Jews in the 1970's and a negative growth rate of at least 0.5% per year since 1970. Now, since he is probably one of the last persons who would tend to exaggerate the size of the Soviet-Jewish population, we are confronted with the following facts: In 1970, the number of Soviet Jews was probably somewhat less than 4 million and today it is around 3.5 million, after several hundreds of thousands of Jews had left the USSR in the interim period.

The Jewish Cost of Lives and Overall Soviet Losses

Obviously, our calculated number of 4.3 million surviving Soviet Jews is confirmed by respectable and knowledgeable Jewish sources. The remaining question is thus how the losses suffered by the Jews in the USSR compare to the overall losses of the Soviet population. The American engineer John Scott, who worked for years in Stalin's armaments industry and was married to a Russian woman, published a book upon his return from Magnitogorsk (*Behind the Urals*, Boston, 1942). There he describes how the inhuman Soviet "work methods" caused millions of men and women in Siberia to die of hunger and cold while further millions succumbed to the unspeakable living conditions.[37]

Following the huge losses of the Red Army, the Soviets mopped industry ruthlessly for men needed in the formation of armies which were to replace those annihilated. In their place, women were mobilized who had to work day and night in two shifts like Stakhanovites. In order to muster the last bit of energy the so-called "Marshall-Plan" honoring Stalin's self-appointment to Marshall of the Soviet Union was initiated: Every Soviet resident aged 14 to 70 regardless of sex was obligated to double his output even if he was working at maximum capacity already. People died like flies.[38]

Willkie, who visited the Soviet Union in September 1942, described the conditions he found there as follows:

> Food in Russia this Winter will be scarce – perhaps worse than scarce. ... Fuel will be little known this Winter in millions of Russian homes. Clothing except for the army and essential war workers is nearly gone. Many vital medical supplies just don't exist. Russian women by the millions side by side with their children – some of them as young as eight and ten – are manning machines in the war factories and running the farms. Every able bodied man is in the army or giving the maximum hours of hard work ...[38a]

The magnitude of this human tragedy was reported in 1943 by Paul Holt, the Moscow correspondent of the London newspaper *Daily Express*. Returning to London after a 15 month stay in the Soviet Union, Holt wrote that *until then* the Soviets had lost 30 million fallen and wounded soldiers, prisoners-of-war and civilians who had died of hunger and illness.[39] It is not known how this huge figure should be divided between military and civilian losses, but certainly the bulk must be attributed to the Red Army. At that time, 5.4 million Red Army men were taken prisoners-of-war by the Germans[40] and a similar number must be allowed for the fallen soldiers. Adding several millions of wounded there remain 10-15 million civilians who died of hunger, epidemics and cold. Further losses running into the millions occurred until the end of the war.

We noted in the Third Chapter that the total population in the Soviet Union numbered at least 202 million at the beginning of the war in June 1941. We do not know its size as of May 1945 since the first post-war census was taken in 1959, followed by a second in 1970. Between 1959 and 1970, the Soviet population increased by 33 million from 209 million to 242 million – a growth rate of 1.3% p.a. But, inasmuch as the Soviet peoples, too, experienced a decline of their fertility following the first baby boom years after WWII, one has to presume that the natural growth rate was somewhat higher between 1945 and 1959 – let us say, 1.5%. This means that there must have been an increase by 39 million in those 14 years; in other words, there could have been no more than 170 million million people in the USSR by the end of the war – 32 million fewer than at the beginning of the war.

Red Army losses during WWII are said to have totalled 13.6 million;[41] accordingly, 18.4 million dead must have been suffered by the civilian population. The respective figures for the Soviet Jews were 200,000 and 830,000 for a total of 1,030,000. In relation to the total population, the Soviet Jews registered a rate of *military* losses of "only" 3.8% (200,000 of 5.3 million) compared to the horrendous 6.7% (13.6 million of 202 million of the overall Soviet population. Obviously, the Soviet Jews were engaged to a much smaller degree in the actual fighting because they were sorely needed in the armaments industry. These facts explain why the census of 1959 showed the overall Soviet population having a considerably smaller percentage of men (of the war generation) than was true for the Jewish segment, namely, 38.4% to 43.4%.

However, the Jews registered a much higher overall and civilian loss:

Civilian losses of the
– entire Soviet population   9.1% (18.4 million of 202 million)
– entire Jewish population   15.7% (830,000 of 5.3 million)

Total losses of the
– entire Soviet population   15.8% (32 million of 202 million)
– entire Jewish population   19.4% (1,030,000 of 5.3 million)

This method of analysis does not pay attention to the fact that large portions of the Slavic and Baltic populations, but only relatively few Jews remained behind in German-controlled territory. We found only about 65 million people in the occupied areas, including almost three-quarters of a million Jews. Looking at it from the other side, 137 million Soviet residents including 4.61 million Jews outside the German sphere of influence were under Soviet domination. Comparing this Soviet-controlled population to the human losses, one obtains the following figures:

Civilian losses of the
– Soviet population *outside* the
  German sphere of influence   13.4% (18.4 million of 137 million)
– Jewish population *outside* the
  German sphere of influence   18.0% (830,000 of 4.61 million)

Total losses of the
- Soviet population *outside* the
  German sphere of influence   23.4% (32 million of 137 million)
- Jewish population *outside* the
  German sphere of influence   22.3% (1,030,000 of 4.61 million)

Thus, while the military losses of the non-Jewish population were considerably larger than those of the Soviet Jews, the civilian losses of the Jews and non-Jews who remained under Soviet control showed the opposite development. Reasons for this phenomenon are not difficult to find: Already in 1940, the Soviets deported a relatively large segment of the Jews from the western territories to Siberia; of the three-quarters of a million Jews in question, hundreds of thousands died on the way and many others of these "foreign elements" lost their lives in Siberian labor and concentration camps due to cold, undernourishment and physical exhaustion. Children especially were affected by this barbarous treatment. In the case, of the evacuated Slavic population in 1941 large portions were men of military age; as a result, the proportion of the very old and children was relatively small. Both factors effected the disproportionately larger civilian losses among the Soviet Jews.

Yet, it is interesting that the total losses of the population remaining under Soviet control were just about equal for Jews and non-Jews – roughly 23%! However, since Stalin had evacuated about 80% of the Jewish population but only a fourth of the other, mainly Slavic residents, the Jewish total losses were noticeably higher (20%) than those of the entire Soviet population (16%). In short, the massive Soviet evacuation during WWII proved to be the single most important cause of the huge human losses suffered by Soviet Jewry.

The calculated number of 4.3 million surviving Soviet Jews thus turns out to be quite realistic: Statements by Dr. Nahum Goldmann, the *Judaica* and the Soviet-Jewish dissidents confirm it. For the purpose of this analysis it is of no significance whether the actual number is closer to 4 or 4½ million. Whatever the case may be, the Jewish losses are quite in line with the decimation experienced by the entire Soviet population as a result of Stalin's evacuation, forced labor and battle strategies.

PART II

THE WESTWARD DRIVE

SIXTH CHAPTER

The Jewish Fate in German-Occupied Europe

France, Benelux countries, Denmark, Norway and Italy

The victory of German arms in the West affected almost half a million Jews in Denmark, Norway, Luxemburg, the Netherlands, Belgium and France, including more than 90,000 refugees, according to the American Jewish Committee.[1] Reitlinger arrives at a similar figure:

> In the six weeks between May 10th and June 25th, 1940, not less than 350,000 Jews of Western Europe passed under German rule. ... a further 130,000 Jews came indirectly under German orders in Vichy territory.[2]

If one adds the 8,000 Jews of Denmark and Norway to these 480,000 in France and the Benelux countries, one does indeed obtain the "nearly half a million" of the American Jewish Committee.

Yet, some reservations are in order as far as the actual number of Jews in these countries is concerned. Before the outbreak of hostilities, Jewish refugees from Greater Germany and eastern Europe were to be found in all western European countries. After the fighting erupted, many Jews – mainly foreigners – fled from Holland to Belgium. Native and other Jews living in Belgium escaped together with those from Holland to France; in many cases, they were rounded up by the Belgians, forcibly interned – affected were mainly male refugees with German passports – and transported by rail to France, where they were put in French concentration camps and subjected to terrible hardships if we may believe Zionist reports.[3] The American Jewish Committee estimated the number of refugee Jews living in Belgium and in Holland before the "invasion" at 25,000 and 23,000, respectively. The total number of Jews escaping from the Benelux countries to France during the few weeks of fighting reached perhaps 30-40,000, but the reports differ greatly from each other.

The Jews in France were augmented in November 1940 by an additional 10,000 German Jews deported from The Palatinate and Baden; it is possible that up to 100,000 German, Czech and Polish Jews lived as refugees in France.[4] In turn, many Jews left France for other countries in the course of time: Switzerland, Portugal, Spain; the Institute of Jewish Affairs places the number of Jews who escaped from France until August 1943 at 30,000.[5]

There are no precise pre-war figures available on the native Jewish population of France and the Benelux countries; only Holland counted its Jews in the census of 1935 and found 111,917[6] and estimates of Belgium's, France's and Luxemburg's Jewish population for the pre-war period – refugees from Germany and eastern Europe excluded – show great differences. In any case, the total number of Jews we are concerned with in the case of these four countries is 460,000 (i.e. 350,000 plus 130,000 plus 10,000 minus 30,000).

Denmark and Norway counted 8,000 Jews; of these, 7,000 fled to Sweden in 1943.[7] Italy's census of 1931 found 47,825 Jews,[8] but in 1938 the figure was much higher at 57,425,[9] because Italy, too, was a target of Jewish migration before the war. Until September 1943, when Germany occupied the peninsula after Italy's defection, the country's Jewish population had decreased by 9,000 to 48,000 as a result of flight and emigration (Switzerland, North Africa, etc.).[10] In total, the number of Jews in these seven countries within the German sphere of influence reached 525,000 in 1941.

If one can believe Reitlinger, the German authorities carried out the following deportations:

Netherlands	110,000 [11]
Belgium	25,437 [12]
Luxemburg	512 [13]
France	65,000 [14]
Denmark and Norway	893 [15]
Italy	10,271 [16]
	212,113

Of these, the following returned:

Netherlands	6,000 [17]
Belgium	1,276 [18]
France	2.800 [19]
Italy	605 [20]
	10,681
Deported Jews (net)	201,432

According to Reitlinger these Jews survived:

Netherlands	36,500 [21]
Belgium	61,000 [22]
Luxemburg	500 [23]
Denmark and Norway	?
France	238,000 [24]
Italy	39,000 [25]
Total surviving Jews	375,000

Reducing the total number of 525,000 Jews (1941) by the 7,000 who fled from Denmark and Norway and by the 9,000 Jews who escaped from Italy until September 1943, only 509,000 remain; if one subtracts from these the surviving 375,000 Jews, the number of "missing" Jews is reduced to "only" 134,000:

France and Benelux countries		460,000
Denmark and Norway		8,000
Italy		57,000
1941 total		525,000
deduct:		
Danish and Norwegian Jews in Sweden	7,000	
Escaped Italian Jews	9,000	16,000
		509,000
Purported survivors		375,000
"Missing" Jews		134,000

Reitlinger, however, asserts that he found at least 201,200 but at most 210,200 "annihilated" Jews and the Anglo-American Committe even claims to have discovered 341,000![26]

The urban Jews of these western European countries showed all the characteristics typical of populations of large cities: Rising mortality rates and falling birth rates. These four countries – France, Holland, Belgium and Italy – are supposed to have had a total Jewish population of 400,000 in the early 1930's. Looking at this figure a little more closely, it begins to evaporate. The *Universal* published the following mortality figures (Norway, Denmark, and Luxemburg were not listed, probably because of the small numerical size of their Jewish populations):[27]

France	1,500
Netherlands	1,000
Belgium	500
Italy	500

Applying a mortality rate of 1.1% per annum, the Jewish populations must have recorded the following sizes:

France	137,000
Netherlands	91,000
Belgium	45,000
Italy	45,000
	318,000

It is unfortunate that the *Universal* rounded these numbers to a full 500. In the case of Belgium and Italy, the computed population size is somewhat lower than is usually given by Zionists, but they are still acceptable. For the Netherlands, the calculated figure of 91,000 compares with the census listing 112,000 – a large gap; but this may be explained by the fact that the mortality figure was rounded off to 1,000.

As for France, it does not matter whether we round up or off, whether the mortality rate is pushed down to 0.9% and whether the number of mortality cases per year is increased even to 1,700, the resulting population figure would always remain below 200,000. Inasmuch as the mortality figures given for other countries by the *Universal* are generally acceptable, there is no reason why we should reject them in this instance. Consequently, one must conclude that the estimates for the Jews of pre-war France – usually given as 240,000-260,000 (excl. refugees) – are completely wrong and that France probably contained 50-100,000 fewer Jews when war broke out than certain people would like us believe. The only other explanation for this discrepancy is that tens of thousands of eastern European Jews had immigrated in France in the early 1930's – at a time when only few Jews had left Germany; if this is the case, we would have another confirmation for the mass emigration from eastern Europe as mentioned by the pro-Zionist Institute for Contemporary History.

Greece and Yugoslavia

Emigration far exceeded the positive growth rate for *Greek* Jews ever since the turn of the century. The result was a continuous decrease in the number of Jews in Greece. This persistent emigration pattern, reinforced by economic misery, probably caused the Jewish population to drop further since the census of 1931 found 67,200 Jews.[28] Precise figures are not available for 1940; for this reason, we assumed only a small decline of the Jewish inhabitants to 65,000 during the 1930's.

How many of them were deported? A report by the International Red Cross mentioned only that all male Jews between the ages 18 and 45 years were registered in July 1942 and, after a temporary incorporation in labor battalions, were deported to Germany in May 1943;[29] nothing in the report was said about Jewesses being deported as well. At the end of the war, the Zionist scholar Hilberg claims to have found only 12,000;[30] the rest of 53,000 is said to have been deported. There is a good probability that this figure is untenable in view of the IRC-report, but we accepted it because we want to base this analysis on Zionist sources if at all possible.

Hilberg insists that *"mass emigration* from eastern Europe *was easiest in* non-Communist *Greece* and in the neighboring states of *Yugoslavia* and *Bulgaria."*[31] Disregarding his own words, this splendid scholar begins to cite statistics which leave no room at all for emigration from these countries between 1945 and 1948. The assumption that tens of thousands emigrated between 1945 and 1948 – in part, already during the war – and that, finally, only 12,000 remained in Greece in the year 1948 probably is not far-fetched; and yet, these 12,000 of 1948 are listed as the only survivors.

The *Yugoslavian* case is not very different. There, too, we find exaggerations regarding the Jewish population size at the beginning of the war, understatements as to the number of survivors, an inflation of the number of deported and, lastly, no figures at all – even no estimates – on the number of those who emigrated right after the end of the hostilities by way of Italy or Austria to Palestine, overseas or to other European countries.

The census of 1931 counted 68,405 Yugoslavian Jews. Reitlinger believes that emigration could have decreased their number until the beginning of the war or, at least, allowed no further growth.[32] Communist post-war Yugoslavia's census of 1946 found only 10,446 Jews. Hilberg, however, who apparently had finished his count prior to this "census", discovered 12,000 survivors.[33]

One can safely assume that many thousands succeeded in fleeing to Italy and from there to Palestine or overseas, as Yugoslavia, too, belonged to those countries where mass emigration was easiest after the war according to Hilberg. Reitlinger admits to this and says that the census of the Communist government of Yugoslavia hardly can be taken seriously because many Jews had lived as gentiles during the war years and did not choose to reveal themselves as Jews after the war.[34]

How many tens of thousands survived for the reasons mentioned and are listed as "missing" in the statistics? And how many emigrated

135

right after the war? We do not know. The number of "missing" Jews for both of these countries adds up to 109,000:

Greece (1939)		65,000 Jews
Yugoslavia (1939)		68,000 Jews
		133,000 Jews
Purported survivors in 1945:		
Greece	12,000	
Yugoslavia	12,000	24,000 Jews
"Missing"		109,000 Jews

Germany and Austria

As of January 1933, the number of Jews living in *Germany* was 522,700;[35] if one adds the 16,600 Jews of the Saar, Memel and Danzig, their total number was 539,300.[36] 281,900 emigrated from the "old" Reich until December 1939, 13,000 from the Saar, Memel and Danzig; another reduction by 38,400 occurred because of an excess of deaths over births. As a result, only 206,000 remained in Germany ("old" Reich) at the end of 1939. The emigrants consisted mainly of the young, most of the elderly remained behind.

The Jewish statistician Dr. Bruno Blau wrote in the *Wiener Library Bulletin* that the Reichsvereinigung Deutscher Juden (Reich Union of German Jews) published data in October 1941 according to which 164,000 Jews were living in Germany at the time.[37] This was prior to the large deportations of German Jews to Russia. Dr. Blau said that of these remaining 164,000 about 13,800 may have died of natural causes. It seems though that the mortality rate of 2.4% per annum for the 3½ years until the end of the war probably is too low. A population mainly composed of older people where births naturally were the exception simply must have had a much greater natural decrease.[38]

Be that as it may, applying the same rate of 2.4% p.a. to the period 1939 to mid-1941, one obtains a natural excess of deaths over births of around 7,000. Thus, if 206,000 Jews lived in Germany in 1939 ("old" Reich), the natural excess of deaths amounted to 7,000 and 10,000 were deported to France in November 1940, then another 25,000 must have emigrated prior to 1941.

19,000 Jews remained at liberty in Germany throughout the war and a mere 8,000 are supposed to have returned from the various concentration camps after Germany's defeat.[39] This leaves 123,000 German Jews unaccounted for.

As for *Austria*, its Jewish population decreased since 1934 because of a negative net birth rate by 10,000 to 181,778 at the time of the unification of Austria with Germany in March 1938.[40] The ensuing massive emigration (117,000) and further excesses of deaths over births (8,000) reduced the Jewish population to 57,000 at the end of 1939.[35]

According to reports in the Zionist press, German statistics published on February 5, 1941 put the number of Austrian Jews at 50,000.[41] Applying Dr. Blau's data for the "old" Reich to Austria, the difference of 7,000 must have consisted of a natural decrease by 2,000 and emigration by another 5,000. Reitlinger, though, mentions 4,000 emigrants after 1939. For the remaining four war years, the mortality excess may well have amounted to a further 5,000 (2.4% p.a. of 50,000 in four years).

As for the survivors, Reitlinger has this to say: "... there survived on October 24th, *1947* [!], some 8,552 Austrian-born Jews in Vienna and a few hundred in Linz and other towns."[42] But he, too, is silent on the number of Austrian Jews who left the camps after the war to proceed directly to Palestine and overseas. The development of the Jewish population in these two German countries appears as follows:

Germany (1933)			539,000
Austria (1934)			192,000
Total			731,000
deduct:			
a) Development until 1939			
– Emigration:			
Germany ("old" Reich)	295,000		
Austria	117,000	412,000	
– Excess of deaths over births:			
Germany ("old" Reich)	38,000		
Austria	18,000	56,000	468,000
– Total in 1939			263,000
b) Development 1939–1941			
– Emigration:			
Germany ("old" Reich)	25,000		
Austria	5,000	30,000	
– Excess of deaths over births:			
Germany ("old" Reich)	7,000		
Austria	2,000	9,000	
– Deportation to France (1940)		10,000	49,000
– Total 1941			214,000

(cont. next page)

c) Development 1941–1945

– Emigration/flight	unknown	
– Excess of deaths over births:		
Germany ("old" Reich)	14,000	
Austria	5,000	19,000
Calculated remainder in 1945		195.000
Purported survivors after the war:		
Germany	27,000	
Austria	9,000	36,000
"Missing" Jews		159,000

Hungary

The census of 1930 recorded a Jewish population of 444,567.[43] In 1941, the census listed 725,007 Jews[44] in Greater Hungary enlarged by the acquisition of neighboring territories. A direct comparison between the two counts is difficult because many districts which had been reduced in size as a result of post-WWI border changes were again reconstituted to their former size. Not affected by border changes were the districts located in Hungary's interior; they contained 147,177 Jews in 1930,[45] but only 132,495 in 1941[46] – a reduction by 10%. Budapest's Jewish population decreased in the same period from 204,371 to 184,453 – also a minus of 10%. Applying this rate to all of Trianon-Hungary's Jews of 1930, there was a reduction by 44,500 to 400,000 in 1941.[47]

From 1930 to 1939, deaths exceeded births by 14,436 and another 1,600 should be allowed for 1940, bringing the total natural decline between 1930 and 1941 to about 16,000 (0.3% p.a.). Changes in religious preference resulted in a loss of 21,125 between 1930 and 1939 and possibly a further 2,000 in the year 1940. On balance, these changes reduced Trianon-Hungary's Jewish population by about 39,000 until 1941. This leaves another reduction of about 5,500 due to emigration.[48] Greater Hungary's Jewish population in 1941 thus was distributed as follows:

Census of 1941		725,007
"Old" Trianon-Hungary		400,000
Newly acquired territories		325,007
Former Slovak areas	42,000[49]	
Banat (from Yugoslavia)	25,000[49]	
Northern Transylvania (from Rumania)	148,621[50]	215,621
Ruthenia (from Czechoslovakia)		109,386

According to the usual post-war version concerning the developments in Hungary, the Germans deported about 400,000 Jews from Greater Hungary by rail between mid-May 1944 and early July 1944 from the areas outside the capital of Budapest, killing almost all of them in Birkenau. The killing was supposedly the main purpose of these deportations. With the exception of Budapest, where Jews were left in peace more or less, this operation "cleansed" Hungary of almost all Jews. On January 31, 1941, the number of Jews in Budapest numbered 184,453,[47] a reduction by 15,000 from the 200,000-figure published by the Jewish statistician Arthur Ruppin for the year 1930.[51]

Now, it just so happened that the International Red Cross (IRC) was represented in Budapest during the war and that the Jewish Senate's headquarters was in the buildings of the IRC. In 1948, the IRC published a report on the events in Hungary during the war, paying special attention to Jewish fate.[52] It is certain that the IRC knew about all the anti-Jewish measures either through its own sources or else through the Jewish Senate quartered in the same buildings. The report mentions some deportations for the period March to October 1944 without specification of figures. It said:

> ... from March 1944 onwards, the position of the [Hungarian] Jews became critical. ... On October 8, the Hungarian authorities, in conformity with the undertaking given to the Committee, announced the final suspension of deportations and made known that the Kistarcea Camp for Jewish intellectuals, doctors and engineers, had been broken up and the internees released.[53]

Only after the arrest of the war-weary Horthy-government by German troops did the real misery of the Hungarian Jews begin. The IRC-report continues:

> A few days later [*after* October 8, 1944] the full tide of the great tribulations of the Hungarian Jews was to set in. ... The replacement in October 1944, of Horthy's Government by one in bondage to Germany, provoked a violent crisis; executions, robberies, deportations, forced labour, imprisonments – such was the lot of the Jewish population, which suffered cruelly and lost many killed, especially in the provinces. ... It was immediately decided to remove them from Budapest and to confiscate their property. Sixty thousand Jews fit for work *were to* be sent to Germany, on foot, in parties of one thousand, by way of Vienna. Moreover, among the able-bodied, men between sixteen and sixty, and women between fourteen and forty were commandeered for forced labour in building fortifications in Hungary. The rest of the

Jewish population, including the disabled and sick, was confined in four or five ghettoes near Budapest. The only Jews to escape evacuation were those in possession of passports with visas for Palestine, Sweden, Switzerland, Portugal or Spain. ... In November [1944], one hundred thousand Jews poured into Budapest from the provinces.[54]

To repeat: There were certain events before October 1944, including deportations, which were too unimportant for the IRC-report even to bother mentioning the figures; but the *IRC-report emphasizes that the really dangerous occurrences for the majority of the Jews began in October 1944.* The maximum number which the report says *were to* have been deported was given as 60,000 and nowhere do we find any trace whatever that this number was exceeded or even attained. To the contrary, there are indications that the actual number of deportees was even less.[55] Still, in this analysis we will assume that, including those deported between March and October 1944, the total number of deported Jews from Hungary reached 100,000, which is probably much too high.

Jews were not allowed to serve in the armed forces; the mobilization law prohibited that. Instead, Jews were drafted into an auxiliary service, the Hungarian military labor force. According to Dr. Rudolf Kastner, the former associate president of the Zionist Organization of Hungary, this labor force included at times 80,000 Jews; all in all, about 130,000 Jews had been drafted into this service. Dr. Kastner estimated that 30-40,000 Jews fell while serving in this force.[56] But the *Judaica* mentioned that in January 1943 alone, after the great Don-breakthrough of the Red Army when the 2nd Hungarian Army practically disintegrated, 40-43,000 of the 50,000 Jews serving in the military labor force lost their lives in the panic that followed.[57] If that many died in this one military catastrophe, further losses certainly occurred during the battles of retreat until Budapest. The total number of fallen Jews in the Hungarian labor force must have exceeded the 50,000-mark by far – if Zionist statistics are correct.

Dr. Zoltan Klar, former elected member of the Council of the Budapest Jewish Community, testified under oath at the hearings of the investigating committee of the US House of Representatives of September 22 and 23, 1954, looking into the treatment of Jews by the Soviets; he said that the Hungarian Minister in Moscow, Prof. Szekfu, visited the Jewish Council in 1946 and declared that 30,000 Hungarian citizens, former members of the military labor force, were still in Soviet prisons as far as he knew; of these, 90% were Jews. Prof. Szekfu thought that they

140

would return home soon. In actual fact, no more than 1,500 ever returned according to Dr. Klar; 25,500 Hungarian Jews had disappeared in Soviet prisons without a trace.[58]

These developments have been summarized in tableform (in 1,000):

	Greater Hungary	Trianon Hungary	Ruthe-nia	Nothern Transyl-vania	Slovak areas	Banat
Jewish population 1941 *deduct:*	–725	400	109	149	42	25
– Deportation to Germany	–100	–55	–15	–21	–6	–3
– Losses in the military labor force	– 50	–27.5	– 8	–10.5	–3	–1
– Members of the military labor force lost in the Soviet Union	–25.5	–25.5	?	?	?	?
Remainder	549.5	292	86	117.5	33	21

The Jewish losses in the Hungarian military labor force were divided proportionately among all the regions because no information is available as to the origin of the victims; the same procedure was followed with regard to the 100,000 (max.) Jews deported to Germany in 1944. But Dr. Klar's testimony was quite specific concerning the Jews who were in Soviet prison and most of whom had disappeared. These were former residents of the "old" Hungary (Trianon-borders) and for this reason we entered the entire figure of 25,500 in the column "Trianon-Hungary." The above table indicates that 292,000 Jews should have been found in Hungary after the war.

As for the natural demographic development during the war, one has to pay due regard to the generally insecure and economically precarious situation of the Hungarian Jews and to the fact that at times up to 22% of the entire male population (i.e. 80,000 of about 360,000 males) was serving in the military labor force. These circumstances must have had a considerable negative impact on the birth rate, which had been too low during the 1930's already.

As was shown in the First Chapter, Greater Hungary's Jewish net birth rate was -0.3% in 1942; this negative figure came about because the relatively high fertility of the Ruthenian Jews was more than offset by the very unfavorable net birth rate in the other regions. In particular, the Jews of "old" Trianon-Hungary had reached a net natural decrease of 0.5% in 1938 already. Also, it is certainly within the realm of possibility that the fatal circumstances of the war effected a further drop in the birth rate. In Germany and Austria, the negative Jewish natural growth rate was much worse before the war and it is safe to assume that the situation of the Hungarian Jews during the war was much more difficult than the one faced by German and Austrian Jews before 1938. Between 1930 and 1935, the annual Jewish excess of deaths over births in Germany and Austria was 5,500 and 2,500 respectively;[59] this is equivalent to an annual decrease of about 1.0 and 1.3%! Following this line of thought, it is probable that the natural decrease of the "old" Hungarian Jewish population during the five war years was near 1% annually causing a decrease totalling 20,000.

We noted above that Jewish sources claim 2,113 Jews had switched annually from the Mosaic to a Christian faith between 1930 and 1939. It stands to reason that many more Jews must have taken advantage of this possibility during WWII in order to secure a greater personal and economic security for themselves and their families. Even assuming only the same annual number of changes, there would still have been 10,000 conversions during the five war years and a corresponding reduction in the number of adherents to the Jewish faith. Another 6,000 have been found after the war in Rumania.[60] It is quite possible that these 6,000 Hungarian Jews in Rumania had tried to reach Turkey by way of Bulgaria or the port of Constanza in Rumania. As we go on, evidence will be forthcoming on the massive emigration via these two channels.

As was pointed out, the number of Jews deported to Germany reached at most 100,000; of these, about 55,000 should be applied to "old" Hungary. We know that thousands returned to Hungary after the war from the German camps. Their number, however, is not known. In this connection, the Hungarian Jew Dr. Klar testified before the US investigating committee that the Soviets prevented many of the returning Jews from entering Hungary after the war; instead, they arrested them at the border and transported them, male and female, to the east. He put their number at 40,000 Hungarian Jews![61]

Today's "official" version of the Jewish fate in Greater Hungary is that, with the exception of the Jews of Budapest, almost all the other Jews were deported *before early July 1944.* Budapest contained 184,453 Jews as of January 31, 1941. But even if one allows for some deportations, natural population decrease, emigrants, proportionate losses incurred in the military labor force, etc. it is still impossible that Budapest was populated by fewer than 150,000 Jews when deportations ceased (July 1944 according to the Zionist version). If one adds those few Jews who survived on the countryside, then it would have been possible indeed that Hungary's Jewish population had shrunk to only 200,000 by war's end as the Anglo-American Committee claims.

This figure is subject to some doubt. First, the International Red Cross was quite clear when it said:

> In November [1944], one hundred thousand Jews poured into Budapest from the provinces.[62]

In other words, these people fled from areas from which according to the Zionist post-war version all Jews supposedly had been removed already! This happened at a period of time when even Zionist reports say the deportations to Germany ("Auschwitz") had ceased. The US War Refugee Board under the leadership of the Zionist Morgenthau admitted that as a result of the negotiations between Saly Mayer from the Joint Distribution Committee and SS-Colonel Kurt Becher the deportation of the *more* than 200,000 Jews living in Budapest in *August 1944* did *not* take place.[63] This means, of course, that *far more than 300,000 Jews must have survived in Hungary* (Trianon-borders) according to the best of sources; we should remember that the IRC-report did not say either that *all* of the Jews had left the provinces and come to Budapest in November 1944.

Secondly, there is no question that thousands of Jews fled west after the war. Hilberg confirms this expressly.[64] Thirdly, figures for the surviving Hungarian Jews as provided by the Anglo-American Committee (200,000) pertained not to the end of the war but to *April 1946*;[65] if the figure of 200,000 for 1946 is correct this would mean that more than 100,000 Hungarian Jews must have left Hungary during the interim twelve months and gone to the West (Austria and Italy)!

Considering all the fallen, deported and escaped, the number of Jews in Hungary should have been expected to be around one-quarter of a million (see the summary below) – about 50,000 fewer than the more than 300,000 who were actually there. The only possible explanation for this discrepancy is that it reflects the Jews who poured into Hungary from other countries – Poland and Czechoslovakia – looking for a place to hide and relative security. Until April 1946 more than 100,000 had left Hungary – if the figure of 200,000 as published by the Anglo-American Committee is correct.

The following is a statistical summary of the Jewish fate in Hungary:

Jewish population at the end of 1939		400,000
deduct:		
– Fallen Jews in military labor force	27,500	
– Missing as Soviet prisoners-of-war	25,500	
– Deported east by the Soviet in 1945	40,000	
– Negative net birth rate during the war	20,000	
– Hungarian refugees in Rumania	6,000	
– Conversions to Christian faiths	10,000	129,000
Remainder		271,000
Purported "survivors" April 1946		200,000
"Missing" Hungarian Jews		71,000

Czechoslovakia

This state, forcibly established by the "Treaty" of Versailles, experienced a very lively history during its short existence. Its subsequent division makes a separate treatment of the various regions mandatory.

The census of 1930 recorded 356,830 Jews on the basis of religion, regionally distributed as follows:[66]

Czech areas (Bohemia and Moravia)	117,551
Slovakia	136,737
Ruthenia	102,542
Total	356,830

Because of low birth rates, the first two regions registered a slow decrease of the Jewish population, whereas the Jews in Ruthenia proved very fertile. After the Munich Accord a huge emigration set in, especially from the Czech areas. Reitlinger, who in turn refers to the Anglo-American Committee, reports that at the end of 1939 only 315,000 Jews lived in the former Czechoslovakian territory.[67]

As was pointed out in the First Chapter, Ruthenian Jews were quite fertile; on the other hand, they suffered from a migratory loss of young males who left for the industrial Czech areas. In any case, the Hungarians found only roughly 109,000 Jews in Ruthenia after the dismemberment of the artificial Czechoslovakian state.

In other words, the Jewish population of the first two regions may have been 206,000 in 1939 (i.e. 315,000 minus 109,000); this means that the Jews of Bohemia, Moravia and Slovakia decreased by 48,288 (i.e. 117,551 plus 136,737 minus 206,000).

Even before the war, Hungary had annexed a section of Slovakia containing 42,000 Jews;[68] the remaining independent Slovak state is reported to have registered 85,045 Jews in 1939 according to the *Year Book* which, in turn, referred to news published in *Der Grenzbote* (Bratislava) of January 18, 1940.[69] Consequently, the total Slovak area must have had 127,000 Jews at the end of 1939. If correct, this would point to a net emigration of 9,700 (a small excess of deaths over births cannot be excluded, though). Thus, the Czech areas cannot have contained more than 79,000 Jews at the end of 1939 (206,000 minus 127,000); emigration, flight and a negative net birth rate added up to a reduction of 38,600 between 1930 and the end of 1939 (i.e. 117,551 minus 79,000). Further population losses ensued in 1940.

Reports in the Zionist press according to which German statistics published on February 2, 1941 put the number of Jews remaining in the "Protectorate" at 70,000 confirm these calculations.[70] Reitlinger adds that until 1942 another reduction of 7,000 Jews occurred because of emigration from Bohemia and Moravia and continuing low birth rates. All in all, 4,000 Jews are said to have succeeded in emigrating during the war.[71] But, as one has to assume that the excess of deaths over births accelerated throughout the war period of 1942-1945 a further deduction of maybe 2,000 should be made. In summary, the Jewish population of the "Protectorate" decreased after 1939 by 4,000 as a result of emigration and by 5,000 as a result of negative net birth rates.

In 1946(!), one whole year following the defeat of Germany, after Jews had left Bohemia and Moravia in huge droves for the American zone of occupation in Germany – we will come back to this later – Reitlinger still found 32,000 Jews in the former "Protectorate."[72]

In *Slovakia's* case, it is somewhat more difficult to trace the development because of the loss of large areas to Hungary just before the war began. At the outbreak of the war, 85,000 Jews lived in the smaller independent Slovakia. Apart from the 52,000 deported, the remaining Jews lived relatively securely until the end of 1944.[73] The IRC wrote:

> ... at certain priods Slovakia was even looked upon as a comparative haven of refuge for Jews, especially for those coming from Poland. Those who remained in Slovakia seem to have been in comparative safety until the end of August 1944, when a rising against the German forces took place.[74]

The consequence of this uprising was that many Jews were deported. In post-war Slovakia – again, including the areas formerly occupied by Hungary – Reitlinger found 45,000 Jews whereas Gregory Frumkin managed to discover even 60,000;[75] let us agree on 50,000. The fate of the Jews in the Hungarian-occupied Slovak regions was covered in the context of the Hungarian Jews.

Part of the Czechoslovakian state until its dismemberment, *Ruthenia* was first annexed by Hungary and, after the war, by the Soviet Union. For this reason, the local Jewish population shared the fate of the Hungarian Jews just like part of the Jews of Slovakia. The human losses of all the Rumanian, Slovak and Serbian Jews under Hungarian domination who were made Soviet prisoners-of-war as former members of the Hungarian military labor force is not discussed in the pertinent literature; all we know is that 27,000 Hungarian-Jewish labor force members were in Soviet prisons and that only 1,500 ever returned. In the case of the Jews of Ruthenia their number would have to be reduced by those who disappeared in Soviet prisons. The remainder of the Ruthenian Jews has been added to the Soviet Union in the Fourth Chapter. Consequentley, we will exclude the Ruthenian Jews on account of the annexation of that region by the Soviet Union after the war. The developments in Czechoslovakia can be summarized as follows:

Czech areas (Bohemia and Moravia - 1930)		117.551
Slovakia (1930)		136,737
Ruthenia (1930)		102.542
Czechoslovakia (1930)		356,830
Ruthenia annexed by the USSR in 1945		102,542
Czechoslovakia without Ruthenia (1930)		254,288
deduct:		
Emigration (incl. excess of births over deaths before the war):		
– Czech areas	38,600	
– Slovakia	9,700	48,300
Jews in Bohemia, Moravia and Slovakia in (1939)		206,000
deduct:		
Changes after 1939:		
– Emigration from Czech areas	4,000	
– Excess of deaths over births in Czech areas	5,000	
– Fallen Slovakian-Jewish members of the Hungarian military labor force	3,000	12,000
Remainder		194,000
Purported "survivors"		82,000
"Missing" Czechoslovakian Jews		112,000

The Rumanian census of December 29, 1930 recorded the population on the basis of language, nationality and religion. Accordingly, the "Jewish" figures were 518,754, 728,115 and 756,930; since many Jews had already given up Yiddish and, despite their Mosaic faith, considered themselves of other than Jewish nationality, the figure of 756,930 represents the best indication of Rumania's Jewish population.[76]

In 1940, three neighboring countries acquired slices of Rumanian territory: The Soviet Union on June 28 (Bessarabia and northern Bukovina), Hungary on August 30 (northern Transylvania) and Bulgaria on September 6 (southern Dobrudja). The remaining Rumanian territory – Core-Rumania – counted 328,930 persons of the Mosaic faith at the time of the last census of 1930,[77] northern Transylvania 148,660, southern Dobrudja 846,[78] Bessarabia 206,958,[79] leaving 71,536 for northern Bukovina; in total, the area seized by the USSR in 1940 thus had a Jewish population of 278,494 as of December 29, 1930. Of course, until mid-1940 these figures were subject to change due to natural growth patterns, emigration and a large migration from the country to the cities, especially to Bukarest.

In the seven-year period from December 1930 until early 1938 an average of 724,600 Jews lived in Rumania;[80] a mean growth rate of 0.2% – as suggested in the First Chapter – would have resulted in an excess of births over deaths of 10,200. Thus, about 74,900 Jews must have emigrated during this time:

Census of 1930	756,930
Excess of births over deaths from December 1930 until early 1938	10,200
	767,130
Jewish population in early 1938[81]	692,244
Emigration 1930 – early 1938	74,900

During these seven years 10,700 Jews left Rumania annually. The Institute for Contemporary History in Munich also counts Rumania among those countries where, because of the poor economic situation, Jews were forced to emigrate in large numbers. It is obvious that the worsening conditions in Rumania in the latter part of the 1930's caused more and more Jews to look for an improvement in their personal lives abroad. Among these were especially the Jews of Bessarabia where many

Jewish refugees from the Russian civil war had fled after WWI. Many other Jews sought to escape from the growing anti-Semitic tendencies by merging into the larger Jewish communities of the big cities.

The size of emigration in the years 1938, 1939 and 1940 is unknown. However, one may be sure that the deteriorating economic and political situation persuaded even more Jews to emigrate. Even if we limit ourselves to the average emigration rate of the years 1931-1937 and apply that to 1938-1940, and if we concede furthermore that the small excess of deaths over births did not expand in 1939 and 1940, then the number of Jews living in Rumania in mid-1940 could have been 665,500 at most:

Jewish population in early 1938	692,244
Emigration from 1938 until mid–1940	26,750
Jewish population in mid–1940	665,500

By 1940, it seems, Rumania's Jewish population had decreased by 91,400, or 12.1% since 1930.

On April 6, 1941, a census found only 315,509 Jews in Core-Rumania, 291,674 of whom were urban.[82] Unfortunately, these figures are not entirely comparable to the census of 1930 because the 1941 census defined "Jews" as including all persons with at least one parent of Mosaic faith. It is unlikely that the latter factor accounted for more than several thousand persons. Deducting this "external" factor from the total of 315,509 only about 300,000 "comparable" Rumanian Jews were left in April 1941.

Thus, whereas Core-Rumania lost 28,930 Jews during the interim ten years, or 9%, Greater Rumania's loss of Jews between December 1930 and mid-1940 totalled 91,430, or 12%. Furthermore, the areas ceded to Hungary, Bulgaria and the Soviet Union in the summer of 1940 recorded 428,000 Jews at the end of 1930 (148,660 in northern Transylvania, 846 in southern Dobrudja and 278,494 in Bessarabia and northern Bukovina combined), but during the 1930's a decrease by 62,500, or 15% had occurred:

Jewish Population in Rumania

	December 1930	B e f o r e the war	Changes number	(%)
Greater Rumania	756,930	665,500 (mid-1940)	– 91,430	– 12
Core-Rumania	328,930	300,000 (April 1941)	– 28,930	– 9
Ceded territories	428,000	365,500	– 62,500	– 15

This considerably smaller decline in Core-Rumania compared to the regions ceded in the summer of 1940 probably has two reasons: First, eastern Rumania contained many Jews who had fled from the Ukraine during the Russian civil war; but Bessarabia's agricultural economy was not developed enough to absorb these people and emigration, therefore, often was the only possibility to escape poverty.

Secondly, the beginning industrialization and the accompanying urbanization lured many rural Jews to migrate to the cities – and in Rumania there was only one with more than 100,000 inhabitants, namely, the capital of Bukarest. The total population of this city had grown from 639,040 (December 1930) to 999,658 (April 1941), i.e. by 56.4%. In the course of the general migration from the rural areas, the Jewish population of Bukarest increased as well although not as rapidly as the Rumanian, because the Jews preferred emigration to a migration to the cities. Still, Bukarest's Jewish population rose by 14,788 from 76,480 (December 1930) to 91,268 (April 1941), that is, by 19.3%.[83] Obviously, the Jewish population of the area where the census was taken in April 1941 (Core-Rumania) would have declined much more than 9% were it not for the internal migration from the regions to Bukarest and other larger central cities.

The admission of tens of thousands of Polish-Jewish refugees in September 1939 poses great difficulties in determining the Jewish population of the ceded territories precisely. To be sure, there is an official Rumanian estimate of 148,621 Jews for the ceded portion of Transylvania as of January 1, 1940[84] compared to the census of 1930 which found 148,660, but it is completely unknown how many Jewish refugees from Polish Galicia were included in the 1940-estimate. Nevertheless, it appears that the Jewish population of Transylvania was stagnant during the previous decades already. The *Jüdisches Lexikon* (Jewish Encyclopedia), for instance, mentions that the censuses of 1910 and 1920 for Transylvania, the Transylvanian foreland and the Banat recorded 172,294 and 181,340 Jews, respectively[85] – an increase of only 9,000 during that decade, or one half of one per cent annually. But the *Jüdisches Lexikon* also says that there had been a large Jewish immigration from Galicia at the time. Without this immigration, Transylvania and the Banat obviously would not have registered any increase at all. For this reason, it is probable that Transylvania – like all the other regions of Rumania – recorded a decrease of its Jewish population until 1940. Even assuming a rate of decrease only half the Rumanian average – i.e. 6% – no more than 140,000 native Jews could have been living in northern Transylvania when it was ceded to

Hungary. But the Rumanians insist that 148,621 Jews populated the area and this figure agrees very well with a similar figure produced by the Hungarians for the Jews in their newly acquired territory.[86] The difference of 8,621 (148,621 minus 140,000) thus must consist of Jewish refugees from Polish Galicia of September 1939.

Given the above information, one can now determine the native Jewish population of the areas ceded to the Soviet Union:

	1930	1940	Changes Number	(%)
All ceded territories	428,000	365,500	– 62,500	– 15
deduct:				
Northern Transylvania (excl.				
Polish-Jewish refugees)	148,660	140,000	– 8,660	– 6
Southern Dobrudja	846	412[78]	– 434	– 51
Territories ceded to the USSR (excl. Polish-Jewish refugees)	278,494	225,088	– 53,406	– 19

A decrease by 53,406 Jews, or 19%, in the areas handed over to the Soviet Union is not particularly large considering that the majority of those 278,494 Jews of 1930 lived in Bessarabia, a poorly developed region.

Yet, it appears, the Soviets acquired many more Jews than those 225,088 when they occupied the Rumanian areas. In September 1939, Polish Jews fled *en masse* not only to the Soviet Union but also to Rumania. Reports on the number of refugee Jews in Rumania are very vague, however. An informative account, but unfortunately poor in statistics, of the flight of Galician Jews to Rumania is J.G. Burg's *Schuld und Schicksal*.

We assumed that at least 100,000 Polish Jews found their way to Rumania because reports in the Zionist press – if true – make this number seem quite realistic. We found 9,000 Polish-Jewish refugees in northern Transylvania. Furthermore, up to 65,000 Jews – apparently consisting mostly of Polish-Jewish refugees – are said to have changed over to Soviet territory when the Soviet Union occupied northern Bukovina and Bessarabia in 1940.[87] These 65,000 Jews must have lived in southern Bukovina and Moldavia since their arrival from Poland, which is not improbable in view of the geographic proximity of Galicia. Many other Jewish refugees from Poland were living in the northern Bukovina and in Bessarabia when the Soviets annexed those areas. For these reasons, it is quite probable that more than 90,000 Polish refugee Jews fell under Soviet domination in the course of the Soviet occupation of large parts of Rumanian territory. Thus, it seems that the Soviets acquired a total Jewish population numbering 316,000 at the time of their acquisition of Bessarabia and northern Bukovina (225,000 native Jews plus 91,000 Polish-Jewish refugees).

But even after the outbreak of hostilities with the Soviet Union (June 22, 1941), there were still many possibilities for Jews to leave Rumania, often taking strange and risky routes. One escape route led from the port of Constanza to neutral Turkey: Many ships left this port – under German protection at times – trying to reach extra-European destinations. In this connection, the tragic fate of the steamer *Struma* comes to mind; this ship had left Constanza for Istanbul on December 16, 1941 and was hit by British mines off the coast of Turkey; except for two saved, all of the 769 Jewish passengers died;[88] other ships met a similar fate.

Reitlinger referred to this route as follows:

> ... it was possible to run a *daily* small steamer from Constanza to Istanbul ...[89]

Even if one allows only 100 persons per trip, a minimum of 100,000 Jews must have left Europe during the war on this route. The composition of the passengers is not known. But since the Jewish population of Rumania still numbered more than 400,000 after "liberation" by the Red Army, it would appear that the majority of the Jewish refugees leaving Constanza by ship during the war must have been of Polish, Hungarian, Czech or Slovak nationality.

A second escape channel ran on land from Rumania through Bulgaria to Turkey and from there to Palestine, Persia or overseas. Reliable figures on the entire exodus by way of Rumanian ports and Bulgaria are not available; all we know is – this will be covered in greater detail in the next chapter – that tens of thousands of European Jews from all countries within the German sphere of influence escaped this way. The *Universal* commented:

> ... during the Second World War ... the State Department of the United States [helped] many Jews fleeing from Roumania to find a haven in Turkey and Palestine.[90]

Assessing the number of Rumanian Jews escaping this way between mid-1940 and the end of the war at only 20,000 is just to keep this exodus on record, because the actual number of Jewish refugees leaving

Rumania during this period must have been much larger, probably many, many times larger.

A comparison of the Jewish population of April 1941 with the purported survivors at the end of the war allows no conclusions as to the extent of flight from Rumania during the war. In 1945, Rumania regained northern Transylvania; the areas annexed by the Soviet Union in 1940 and reconquered in 1941, however, were again occupied by the USSR. The post-war "estimates" thus refer to the Rumania within its post-war borders – an area which contained maybe 451,000 Jews in August 1939:

Jewish population in early 1938	692,244
Emigration from 1938 until mid-1939	app. 16,000
mid-1939 (borders of 1939)	676,244
Rumanian Jews in the areas ceded to the USSR	225,088
Jewish population in mid-1939 (borders of 1945)	451,000[91]

The number of Jews found in northern Transylvania after the war is not known. Our calculations show that 21,000 were deported to Germany during the war, but according to Reitlinger 20,000 returned from German camps.[92] On the other hand, is is probable that at least 10,000 died in the Hungarian military labor force and the number of those who disappeared in Soviet prisoner-of-war camps – as in the case of the Hungarian Jews – is a total mystery. Reducing the original figure of 148,621 for Transylvania by those 1,000 failing to return from German camps and the 10,500 killed in action, the remainder of 137,000 probably is still too large; but this is the best one can do.

As for the "survivors", Dr. Isaac Glickman, former member of the executive committee of the Federation of the Jewish Communities of Rumania, gave evidence before the investigating committe of the US House of Representatives in 1954 – Dr. Glickman says he left Rumania at the end of 1947 – estimating their number at 425,000 at the "time of liberation."[93] Mr. Hilberg, though, found 430,000 in post-war Rumania.[94]

It is all but certain that the figure of 430,000 Jews in Rumania is too low by several tens of thousands. If Dr. Glickman put the number of Jews in Rumania *at* the "time of liberation" at 425,000, this must be a low figure. After all, Reitlinger mentioned 20,000 who returned from German camps after the war, i.e. *after* the "time of liberation", and further thousands are supposed to have returned from the USSR *after* the war.

All of this adds up to far more than 450,000 – at least 20,000 more than Hilberg claims to have found.

Following our own cautious calculations, we should have found 433,000 Jews (or even less, because we had no clues as to the number of former members of the Hungarian military labor force who did not return from Soviet prisons and our imputed figure of only 20,000 emigrants between 1941 and the end of the war is probably only a fraction of the real number). In other words, when war drew to a close in Rumania, tens of thousands of Jews were living in that country who had arrived there *during* the war. And, indeed, there is a report by the International Red Cross published in 1948 about its activities during the war, saying that after the retreat of the Germans 6,000 Hungarian Jews had been found in northern Transylvania in December 1944. This obviously vast immigration of non-Rumanian Jews during the war is another indication that Rumania was a real gateway for untold numbers of European Jews to leave Europe by water and by land. Statistically the development looks like this:

Jewish population in early 1938		692,244
Emigration from 1938 until mid-1939		16,000
mid-1939		676,244
Admission of Polish-Jewish refugees (1939)		100,000
September 1939		776,244
Taken over by the Soviet Union:		
– Polish-Jewish refugees	91,000	
– Native Rumanian Jews	225,088	
	316,088	
Acquired by Hungary	148,621	
Acquired by Bulgaria	412	
Emigration 1940	10,700	475,821
		300,423
Persons considered Jewish according to the changed census definitions of 1941 (est.)		15,086
Jewish population – census of April 6, 1941		315,509
Emigration: April 1941 – end of war		20,000
Jews in Core-Rumania at end of war (maximum)		295,509
Recovery of Transylvania	148,621	
Recovery of southern Dobrudja	412	
	149,033	
Fallen Jews in Hungarian military labor force	10,500	
Jews failing to return from German camps	1,000	137,533
Calculated number of Jews in post-war Rumania		433,000
Purported "survivors" according to Hilberg		430,000
"Missing" Jews		3,000

The census of 1934 recorded 48,398 Jews.[95] In 1947(!), their number had been reduced to 46,500 according to the *Year Book*;[96] the difference of 1,898 must be attributed either to emigration or an excess of deaths over births, because not a single Jew was deported from Bulgaria during the war.[97]

We will show in the next Chapter that 48,642 Jews emigrated to Israel from Bulgaria between May 15, 1948 and December 31, 1970. The number of Bulgarian Jews who might have left their country during or immediately after the war is completely unknown. But Bulgaria, too, belonged to those countries where large-scale emigration was easiest after the war according to Zionist scholar Hilberg; it is thus not far-fetched to assume that thousands (or tens of thousands?) made use of this possibility *before* 1947 in order to emigrate to Palestine and overseas. Also, there is no reason to believe that *all* of the Bulgarian Jews had left for *Israel* after May 15, 1948.

In 1970, there were still 7,000 Jews in Bulgaria.[98] Since Bulgarian Jews were not known for their great fertility, it becomes quite obvious that Bulgaria's Jews did not number 46,500 at the end of the war as Zionists want us to believe, but many thousands even tens of thousands more; in any case, 56,000 (48,642 plus 7,000) is a minimum figure. This is another piece of evidence that Bulgaria – just like Rumania – was a transit country during the war for Jewish refugees from Yugoslavia, Hungary, Rumania, Slovakia and Poland! More than that, these contradictory figures show the relative magnitude of understatement contained in the "survivor"-figures as published by Zionist sources.

Jewish population (1934)	48,400
"Survivors" (1947)	56,000
"Immigrants"	7,600

Summary

At the beginning of the 1930's all the European countries (excl. the USSR and the Baltic countries) which later fell within the German sphere of influence contained about 6 million Jews (*Table 11*). Anti-Jewish measures and economic misery resulted in a massive emigration of over 1.1 million Jews from just five countries – Poland, Germany, Czechoslovakia, Hungary and Rumania (see also First Chapter). The largest part of this emigration was directed toward Palestine and overseas (more about that in the next chapter) and, to a smaller degree, to western Europe. Other unfavorable developments (negative population growth in Germany and Hungary, conversions in Hungary) more than compensated for the relatively meager excess of births in other parts of Europe – if there was any at all. At the outbreak of the German-Polish war (end of 1939) the Jewish population in these European countries had dropped to about 5 million.

The *Year Book* committed a serious error when it placed the number of Jews in these countries at 6 million for the year 1939.[99] A comparison would show that the *Year Book* did account for emigration from Germany and Hungary (in part, at least), but not for that from Poland, Rumania and Czechoslovakia. To the contrary, the Jewish populations of these latter three countries were "increased" by assuming unrealistically large birth rates. The result is grave. In actual fact, Poland, Rumania and Czechoslovakia contained only 3.6 million Jewish inhabitants at the end of 1939, but the *Year Book* insists on 4.5 million! Since there were 956,000 fewer Jews in the area of the subsequent German sphere of influence in 1939 (*Table 11*), 90% of this difference must be attributed to just those three countries. In other words, here we have almost one million Jews who were not even in Europe at the start of WWII, but who are nevertheless included in the "Final Solution" according to Zionist statistical methodology.

However, in 1941 – just prior to the German invasion of the USSR – only 2.8 million Jews lived within the German sphere of influence. The decrease by 2.2 million was largely the result of the annexation of large parts of Rumanian and Polish territory by the Soviet Union in 1939 and 1940 when those regions' numerous Jewish populations together with many hundreds of thousands of Jews fleeing before the German armies disappeared into the Soviet empire. It is well known today that the Soviets succeeded in keeping the vast majority of their Jews outside the reach of German military power – for reasons of self-interest. Therefore, it is simply misleading to calculate the number of "missing" Jews by deducting the "survivors" after WWII – in most cases figures are available only for 1946 and 1947(!) – from 1939-figures which, to make it worse, are exaggerated by 1 million. There have been many changes between 1939 and 1945 due to emigration, low birth rates, conversions, deaths in combat, evacuation etc. Also, Poland and Rumania had suffered large losses of territory and population to the Soviet Union.

Table 11

Jewish Population in the former German Sphere of Influence in Europe (exl. USSR and Baltic States) from the early 1930's until the End of WWII (in 1,000)

Country	Early[a] 1930's	1939[b]	1941[b]	"Survivors" 1946/47[b]	"Missing" in Europe[b]	Acquired by the USSR[b]
Italy, Benelux, France, Denmark, Norway	470	545	525	375	134	
Greece	73	65	65	12	53	
Germany and Austria	731	263	214	36	159	
Former German-occupied western Europe	1,274	873	804	423	346	
Yugoslavia	68	68	43	12	56	
Hungary, of which:	445	(551)	(725)	200	71	66
– Hungary (Trianon-borders)		400	400			
– Slovak areas		42	42			
– Ruthenia		109	109			86
– Northern Transylvania			149			
– Serbian Banat			25			
Czechoslovakia, of which:	(357)					
– Bohemia-Moravia (Protectorate)	118	79	70	32	38	
– Slovakia	137	85	85	50	74	
– Ruthenia	102				15	

(continued on next page)

Table 11 (concluded)

Rumania	757	676	315	430	3	225
Bulgaria	48	48	48	56	- 8	
Poland/Government General[c]	3,114	2,664	757	83	674	1,867
Former German-occupied eastern Europe	4,789	4,171	2,043	863	923	2,244
Jewish refugees returned to Poland from the USSR				+157		- 157
						2,087
Former German-occupied Europe:						
– according to our analysis	6,063	5,044	2,847	1,443	1,269	
– according to AJYB-figures[d]		6,000		1,410	4,590	
Difference		- 956		+ 33	-3,321	

Sources:

(a) With the exception of Germany and Austria all figures in this column have been taken from *Table 16* (Eighth Chapter). Germany (incl. Danzig, Memel and the Saar) had 539,265 Jews in 1933 and Austria's census found 191,781 Jews according to the *AJYB*, 1940, Vol. 42, p. 600.

(b) With the exception of the lines "Poland" and "AJYB-figures" all of the figures listed in this column have been taken from the country-specific details in the Sixth Chapter.

(c) See First and Second Chapter.

(d) *AJYB*, 1947, Vol. 49, p. 740.

Our investigation in the Second and Sixth Chapters found 1,443,000 "surviving" Jews compared to 1,410,000 of the *Year Book* (*Table 11*). These "survivors" should be compared with the Jewish population in the European countries in 1941 taking into account the many changes which occurred in those countries during the war; on this basis, we arrived at a "missing"-figure of 1,269,000. This number is about 3.3 million smaller than that of the *Year Book*. The reason is clear: The *Year Book's* pre-war figure is too large by almost one million and did not take into account the Soviet net acquisition of 2.1 million Rumanian, Polish, Hungarian and Ruthenian Jews; just these two "mistakes" added up to an exaggeration of about 3.0 million "missing" Jews.

Let us summarize: In 1941, 2,847,000 Jews lived within the German sphere of influence in Europe (excl. the USSR and the Baltic countries). After allowing for war losses, the missing in Soviet prisons, emigration and very low birth rates during the war, annexation of Ruthenia by the USSR in 1945 and the return of Polish-Jewish refugees from the USSR after the war, 2,712,000 (1,443,000 plus 1,269,000) Jews should have been counted in those countries after the war. On the basis of Zionist statistics – which refer to a large extent to 1946 and 1947, not to 1945 – we arrived at only 1,443,000 "survivors". A similarly large number of Jews, namely 1,269,000, is not accounted for.

SEVENTH CHAPTER

Jewish Emigration after World War Two

Following the defeat of Germany a flood of non-German refugees poured from the East into the three Western zones of the occupied and divided country. Among them were many Jews. British General Sir Frederick Morgan, head of the UNRRA operations in Germany, declared in a press conference in Frankfurt/Main at the end of 1945 that an unknown Jewish organization was bringing masses of Jews from the East to Germany and that all of them were well fed and well dressed. The Zionist Hilberg, too, commented:

> In Poland, Czechoslovakia, and Hungary many Jews chose not to wait; they decided to embark on their journey. ... From Poland the exodus began through Czechoslovakia to the American zone in Germany. From Hungary and even Roumania the Jews began to arrive in Austria. By November 1945, the flow was beginning to thicken, and thousands of refugees were spilling over into Italy.[1]

In this connection, one should always keep in mind that the statistics on Jewish "survivors" do not pertain to May 8, 1945, but to the years 1946 and 1947; the 1.4 million "survivors" thus cannot possibly include this huge number of refugees leaving their native countries in eastern Europe.

Immediately after the war, more than 250,000 Jews inhabited the DP-camps in Germany and in July 1947 more than 400,000 refugee Jews are said to have remained in western Europe.[2] These figures apply only to certain fixed points in time because in the interim periods hundreds of thousands of Jews left Europe in the direction of Palestine, North and South America and other places!

These uncontrolled arrivals and departures in the chaotic post-war

159

period prevented an official count of the wandering, fleeing and uprooted Jews. The only possibility to obtain a somewhat reliable picture of this mass migration is to determine the post-war Jewish *immigration* in the main countries of destination.

United States

Official US statistics put the number of Jews in 1926 at 4,081,242; another official count in 1936 found 4,641,184.[3] Both figures refer only to communities with synagogues. As Special Agent of the United States Bureau of the Census, Dr. Harry S. Linfield made a study of all the communities without synagogues and found that 4,228,029 Jews lived in the United States at the end of 1927;[4] a similar investigation by Dr. Linfield in the same capacity produced 4,770,647 Jews for 1937.[5]

It is not certain to what extent immigration and natural growth contributed to the population increase of 543,000 in the ten-year interval. In the previous decades millions of Jews had entered the United States: About 1.8 million between 1899 and 1924. At least three-fourths of them originated in Poland and Russia, countries with a very fertile Jewish population in those days. A large portion of the other fourth, too, hailed from countries such as Rumania, whose Jewish population had shown large natural growth rates.[6] But the changes in the US immigration laws in the 1920's are supposed to have led to a drastic reduction in the flow of Jewish immigration from eastern Europe.

Besides, the new urban American environment soon began to show up in sharply dropping birth rates. It is thus quite reasonable to assume that the annual natural increase of American Jews amounted to 0.5% at most between 1927 and 1937. Even this rate seems somewhat high, particularly in view of the 0.8% net growth rate of the total US population – with its large and fertile colored and white rural sections – between 1930 and 1939.[7] It would seem that an excess of births over deaths could have increased the US Jewish population from 4,228,029 in 1927 to at most 4,444,000 in 1937. In actual fact, however, 4.77 million Jews were found in 1937 – 326,000 more than natural growth would have warranted. A check of US immigration statistics reveals, though, that only 81,212 Jewish immigrants were recorded in this period.[8] An explanation for this wide discrepancy will be forthcoming below.

The *Year Book's* post-war American-Jewish population statistics are as follows:

1946 until 1956	5,000,000
1957 and 1958	5,197,000
1959	5,367,000
1960 until 1967	5,532,000
1968 until 1970	5,869,000
1971	6,060,000

These figures are fictitious. The purported population size for 1946 was simply maintained without change for ten years, at a time when hundreds of thousands of central and Eastern European Jews found shelter in the United States. Finally, when it was decided to proceed with the long overdue correction, the increase by just 197,000 was barely enough to explain the net natural growth between 1946 and 1957. Obviously, these figures are politically inspired.

Already in 1943, the Jewish historian and former secretary of the Hilfsverein der Deutschen Juden (Relief Association of German Jews), Dr. Mark Wischnitzer, who was employed by the American Jewish Joint Distribution Committee since 1938 and figured prominently in the edition of the *Universal Jewish Encyclopedia*,[9] wrote in an article in *The Jewish Quarterly Review* that the Jewish population of the United States had reached 5,199,200.[10] The rise by 429,000 from 4.77 million since 1937 amounts to an annual growth of 1.45% (!) – much too large for any possible natural increase. The answer to this contradiction was provided by Assistant Secretary of State Breckinridge Long.

In March 1943, Long declared in the name of the US Government that 547,775 refugees had entered the United States since 1933.[11] Eight months later, on November 26, Long testified before an investigating committee of the US House of Representatives, the House Foreign Affairs Committee:

> The United States has admitted about 580,000 victims of persecution by the Hitler regime since it began ten years ago. ... the majority of the refugees admitted were Jews ...[12]

It is not known what was meant by the term "majority." If he meant at least 70%, 406,000 of the 580,000 victims of persecution accepted by the United States must have been Jews. Unfortunately, the official immigration statistics show only 163,583 immigrant Jews between 1933 and 1943, which is about 240,000 fewer.[13] The explanation for this further discrepancy is very simple.

First, the Jewish statistician Arthur Ruppin pointed out that US immigration statistics for Jews do not mean very much; the reason is that they do not include those Jewish immigrants whose culture and ordinary language makes them appear as members of the people of their country of origin. The Jewish immigrants from Germany, for example, were not registered as "Hebrews" but as Germans, whereas Galician Jews from Poland often appeared very "Jewish" because of their everyday language, looks, etc. and thus were registered in the column for "Hebrews."[14]

Secondly, Long told the investigating committee that the United States allowed Jews to enter the United States on *visitors'* visas before and during the war. This is of course another very important reason for the fact that US immigration statistics show only 165,583 Jewish immigrants between 1933 and 1943 instead of more than 400,000.[15]

One to way to arrive at the real number of Jewish immigrants before and after 1937 may be – despite unavoidable inaccuracies – to divide those estimated 406,000 immigrant Jews on the basis of the registered Jewish immigrants between 1933 and 1943:

Jewish Immigrants in the United States: 1933–1943

Period	Registered	Calculated
1933–1937	27,374	67,000
1938–1943	138,209	339,000
1933–1943	165,583	406,000

Adding the calculated Jewish immigrants numbering 339,000 between 1938 and 1943 to the 4,771,000 Jews of 1937, one obtains a total of 5.11 million, or 89,000 fewer than mentioned by Dr. Wischnitzer for the year 1943. This difference is equivalent to a natural growth rate of about 0.3% p.a. – possibly somewhat low, but still quite plausible for an urban population whose birth rate was negatively affected by economic need during the Great Depression (1937-1940) and men absent on military duty (1941-1943).

According to the *Year Book*, however, the American Jewish population reached only 5,197,000 in 1957; this figure is still smaller than found in 1943 by Dr. Wischnitzer who was in an excellent position to judge the actual size of Jewish immigration. Meanwhile, though, further hundreds of thousands of homeless European Jews entered the United States since 1943. Also, it is a matter of statistical record that the Jewish population, too, was affected by the baby-boom following WWII, although for a much shorter time period. The figure produced by the *Year Book* for 1946, therefore, is just plain *wrong*.

In 1970, the Council of Jewish Federations and Welfare Funds sponsored a nationwide sampling survey of the Jewish population, the so-

162

called National Jewish Population Study (NJPS). The survey did not aim at tracing all American Jews but only those who were still connected with Jewry in any form whatever.[16] Jews who had broken completely with their Jewish past and retained no further ties to their Jewish identity were not included. We shall attempt to obtain some answers from this study to questions regarding immigration, natural growth and assimilation.

NJPS found 5,731,685 persons in Jewish households – defined as households with at least one Jewish person; among these there were 5,370,000 Jews. If this number would have included all the American Jews, the increase over 27 years earlier would have been only 171,000! An analysis of the age structure (*Table 12*) proves that such a tiny growth is totally impossible.

Table 12
Age Structure of American Jews: 1970

Year of Birth	Age	Share in %	Share per Year of Birth (%)
1966–1970	0– 4	5.7	1.14
1961–1965	5– 9	6.7	1.34
1956–1960	10–14	10.1	2.02
1951–1955	15–19	9.4	1.88
1946–1950	20–24	8.7	1.74
1941–1945	25–29	5.7	1.14
1936–1940	30–34	4.7	0.94
1931–1935	35–39	5.8	1.16
1926–1930	40–44	6.0	1.20
1921–1925	45–49	7.1	1.42
1916–1920	50–54	6.7	1.34
1911–1915	55–59	6.4	1.28
1906–1910	60–64	5.0	1.00
1901–1905	65–69	4.3	0.86
1896–1900	70–74	3.2	0.64
1891–1895	75–79	2.1	0.42
prior to 1891	80 and older	1.5	
	unknown	0.9	
		100.0	

Source: *AJYB*, 1973, Vol. 74, S. 271.

It is evident that the incidence of births was not very great from 1941 to 1945 but between 1946 and 1960 it was considerable; after that it fell rapidly. The table points to a net growth rate between 1946 and 1960 of possibly around 0.8% per year. The decade of 1961-1970 saw a drastic reduction in the number of births; it may be assumed that the rate of natural increase fell to as low as 0.2% p.a. on average.[17] Given these growth rates, the Jewish population would have had to pass the 6-million-mark by 1970 even without the post-war immigration flows.

The absolute impossiblity of just 5.37 million American Jews in 1970 was supported by other information made available by the NJPS. The study noted that 8.6% of all heads of households aged 20 to 24 years – born 1946 to 1950 – were foreign-born.[18] There is no reason to assume that the heads of households showed very different characteristics from the rest of the Jewish population; thus, we can apply that rate to the entire Jewish population as well.

While there is no information on the percentage of those born abroad in the years 1946-1950 among the post-war Jewish migrants to the United States, the population statistics of the immigrant nation of Israel provide a rather good indication of the relative number of Jewish immigrants born in Europe during the first few post-war years.

As of December 31, 1954 there were 37,279 Jews in Israel born in Europe[19] between 1945 and 1949 (age 5-9 years).[20] From 1945 until May 15, 1948 a total of 73,282 Jews entered Israel, 90%, or roughly 67,000, of them from Europe.[21] Between May 15, 1948 and December 31, 1954 another 346,000 Jews arrived from there.[22] The total number of immigrants from Europe may have reached 413,000 between 1945 and 1954, about nine-tenths of them in the years 1945-1950. A relatively small number either returned or moved on to America, Australia, etc. Of all the Jews entering Israel between May 15, 1948 and the end of 1955, 7% are supposed to have left again;[23] the extent to which these emigrants consisted of European, North African or Near Eastern Jews is not known. Applied to the 413,000 European Jews who emigrated between 1945 and 1954, one may argue that the net immigration from Europe between 1945 and 1954 amounted to only 384,000 (93% of 413,000).

Evidently, the age groups 1945 to 1949 amounted to only 9.7% (37,279 of 384,000) of the European Jews who immigrated in Israel between 1945 and 1954. There is no reason to suppose the Jewish immigrants in the United States displayed a radically different age structure – after all, they too came from Europe. The implications for the American Jews are as follows:

1. The age group "20-24 years" in the *purported* Jewish population of 5.37 million amounted to 8.7% according to *Table 12*; in numbers, 467,000.
2. Of these, 8.6% or about 40,000 were born abroad in the years 1946-1950.
3. These 40,000 immigrant Jews born abroad in the years 1946-1950

constituted 10% of all immigrants; thus, total immigration must have numbered about 400,000!

Using the age structure as provided by NJPS and the natural growth rate which may be estimated from it, the total natural increase must have been around 700,000 between 1946 and 1970. Deducting these excess births and immigration from the 5.37 million (1970) one should obtain the level of the Jewish population in the United States at the end of the war: Not surprisingly, the remainder of 4.27 million is even half a million *below* the semi-official figure of 1937!

The conclusion to be drawn from this exercise is *not* that the data gathered by NJPS are worthless. They are probably quite correct. The problem is that the NJPS-study was only concerned with those Jews with continuing ties to the Jewish community; the assimilated Jews remained outside the study. In effect, the study shows the magnitude of the losses suffered by American Jews during the past decades through assimilation!

But just how large was the American Jewish population really in 1970? Publishing the Zionist population figures for the United States in 1957, the *World Almanac and Book of Facts* apparently believed them to be far too anachronistic. To be sure, the *Almanac* cited the "official" Zionist figure of just 5.2 million but added that "an independent study places the percentage [of Jews] at 3.69%, and the possible number of Jews in the United States at 6,290,000."[24]

Starting from these 6.29 million (1957) and projecting them until 1970 on the basis of the growth rates implicit in *Table 12*, one obtains 6.6 million; this figure includes, of course, the assimilated Jews as well. If the latter did not exhibit drastically different characteristics, which is not likely, 8.7% of them were also born in the years 1946-1950 and 8.6% of these, in turn, were foreign-born; the relationship of this age group to all of the Jews immigrating after the war also must have been 1 to 10. The resulting alternative development looks like this:

Jewish population in the United States – 1970		6,600,000
deduct:		
– Natural increase 1946–1970[25]	865,000	
– Post-war immigration until 1970[26]	490,000	
Total demographic changes after the war		1,355,000
Jewish population in the United States – 1945		5,245,000

This calculated 1945-figure is just barely above the one mentioned by Dr. Wischnitzer for the Jewish population of the United States in 1943. If one deducts, furthermore, the semi-official figure of 4.77 million for

1937, it becomes apparent that Long's testimony regarding the immigration of hundreds of thousands of Jews until 1943 fits neatly into the difference.

The composition of the Jewish population in the United States by age and origin – as published by NJPS – provides the following conclusive results:

A. In *1945*, 5.25 million Jews inhabited the United States;

B. Their number increased to 6.6 million by *1970*.

C. About 0.5 million Jews entered the United States *between 1945 and 1970*.

At the same time, NJPS admitted unintentionally that 1¼ million Jews, or one Jew in five, renounced their Jewish identity:

Actual Jewish population 1970	6,600,000
Jews found by NJPS 1970	5,370,000
Assimilated Jews 1970	1,230,000

Such a high assimilation rate among American Jews cannot surprise. Today, more than 40% of all American Jews marry gentiles – four times as many as just a few decades ago. Only one third of these mixed couples raise their children in the Jewish tradition. In a study on "Intermarriage and the Jewish Future" the American Jewish Committee complained that the United States' Jewish population would drop below one million within fifty years unless these losses can be stopped.[27]

Israel

The census of 1931 found 174,610 Jews in Palestine; by 1944, their number increased to 553,600[28] and to 649,600[29] on May 15, 1948. Officially, Jewish immigration – most of the immigrants came from Europe at the time – numbered 292,779 between 1932 and 1944 and 73,282 between 1945 and May 15, 1948.[30] But these statistics are not as reliable as they seem. They represent only gross numbers because comparable emigration figures appear not to exist for Palestine. Also, it is questionable whether the authorities really succeeded in keeping statistics on the considerable number of illegal immigrants. It is possible that emigration and illegal immigration cancelled each other; but it seems that the remaining difference, implying a natural increase of about 2% p.a., is too high even for the young Jewish immigrant population of those days.

166

Between May 15, 1948 and December 31, 1970 another 1.4 million Jews entered the country, mainly from Europe, Africa and the Near East.[31] The immigration figures shown in *Table 13* according to countries of origin should not be taken at face value. Ostensibly, Israeli immigration statistics are kept on the basis of the country of origin. But there is good reason for doubt as the following examples indicate.

It can be shown that among the 60,581 Jews from Persia, there were few Persian Jews; almost certainly, most of them originated from eastern Europe or the Balkans. Another explanation is impossible: Before the war, Iran's Jewish population numbered 40,000;[32] by 1970, 60,581 Jews had left Persia for Israel and, yet, in 1971, there were still 80,000 Jews in Persia.[33] A natural increase of this size is unthinkable, leaving only one logical conclusion: They must have entered Persia between 1939 and the end of the war coming from eastern Europe and the Balkans. The Soviet Union, Great Britain and the United States violated Iran's proclaimed neutrality by force of arms and occupied that country against its will in World War Two. Persia was powerless to stop the immigration of Jews who had escaped from the German sphere of influence but whom no country wanted to accept.

In theory, two roads existed for the fleeing Jews to reach Iran: One was by way of the Soviet Union and may have been used by a few Polish and Rumanian Jews – provided the Soviets allowed it. The second, more important route, led from Rumania through Bulgaria and neutral Turkey to the Anglo-Saxon occupied part of Persia. Now, if Israel alone obtained 60,000 non-Iranian Jews from Persia it would be only logical to assume that many other tens of thousands migrated to other countries and continents as well, for instance, to North and South America. The exact number is of no great importance, although it would be helpful, because if Iran accepted that many Jewish refugees during the war from eastern Europe, the bridge from the Balkans across Turkey must have been used by more than one hundred thousand, possibly even two hundred thousand refugee Jews. One should keep in mind that the official immigration in Palestine between 1940 and 1944 amounted to 45,066[34] and to this must be added the many thousands of "illegal" entries. Almost all of these immigrants had come from eastern Europe and the Balkans.

The census of 1936 listed 161,312 Jews in French-Morocco.[35] The high fertility of these Jews was offset, however, by a very high infant mortality rate meaning that their natural increase was not all that different from that in other Oriental countries. In the early 1930's, the excess of

Table 13
Jewish Immigration in Israel: 1948–1970

Countries of Origin	5/15/48–1970	1952–1970	5/15/48–1951
Bulgaria	48,642	11,411	37,231
Hungary	24,255	10,624	13,631
Yugoslavia	8,063	468	7,595
Poland	156,011	52,279	103,732
Czechoslovakia	20,572	2,355	18,217
Rumania	229,779	110,839	118,940
Others	4	4	
Eastern Europe (excl. the Soviet Union)	487,326	187,980	299,346
England	14,006	11,863	2,143
Greece	2,722	717	2,005
France	26,295	22,287	4,008
Germany	11,552	2,696	8,856
Austria	4,120	1,126	2,994
Others	16,342	11,343	4,999
Western Europe	75,037	50,032	25,005
Soviet Union	21,391	16,693	4,698
Canada	4,004	3,771	233
United States	34,288	32,379	1,909
Argentina	19,964	18,830	1,134
Brazil	5,590	5,148	442
Chile	2,782	2,782	–
Uruguay	2,743	2,743	–
Others	6,001	5,131	870
Americas	75,372	70,784	4,588
Iraq	124,647	3,135	121,512
Iran	60,581	35,777	24,804
Yemen	46,447	1,248	45,199
Aden	3,912	757	3,155
Turkey	53,288	19,075	34,213
Others	33,871	25,531	8,340
Asia	322,746	85,523	237,223
Algeria	13,119	11,596	1,523
Tunisia	46,255	33,116	13,139
Libya	34,265	3,783	30,482
Morocco	252,642	221,892	30,750
Egypt	37,867	21,359	16,508
South Africa	6,845	6,261	584
Others	1,450	1,259	191
Africa	392,443	299,266	93,177

Other countries	24,797	4,633	20,164
Total	1,399,112	714,911	684,201

Source: *Encyclopaedia Judaica*, Vol. 9, S. 535 und 541.

births of Oriental Jews amounted to 5,000 according to the *Universal*.[36] Applied to a total Jewish population in Africa of perhaps 550,000, this excess is equivalent to a net growth rate of 0.9% p.a. For the period 1939-1945 the *Year Book* suggests an increase of the African Jews (excl. South Africa and Rhodesia) by 27,000 or 4,500 annually; this, too, would correspond to a net growth rate of 0.9% for an African-Jewish population (again excl. South Africa and Rhodesia) averaging barely more than 500,000.[37] Given a natural increase of, let us say, 1% p.a. Morocco's Jewish population could have increased to reach at most 200,000 by the early 1950's when most of the Jews left the country. Almost 50,000 Moroccan Jews (1971: 48,000)[38] however decided to stay.

In other words, the total number of Jews who could possibly have left Morocco for Israel was 150,000 – provided that *all* of them decided to go to Israel. Israeli immigration statistics, however, list more than 250,000 immigrant Jews from Morocco. The only explanation is that Morocco, a French protectorate during and after the war, was an intermediate station for Jewish refugees from devastated Europe. Western Europe's resident Jews certainly saw little reason to move into Moroccan DP-camps after the war and those 100,000 "surplus" Jews in Morocco, therefore, can only have originated in eastern Europe or they consisted of western European Jews who returned from German deportation camps and who were neither willing nor capable of adjusting to a new life in their native countries.[39]

We can observe a similar development in Tunesia. The 1936 census registered 59,485 Jews,[40] but in 1950, 105,000 Jews inhabited the country[41] and 13,000 had left Tunesia meanwhile for Israel (*Table 13*). Even conceding a natural increase of 1%, as in the case of the Moroccan Jews, Tunesia's Jewish population could not have grown to more than 73,000 by the mid-1950's when the majority of the Jews left the country. Obviously, Tunesia, too, had "surplus" Jews numbering 45,000 (105,000 plus 13,000 minus 73,000). 10,000 were still living in Tunesia in 1971, about 46,000 had left for Israel and the largest part of the rest of the remaining 60,000 had moved on to France.

Without question, other countries in the Near East and North Africa also gave shelter to refugee Jews, most of whom left for Israel after

May 15, 1948, but never appeared as European Jews in Israeli statistics.

All of the western European countries were affected by the Jewish drama. But it was the uprooted Jews looking for a new beginning who constituted the bulk of the immigrants in Israel. Almost certainly, the 75,037 Jews who immigrated from western Europe either were eastern European in origin or else they belonged to those Jews returning from deportation camps; it is quite unlikely that western European Jews who survived the war in their home countries would have departed in large numbers for Israel.

The 75,372 immigrants from the Americas also provide some food for thought. A resident population does not migrate abroad very eagerly. All of the listed American countries were prime destinations for Jewish immigrants before, during and after the war. It is probable that the majority of these Jews also hailed from eastern Europe; but there is no direct evidence.

The following summary of the immigrant European Jews in Israel after May 15, 1948 represents a minimum number:

(Eastern) European Jews from Tunesia	45,000[42]
(Eastern) European Jews from Persia	60,581
(Eastern) European Jews from Morocco	100,000
(Eastern) European Jews from western Europe	75,037
Jews from eastern Europe (excl. the USSR)	487,326
Immigration of European Jews 1948-1970	767,944

Not all of the 1.4 million immigrants between 1948 and 1970 remained in Israel. For the same period, the *Statistical Abstract of Israel 1971* listed a net immigration figure of 1,155,100.[43] This means that 244,000, or every sixth immigrant left the country; it is not known how many of them were of European origin. But inasmuch as the European Jews were considerably better educated than the Jews from North Africa and the Near East and also had, in many cases, close ties of kinship to Jews in other Western countries, it is probable that the majority of the emigrants, let us say 75%, were of European origin, i.e. 183,000 of 244,000. On balance, the net number of European Jews immigrated in Israel between 1948 and 1970 must have numbered 585,000 (768,000 minus 183,000).

170

The other countries serving as main immigration countries besides the United States, Israel and France, which will be covered subsequently, are listed below:[44]

	Jewish Population		
	Pre-war	1943	Post-war
Argentina	260,000 ('35)	350,000	500,000 ('70)
Brazil	40,000 ('33)	110,750	150,000 ('70)
Chile	3,697 ('30)	25,000	40,000 ('50)
Colombia	2,045 ('35)	5,800	10,000 ('70)
Mexico	20,000 ('35)	20,000	35,000 ('70)
Peru	1,500 ('35)	2,150	5,300 ('70)
Uruguay	12,000 ('30)	37,000	50,000 ('70)
Venezuela	882 ('26)	1,600	12,000 ('70)
Latin America	340,124	552,300	802,300
Canada	155,614 ('31)	170,241 ('41)	296,945 ('71)
Australia	23,553 ('33)	32,500	72,000 ('70)
South Africa	90,662 ('36)	99,000	119,900 ('70)
England[45]	300,000 ('31)	365,000	450,000 ('50)
Anglo-Saxon countries	569,829	666,741	938,845
Total	909,953	1,219,041	1,741,145

Until 1943, Latin America's Jewish population of 340,000 had increased by 210,000; of this total, no more than 30,000 may be attributed to a natural increase and the remainder of 180,000 thus represents Jewish immigration. In the post-war period, the Jewish population increased to over 800,000 – an additon of 250,000. Since Latin America's Jews are mostly urban dwellers, especially in Argentina and Brazil, it is quite improbable that the excess of births over deaths even reached 100,000; this means that at least 150,000 must be due to immigration.

In the case of the Anglo-Saxon countries, excl. the United States, there was an increase of 97,000 until 1943. In all four countries, however, the Jewish population was rather infertile. Between 1933 and 1943, the following immigration occurred:[46]

Canada	8,000
Australia	9,000
South Africa	8,000
England	65,000
Total	90,000

In other words, the natural increase cannot have been larger than 7,000. After the war, the Jewish population rose by 272,000; because of the relatively low birth rate and, in the case of England, because of the short time interval immigration must have been at least 250,000.

France

France is a special case in the group of the main immigration countries for Jews; it was the only country occupied by Germany during the war, and after the war it not only recorded a huge immigration from eastern Europe but from North Africa as well. As mentioned in the Sixth Chapter, only 238,000 Jews are supposed to have survived the war in France. In 1970, it is claimed 550,000 Jews were living there.[47] Up to 60,000 Jews had entered the country from Tunisia in the 1950's and in the years 1962/1963 most of the 130,000 Algerian Jews decided to go to France; only 13,000 moved to Israel and 1,500 remained in Algeria after independence.[48] Without any natural growth at all, there would have been almost 400,000 Jews in France by 1970. But whatever their natural increase was, 150,000 would have been out of reach.

Unfortunately, the 550,000-figure published by the *Year Book* turns out to be much too low! In the mid-1970's, an official investigation discovered 700,000 Jews living in France. The *International Herald Tribune* commented: "... a census report showed there were 700,000 Jews in France, at least 150,000 more than had been believed."[49]

It is true that the North African Jews proved relatively fertile, but the native European Jews exhibited the low birth rate usual for Europe. It may be assumed that this mixed Jewish population was not much larger than 670,000 in 1970 – seven years prior to the official count; of these, in turn, 185,000 may have been of North African origin (see footnote to *Table 15*). Consequently, the number of European Jews in France probably was 485,000 in 1970. In view of the "original" 238,000 of the year 1945 and the relatively small growth rate, immigration from eastern Europe must have amounted to 230,000 Jews after the war.

As for the pre-war immigration in France, a number of "estimates" exist. But the number of 90,000 (Sixth Chapter) also contained the – mostly foreign – Jews who fled from Belgium and Holland.

Summarizing we may say that from the end of WWII until 1970 1,778,000 Jews found shelter in the main Jewish immigration countries; this number is about half again as large as the 1.1 million Jews who entered the same countries during the 1930's (*Table 14*). In analyzing Jewish emigration from the countries occupied by Germany during the war, however, we must disregard France because this country, even though it was one of the large immigration countries for Jews both before and after the war, was in the German sphere of influence during WWII. Thus, Jewish immigration in all the above mentioned main immigration countries *outside* the former German sphere of influence totalled 1,548,000 after the war (until 1970). The only possible countries of origin of these more than 1.5 million Jewish immigrants are those European countries (excl. the USSR in today's borders) which were occupied by Germany during WWII.

Table 14
Immigration of EUROPEAN Jews
in the Main Countries of Immigration
b e f o r e and a f t e r World War Two

	Before the war	After the war
Palestine	293,000 ('32–'44)	73,000('45–'48)
Israel		585,000('48–'70)
United States	406,000 ('33–'43)	490,000
Latin America	180,000 (30er J.)	150,000
Canada, Australia,		
England, South Africa	90,000 (30er J.)	250,000
France	90,000 (30er J.)	230,000
Main immigration		
countries	1,059,000	1,778,000
deduct:		
France	90,000	230,000
Main immigration countries outside the German sphere of influence during World War Two	969,000	1,548,000

Source: Seventh Chapter.

In 1970, 860,000 Jews of European origin lived in these very same countries (*Table 15*). If one adds them to the 1,548,000 Jews who left these countries after the war for the main immigration countries (excl. France), one obtains the minimum number of Jews who must have been living in the former German-occupied European countries (excl. the USSR and the Baltic states) at the close of World War Two, namely, 2,408,000. Probably their number was larger yet because European Jewry was subject to considerable attrition during the interim 25 years on account of low birth rates and assimilation.

Table 15

Jewish Population of EUROPEAN Origin in the former German-occupied European Countries in 1970[50]

Bulgaria	7,000	
Yugoslavia	7,000	
Poland	9,000	
Rumania	100,000	
Czechoslovakia	14,000	
Hungary	80,000	
Communist countries excl. the USSR		217,000
Belgium	40,500	
Denmark	6,000	
Greece	6,500	
Italy	35,000	
Luxemburg	1,000	
Netherlands	30,000	
Norway	750	
Austria	8,000	
Germany	30,000	
France*	485,000	
Western European countries app.		643,000
Approximate total		860,000

Note: (*) In 1977, 700,000 Jews were found in France;[44] the native Jewish population was stagnant, but the younger immigrant Eastern European Jews might have had some growth. Much larger excesses of births over deaths were recorded by the app. 170,000 immigrant North African Jews who arrived in the 1960's. Applying an average rate of growth of at most 0.8%, there were 670,000 Jews in France in 1970. It may be possible that the North African Jews recorded an excess of births amounting to 15,000; if true, 485,000 Jews of European origin were living in France in the year 1970.

However, highly regarded Zionist organizations like the American Jewish Committee put the number of Jews in those European countries in 1946/47 at only 1.41 million; thus, the missing million Jews (2,408,000 minus 1,410,000) must have left Europe either during the immediate post-war period or – disregarding the possibility that we were given "political" figures – the count in 1946/47 was incomplete.

The improbability of just 1.41 million "survivors" (1946/47) as published by the *Year Book* is highlighted by the fact that in that case only half a million Jews (1,410,000 minus 860,000) from the former German-occupied countries could have entered the main immigration countries between the end of the war and 1970. The fact is that Israel alone received more than half a million immigrants from these countries after 1948.

Insisting on the 1.41 million figure is to deny the huge Jewish immigration in the Western Hemisphere after World War Two. That, of course, is nonsense. Which European countries these surviving, but statistically "missing" European Jews should be allocated to, cannot be reconstructed today. During the first post-war years, Jewish refugees were streaming week after week, month after month from the East to the West, being transported from camp to camp and it often lasted years until they finally found their place of final residence. Hundreds of thousands were literally moving "between" the countries and thus were not recorded in the statistics for individual countries. Certainly, the *Year Book* published figures on the number of Jewish DP's for 1947 in the case of Italy, Germany and Austria; but not for other countries. For instance, one cannot detect Cyprus – where the British held tens of thousands of Jews wanting to migrate to Palestine – or Morocco and Tunesia.

By proving a large-scale immigration in many countries outside the former wartime German sphere of influence, it was possible to demonstrate that   1,548,000
Jews left Europe between the end of the war and 1970 (*Table 14*). In 1970, these European countries still contained   860,000

European Jews (*Table 15*). Consequently, the number of Jews who survived must have been at least   2,408,000.
On the basis of largely Zionist or pro-Zionist data, however, the number of surviving Jews found was only (*Table 11*)   1,443,000.

This means that the difference constitutes additional survivors in, and/or emigrants from, former German-occupied Europe; their numbers are   965,000.

Thus, while the real number of Jewish survivors in former German-occupied Europe (excl. the USSR in today's borders) was almost 2½ million, the sum of the actually missing Jews was much smaller. Based on Zionist statistics we arrived in *Table 11* at   1,269,000
"missing" Jews. Deducting the additional   965,000

survivors from them, European Jews not traceable statistically
number   304,000.

The extent to which these 304,000 represent actual missing persons is difficult to judge. It is known that the Jewish population of German-occupied Europe suffered from an extremely low birth rate; the resulting excess of natural deaths over births was not taken completely into account in the above analysis due to lack of data. In addition, we only considered Jewish immigration in fourteen countries which accepted the bulk of the large number of Jewish emigrants after the war; an investigation of some of the smaller countries of destination certainly would discover further emigrants.

It is thus obvious that the figure of 1.3 million "missing" Jews arrived at on the basis of Zionist information for former German-occupied Europe (excl. the USSR in today's borders) in no way reflects reality. The huge flow of Jewish immigrants from Eastern Europe after the cessation of hostilities – as described by General Morgan and even Zionist sources – must have exceeded 1.5 million until 1970; this flow also included the majority of the deportees and the Polish Jews under wartime German control.

Organized Flight

It was pointed out before that many Jews managed to escape during the war from the German sphere of influence. They, too, belong to the 965,000 surviving, but statistically unaccounted for European Jews. The exact number of Jews who fled after the start but *before* the end of the Second World War to neutral or Allied countries and regions is not known; it must have reached several hundreds of thousands.

To be sure, the Institute of Jewish Affairs reported that 180,000 Jews escaped from the countries controlled by the Axis powers between the beginning of the war and 1943, but their countries of origin and routes of escape are largely clouded in mystery.[51]

Hidden indications can be found here and there pointing to Turkey as an important receiving and transit country for fleeing Jews who tried to reach neutral or Allied overseas countries by ship via the port of Constanza (Rumania) or by rail via Bulgaria. Even more mysterious are the temporary receiving stations for these refugees. The *Year Book*, for instance, does list figures for the Jewish DP-camps in post-war Germany, Austria and Italy, but none for Cyprus, Persia or Morocco where – as was shown in this chapter – many Jewish refugees were admitted before and just after the end of the war.

An invaluable piece of evidence describing the extent and organization of this refugee movement during the last 16 months of the war is furnished by the U.S. War Refugee Board. The Board was established by Roosevelt on January 22, 1944 for the purpose, *inter alia*, of aiding the escape of as many Jews as possible from areas under German control. Special Representatives of the Board were stationed in all "strategic" places important for the reception, shelter and transport of these refugees, such as Turkey, Switzerland, Sweden, Portugal, Great Britain, Italy and North Africa.[52]

The diplomatic status of these Representatives enabled them to negotiate with all friendly and neutral governments in the name of the US Government and even to contact German authorities for the purpose of obtaining the release of Jewish prisoners. The number of Jews freed from German control as a result of these direct negotiations is not specified, but the last German-American exchange is supposed to have taken place in February 1945; the released Jews "were taken to an UNRRA camp in North Africa to await ultimate resettlement."[53]

Of much greater importance for the escape of Jews from the German sphere of influence – especially during the last 1½ war years – was their flight to Turkey and, to a smaller degree, to southern Italy. To be sure, the United States had no need to pay attention to a sovereign Italian government, but in the case of neutral Turkey an agreement had to be reached. In order to transfer the escaped Jews on to Palestine and to transit camps in the Near East and North Africa, the consent of Great Britain and France, i.e. deGaulle's, was necessary. The United States Government

> assured the neutral governments that it would arrange for the maintenance of newly arrived refugees and for the evacuation to other places of safety as soon as possible.[54]
> Representations were therefore made to the Turkish Government for consent to admit into its territory all refugees from Axis areas

who might reach the Turkish border. Assurances were given the Turkish Government that the Board would arrange for maintenance of refugees in Turkey as well as for their eventual removal to other places. ... the Turkish Government finally agreed to grant increased numbers of entrance and transit visas and transportation facilities, and generally to cooperate in this [US] Government's program to rescue Nazi victims.[55]

In order to carry out this far-flung escape operation the services of the UNRRA were utilized, which provided temporary shelter for the Jewish refugees and their transport and maintenance on the way to makeshift camps. UNRRA camps sprouted in the Near East, Italy and North Africa ready to accept thousands of these refugees.[56]

The possibility to escape from the Balkans via Turkey to Palestine and other allied territory existed for Jews since the beginning of World War Two. The route of escape led from the port of Constanza (Rumania) across the Black Sea to Istanbul or by rail through Bulgaria. The Board assumed the task to systematically improve and expand these routes to "develop a steady flow of refugees over these routes through Turkey."[57]

For this purpose, lesser German and other border officials were bribed, false identification papers were supplied, exit and entry visas were procured and transportation by boat and by rail was provided for evacuation to safe areas. "*Tens of thousands* were rescued from the Nazis by these clandestine means," the Board wrote.[58]

> ... refugees were collected, concealed from the Nazi-controlled Rumanian officials and placed in small vessels in the port of Constanza. ... [The refugees] were herded by the hundreds on ships built to carry 20 to 50 passengers. ... late in March 1944, 48,000 Jews were moved from Transnistria to Rumania. Many of them, mostly children, were transferred *with other* [Jewish] refugees from Rumania to Palestine.[59]

A second route of escape from the Balkans to Allied territory led from Yugoslavia by boat across the Adriatic Sea to southern Italy. Partisan and other underground units in Slovakia, Hungary and Yugoslavia smuggled Jewish refugees to the coast where boats organized by the Board waited to receive and transport them to southern Italian UNRRA camps. Approximately 7,000 Hungarian Jews are supposed to have escaped this way, but it is not known whether they were Jews from Greater Hungary or from the Hungarian territory within post-war borders.[60]

In southern Italy the UNRRA maintained numerous camps for the

Jews streaming across the Adriatic Sea. Soon, these facilities became overtaxed and the inmates were transferred to "havens in other Allied territory."[61] The reference was to the UNRRA camps in North Africa like, for instance, Camp Marechal Lyautey near Casablanca or Camp Philippeville in Algeria.[62]

The financial means to bribe officials, procure false identity papers and obtain ship and rail transport in German-occupied areas was paid for by funds channelled through "neutral" Switzerland and from there to the Jewish organizations in Hungary and elsewhere.[63]

It is unfortunate that the Board made no references as to the total number of Jews who escaped from Axis territory through its assistance. Here and there the report mentions some figures for particular national Jewish groups, but generally the Board just mentions hundreds, thousands and tens of thousands coming out of German-occupied Europe. The fact that

– at the end of the war, there were 8,000 more Jews in Bulgaria than at the beginning,
– 6,000 Hungarian Jews were found stranded in Rumania after the war,
– 60,000 and more than 100,000 *European* Jews, respectively, arrived in Israel from Persia and Morocco between 1948 and 1970,
– the Jewish population of Palestine increased by about 100,000 between 1939 and 1945, with only a fraction thereof accounted for by natural net growth,
– the Institute of Jewish Affairs reported 180,000 escaped Jews between the beginning of the war and 1943,
– the US Government's War Refugee Board and the UNRRA had systematically organized the escape of a stream of refugees through Turkey and southern Italy,

permits us to assume a gigantic flight and evacuation during the war from areas of former German-occupied Europe: It numbered many hundreds of thousands.

EIGHTH CHAPTER

The World Jewish Population

The Demographic Development before the War

As late as the early 1930's 9.5 million Jews lived in Europe (incl. the Soviet Union);[1] almost two-thirds of them either were never in the German sphere of influence or escaped from it. On the other hand, Europe's Jewish population was in the midst of a process of dissolving its former concentration long before Hitler's ascension to power. This dissolution was the consequence of a large flow of emigration from eastern European countries, negative net birth rates, conversions and general assimilation tendencies. The economic crisis of the 1930's and the officially managed anti-Jewish measures in Greater Germany, Poland, Rumania, etc. intensified the efforts of Jews to turn their backs on Europe. The outbreak of World War Two, finally, destroyed their one-time stronghold in Europe excepting a few remnants on the western rim of the Occident.

About one million Jews left Europe before the war; roughly half a million lived anyway in European countries never occupied by Germany and between September 1939 and mid-1940 more than two million Jews disappeared in the Soviet Union and shared the fate of the other three million Soviet Jews. Consequently, only 2.8 million Jews remained in the countries that were to come within the German sphere of influence until June 22, 1941. Another three-quarters of a million Jews fell into German hands when Axis troops struck in order to forestall a Soviet attack, bringing the total number of Jews in the German sphere of influence in Europe during the Second World War to 3.5 million.

Of the 5-5.5 million Jews in the USSR (1940), one million inhabited from the start the territories outside the maximum German expansion in Russia, close to another million were deported by the Soviets from the western frontier areas to Siberia in the spring of 1940 already, and four-fifths of the remaining 3.5 million Jews withdrew more or less voluntarily with the Red Army in 1941.

After World War Two, 2.4 million Jews were found to be alive in the former German-occupied European countries (excl. the USSR);

181

Table 16
World Jewish Population in the 1930's
– by Countries –

Europe

England (1931)	300,000	
Gibraltar (1931)	886	
Ireland (1926)	3,686	
Malta (1920)	35	
Portugal (1931)	1,200	
Spain (1934)	4,000	
Sweden (1930)	6,653	
Switzerland (1930)	17,973	
Unoccupied Europe		334,433
Albania (1930)	204	
Belgium (1934)	60,000	
Bulgaria (1934)	48,398	
Czechoslovakia (1930)	356,830	
Denmark (1930)	5,690	
Finland (1937)	1,755	
France (1936)	240,000	
Germany (1939)	250,448	
Greece (1928)	72,791	
Hungary (1930)	444,567	
Italy (1931)	47,825	
Luxemburg (1935)	3,144	
Netherlands (1935)	111,917	
Norway (1930)	1,359	
Poland (1931)	3,113,900	
Rumania (1930)	756,930	
Yugoslavia (1931)	68,405	
Former German-occupied Europe		5,584,163
Estonia (1934)	4,302	
Latvia (1935)	93,479	
Lithuania (1923)	155,125	
Soviet Union (1939)	3,020,141	
Soviet Union and Baltic states		3,273,047
Europe		9,191,643

Africa, Asia, Australia

Algeria (1931)	110,127
Congo (1923)	177
Egypt (1934)	72,550
Ethiopia (1936)	51,000
Kenya (1931)	305
Libya (1938)	30,046
Marocco (French) (1936)	161,312

Marocco (Span.) (1936)	12,918
Portug. East Africa (1923)	100
Rhodesia (1931)	2,447
South Africa (1936)	90,662
S.W. Africa (1925)	200
Tanganyika (1931)	10
Tangier (1936)	7,000
Tunesia (1936)	59,485

Africa		598,339

Aden (1931)	4,151
Afghanistan (1929)	5,000
Arabia (?)	25,000
China (1935)	19,850
Cyprus (1931)	75
Hong Kong (1935)	250
India (1931)	24,141
Indochina (1924)	1,000
Iraq (1935)	90,970
Japan (1938)	200
Malaya (1921)	703
Palestine (1939)	424,373
Persia (1935)	40,000
Philippines (1934)	500
Syria/Lebanon (1931)	26,051
Transjordan (1934)	200
Turkey (1935)	78,730

Asia		741,194

Australia (1933)	23,553
New Zealand (1936)	2,653

Australia and New Zealand		26,206

Africa, Asia and Australia		1,365,739

North and South America

Argentina (1935)	260,000
Brazil (1933)	40,000
Chile (1930)	3,697
Columbia (1935)	2,045
Costa Rica (1939)	500
Cuba (1933)	7,800
Curacao (1929)	566
Dominican Republic (1940)	756
Guatemala (1938)	350
Guiana (Brit.) (1938)	1,000
Haiti (1936)	150
Honduras (1938)	25
Jamaica (1935)	2,000
Mexico (1935)	20,000
Nicaragua (1938)	100

Panama (1930)	850		
Panama Canal Zone (1938)	74		
Paraguay (1930)	1,200		
Peru (1935)	1,500		
Salvador (1939)	120		
Surinam (1938)	799		
Uruguay (1930)	12,000		
Venezuela (1926)	882		
Latin America		356,414	
Canada (1931)	155,614		
United States (1937)	4,771,122		
North America		4,926,736	
Americas			5,283,150
World Jewish population			15,840,532

Source: *AJYB*, 1944, Vol. 46, p. 501 for all countries except Rumania and the Netherlands; for these two countries "estimates" were provided by the *Year Book*, even though the Dutch census of 1935 registered 111,917 Jews (*AJYB*, 1940, Vol. 42, p. 602) and Rumania's census of 1930 found 756,930 Jews (Hilberg, *Destruction of the European Jews*, p. 486).

about 300,000 are statistically unaccounted for. Over one million of the more than five million Jews died during the war in the Soviet Union, the largest part either as Red Army men or in Siberian labor and concentration camps. Probably up to 4.3 million Jews survived the war in the Soviet Union and as late as 1980 prominent Zionist personalities like Dr. Nahum Goldmann estimated the number of Soviet Jews at up to 3.5 million; but meanwhile hundreds of thousands had left the Workers' Paradise during the past three and one-half decades and considerable negative net birth rates and numerous mixed marriages caused Soviet Jewry to suffer great losses.

Fitting the numerical development of the Jewish population in Europe into that of world Jewry is aggravated by the fact that there are no reliable figures on the actual number of Jews throughout the world. In most countries, Jews are still not considered an ethnic, but a religious minority and, strangely enough, political Zionism was unable so far to persuade the governments of the Western countries with the largest Jewish populations to include them separately in the periodic censuses.

This situation led to large differences in the estimates of the world Jewish population even before the Second World War; as a rule, the Jewish population estimates were too low for the immigration countries, too high for the countries of emigration and, generally, Jewry was endowed with far too large rates of natural increase. This is particularly a problem for the last pre-war figure, namely, the world Jewish population estimated at 16.7 million in 1939. The huge shift of millions of Jews to the East, West and South caused by the war and its aftermath, and the political interest in keeping the pre-war figure high, made it impossible so far to attain an objective correction of this number; yet, historical truth demands it.

For most of the countries of the world the latest official and semi-official pre-war figures are available only for the early or the middle 1930's. Exceptions are the United States, Palestine, the Soviet Union and Greater Germany. On the basis of the last censuses or estimates for the countries listed on *Table 16* one obtains the following summary:

North and South America	5,283,150
Asia, Africa, Australia	1,365,739
European countries not occupied by Germany during World War Two	334,433
Countries *outside* the area of wartime German influence	6,983,322
Countries *inside* the area of wartime German influence	5,584,163
World Jewry *outside* the USSR and the Baltic countries	12,567,485
Soviet Union and the Baltic states	3,273,047
World Jewry	15,840,532

In *Table 17* we listed the census years when the Jewish population of the individual countries was counted or estimated last before the war. Classified by periods of time the summary is as follows (in 1,000):

	A	B	C	D	E	
	1923/25	1926/32	1933/35	1936/38	1939	Sum
North and South America	0	175	333	4,774	1	5,283
Asia, Africa, Australia	2	172	352	415	424	1,366
Europe	0	5,199	227	242	250	5,918
World excl. USSR and Baltic states	2	5,546	912	5,431	676	12,567
Soviet Union and Baltic states	155	0	98	0	3,020	3,273
World Jewry	157	5,546	1,010	5,431	3,696	15,841
Years until 1939 (average)	15	8	5	2	1	
Average percentage increase	0.2	0.2	0.7	0.5	0.3	
Possible Jewish population at the end of 1939	162	5,635	1,046	5,485	3,707	16,035

185

The main countries listed in columns A and B are Lithuania, Poland, Hungary, Czechoslovakia, Rumania and England. Poland registered a very small natural increase of only 0.2% for its Jewish population before the war already; Hungary's Jews suffered a negative net growth rate. In Czechoslovakia and probably in England, the Jewish population was stagnating and Rumania's Jews, too, recorded just a very small natural growth (0.2%) in the 1930's. The relatively high rate of growth of the small number of Asian and African Jews cannot possibly have affected the overall rate for these columns; an average rate of 0.2% seems ample under the circumstances.

The countries listed in column C are distributed quite evenly among the Western Hemisphere, Europe and Asia/Africa. The small or even totally absent growth rates in Europe were more than offset by the large growth rates in Asia; still, the applied average rate of 0.7% seems somewhat high. American Jews dominate column D almost completely; their rate of natural increase is not certain. But we do know that the highly urbanized American-Jewish population recorded much lower net growth rates than the American average; also, other US population sections (for instance, the non-white and the rural white population) were blessed with a growth rate far in excess of the American average of 0.75% (1935-1939).[2] Thus, an average rate of 0.5% in column D is probably exaggerated. Column E also was provided with a growth for one year because the Soviet census took place in January of 1939; here too, it seems the applied increase of 0.3% is rather generous, because the Soviet-Jewish population stagnated long before the war, as Prof. Lorimer pointed out.

The maximum size of the world Jewish population thus cannot have exceeded 16.04 million in 1939. A scrutiny of *Table 17* shows that the census dates of the countries receiving Jewish immigrants in the Western Hemisphere and Palestine happened to fall into the second half of the 1930's, whereas those of the European emigration countries, excepting Germany, were to be found at the beginning of the decade, generally 1930/1931. No question, the census count of many immigration countries included Jews who were also covered by the population statistics of Poland, Rumania, the Baltic, Hungary, Czechoslovakia, Greece, etc. Considering the half a million Jewish emigrants from Poland in the 1930's and the many tens of thousands from other European countries, it is certain that double counting must have amounted to at least 100,000, probably more. We can be sure that the Jewish world population of 1939 never reached the 16-million mark; it was at least 700,000 smaller than is usually assumed.

Table 17
World Jewish Population in the 1930's
– by Census Years –

Year	Europe +	Asia +	Australia +	Africa +	Americas =	World
Unknown		25,000				25,000
1920–1925	155,160	1,703		477		157,340
1926	3,686				882	4,568
1928	72,791					72,791
1929		5,000			566	5,566
1930	1,590,206				17,747	1,607,953
1931	3,532,216	54,418		112.889	155,614	3,855,137
1933	111,917		23,553		47,800	183,270
1934	116,700	700		72,550		189,950
1935	96,623	229,800			285,545	611,968
1936	240,000		2,653	382,377	150	625,180
1937	1,755				4,771,122	4,772,877
1938		200		30,046	2,348	32,594
1939	250,448	424,373			620	675,441
1940					756	756
World excl. USSR	6,171,502	741,194	26,206	598,339	5,283,150	12,820,391
1939 USSR	3,020,141					3,020,141
World	9,191,643	741,194	26,206	598,339	5,283,150	15,840,532

Source: *Table 16.*

The elusiveness of the figure of 16.64 million[3] published by the *Year Book* can be demonstrated another way: For this figure to be true, the Jews would have had to grow by an annual average rate of 1.2% until 1939 since the last count in the individual countries. This rate is 50% larger than the populations of North America and Europe with their very large rural population were able to show! This is obvious nonsense.

In the official *Statistical Abstract of Israel* a similar unreal number may be found for 1939, namely, 16.7 million. The same source also mentioned the worldwide Jewish population for the years 1914 and 1925:[4]

1914	13,5 Millionen
1925	14,8 Millionen

An increase by 1.3 million from 13.5 million to 14.8 million within eleven years is equivalent to an annual rate of 0.85%. Before and after these dates millions of Jews left eastern Europe and emigrated mainly to North America, where their natural increase soon began to decelerate in the new urban commercial environment. Also, the economic crisis of the 1930's produced the same trend to lower birth rates among the Jews as was true for all industrial nations. But an increase to 16.7 million in 1939 would correspond to an average rate of +0.9% per year. Not only would the Jews have had an actual rise in their rate of natural increase, but – contrary to the trend of those years – their fertility would have been considerably larger than was recorded for central and western European countries. This is absurd!

However, an increase by 1.2 million from 14.8 (1925) to 16 million in 1939 would amount only to an average rate of growth of 0.55% per annum. Even this rate would seem rather high in view of the drastically falling Jewish birth rates in eastern Europe, the negative tendencies in some central and southeastern European countries and a moderate growth in the United States; still, considering the whole development since 1914 it appears much more realistic. By way of comparison: The US population recorded an average net growth rate of only 0.8% between 1930 and 1939 despite a fast growing non-white and white rural population;[5] in Germany the net rate was 0.7-0.8% (however, there was a decline from 0.9% in 1925 to 0.66% in 1930 and a rise from then on to 0.8% by 1939).[6]

To be sure, the much publicized emigration from Germany and the immigration in Palestine was reflected in the *Year Book's* figures, but the considerably larger emigration from eastern Europe was disregarded almost entirely. The fact that the United States had accepted more than

400,000 Jewish refugees and immigrants was made public only in 1943 during hearings of an investigating committee of the US House of Representatives; but those hearings did not receive particular notice. Thus, while Jewish immigration showed up to a small extent in the statistics for the immigration countries, emigration was disregarded in the statistics for eastern Europe. This situation had dire consequences for the ascertainment of the total number of the pre-war Jewish population and the number of missing persons; to all appearances, the overseas immigration countries displayed fewer Jews than actually were present before and after WWII and the eastern European emigration countries were assigned numbers that were exaggerated by 800,000!

The country-specific investigation in the First and Sixth Chapter points to a net emigration *before* and during the war of at least 1,121,000 (*Table 18*). It is possible though that this figure does include some negative net growth because sometimes the data available was just too scanty.

Table 18
Jewish Emigration
before and during World War Two

Czechoslovakia	52,300
Germany and Austria	442,000
Hungary	5,500
Poland	500,000
Rumania	121,600
Total	1,121,000

Source: First and Sixth Chapter. The escape of about 30,000 Jews from France in 1940 was not taken into account; they consisted mainly of refugees from Germany, Poland and Czechoslovakia and thus would in effect constitute a double counting.

Analyzing immigration in the main immigration countries – i.e. Palestine, the United States, Canada, Australia, England, South Africa, France and seven Latin American countries – *before* the end of WWII, we found 1,059,000 Jews in the Seventh Chapter (*Table 14*). In addition, there were many other smaller countries which also accepted thousands of Jewish refugees, Switzerland, Sweden, New Zealand, China, for instance.

It is apparent that the emigration and immigration figures for the period before the end of WWII as developed in this study are more or less balanced, each in effect confirming the other.

189

In order to check on the accuracy of the world population figures as published by the *Year Book* for the post-war period (1946), we established two groups which will be looked at separately: The Soviet (or those living in the Soviet Union) and the non-Soviet Jews.

As mentioned above, the world Jewish population of 1939 numbered less than 16 million; of these, 3.02 lived in the Soviet empire; the non-Soviet Jews thus counted fewer than 13 million in 1939. Within a few months the Soviets acquired millions of Polish, Baltic and Rumanian Jews. On balance, the division looked like this one year later:

World Jewish population 1939 (maximum)		16,000,000
deduct:		
– "Old" Soviet Jews(1939)	3,020,000	
– Former Polish Jews (1939/1940)	1,867,000	
– Former Baltic Jews (1940)	225,000	
– Former Rumanian Jews (1940)	225,000	
Total Soviet Jews		5,337,000
Jews *outside* of the Soviet Union 1940 (maximum)		10,663,000

Early in WWII, the rough distribution of these 10.7 million non-Soviet Jews was as follows:

United States (1943)[7]	5,200,000
Canada (1941)[8]	170,241
Latin America (1943)[8]	584,384
Western Hemisphere	5,954,625
Palestine (1939)[9]	424,373
Asia (incl. Turkey) (1939)[10]	376,500
Africa (1939)[10]	609,800
Australia/New Zealand (1939)[10]	33,000
European countries *not* occupied by Germany during the Second World War[11]	384,500
Countries *outside* the subsequent German sphere of influence	7,782,798
European countries *inside* the subsequent German sphere of influence 1939[12]	2,952,000
Jews *outside* the USSR 1939/1943 (maximum)	10,735,000

For the Western Hemisphere no figures were obtainable for 1939; they are therefore somewhat too high and reflect the immigration during the first war years. On the other hand, the population of 384,500 for the unoccupied European countries probably is too low by several tens of thousands. Generally though, the total of 10,663,000 is quite in line with the sum of the individual country groups for the years 1939/1943. It is rather improbable that the post-war figure for the Jews living *outside* the Soviet Union exceeded the pre-war figure because possible negative net growth rates in Europe during the war, direct war losses (soldiers and partisans killed in combat), chaotic conditions in the German camps during the closing months of the war, Allied bombing raids, etc. may have pushed the total down to at least 10.6 million or below.

Comparing these 10.6 million survivors with the 9 million outside the Soviet Union as published by the *Year Book* for 1946 (*Table 19*), there is a gap of 1½ million.

Table 19 .

Purported World Jewish Population: 1939 and 1946
– according to the American Jewish Year Book[13] –

	1939	1946[x]	Difference
A. World *outside* the German sphere of influence in World War Two			
– North and South America	5,489,620	5,756,700	+ 267,080
– Asia, Africa, Australia	1,494,300	1,647,000	+ 152,700
– Non-occupied Europe	384,500	419,000	+ 34,500
	7,368,420	7,822,700	+ 454,280
B. German sphere of influence *outside* the Soviet Union:			
– Poland	3,250,000	120,000	–3,130,000
– Czechoslovakia	360,000	55,000	– 305,000
– Rumania	850,000	300,000	– 550,000
– Other European countries	1,539,700	669,600	– 870,100
	5,999,700	1,144,600	–4,855,100
C. World *excl.* the USSR	13,368,120	8,967,300	–4,400,820
D. Soviet Union and Baltic states	3,275,000	2,032,500	–1,242,500
E. World Jewish Population	16,643,120	10,999,800	–5,643,320
of which:			
F. Jewish population in the German sphere of influence (B + D)[y]	9,274,700	3,177,100	– 6,097,600

Note: [x] The *Year Book* listed the world Jewish population for 1946 as 11,123,800, but an addition of the individual countries totalled only 10,999,800; it is not clear where the difference of 124,000 should be looked for, but it seems the Rumanian figure may be wrong.

[y] In this table the entire Soviet Union appears as having belonged to the German sphere of influence; in reality, in 1939 one million Jews lived already outside the territory later occupied by German troops.

191

The *Year Book* figure of 9 million for 1946 includes only 5.75 million Jews in North and South America. But the *Year Book* itself admitted to 5.95 million Jews in this region in the year 1943, and in 1945 and 1946 other hundreds of thousands of Jews coming from devastated Europe had arrived in the New World. Evidently, the *Year Book* understated the 1946-figures for Western Hemisphere by half a million persons.

In Asia, Africa and Australia, too, the actual number of Jews in 1946 was not 1.67 million as the *Year Book* would like us to believe, but hundreds of thousands more. As we mentioned already, the Jews coming from eastern Europe were moved from camp to camp in western Europe and many were quartered temporarily in UNRRA camps in the Near East, Cyprus and North Africa. We know, for instance, that about 200,000 *European* Jews immigrated in Israel after May 15, 1948 coming from Persia, Morocco and Tunesia (see Seventh Chapter).

The figure of 1.6 million Jews in all of Europe (1,145,000 plus 419,000) as published by the *Year Book* for 1946 also is much too low; we have seen in the Seventh Chapter that roughly one million more Jews had survived in the countries within the former German sphere of influence (excl. the USSR) than was admitted to by the *Year Book*. In addition, the *Year Book* committed an obvious mistake in the case of the Rumanian Jews, because in the following year already the figure for the Jewish population of Rumania was increased by 130,000.

The statistical data published by the *Year Book* become even more doubtful when one realizes that the figure of 11.33 million for 1970 (excl. the USSR) is too low by several hundreds of thousands – despite the huge jump by 30% within only 24 years! The *Year Book* listed only 5.9 million American and 550,000 French Jews. In realtiy, there were 6.6 million in the United States and almost 700,000 in France.

For 1970, the *Year Book* mentioned the following Jewish population[14]

in Europe (excl. France)	837,150
in Asia (incl. Turkey and Israel)	2,707,200
in Africa	196,600
in Australia and New Zealand	77,000
in Latin America	812,925
totalling	4,630,875.
Furthermore, the Canadian census of 1971 listed[15]	296,945.
In the United States we found (Seventh Chapter)	6,600,000
and in France (Seventh Chapter)	670,000.
In 1970, the world Jewish population outside the Soviet Union was at least	12,200,000.

It is almost certain that this figure of 12.2 million for 1970 is too low as well. As mentioned already, an official investigation in France found 150,000 more Jews than was admitted to by the *Year Book*. In other countries the situation may be very similar. The Zionists themselves admit that the Jewish population is suffering from attrition through assimilation in all European countries – in East and West. The number of Jews who fail to appear statistically as Jews because of this development is not known, but the examples of France, where the *Year Book's* estimate is 20% below the official figure, and of the United States, where more than one million Jews disappeared from the statistics, provide some food for thought. We may be sure that the real number of Jews outside the USSR exceeded 12.3 million in 1970.

In this connection, we find a very interesting piece of information in the *Israel Almanach* (1958-1959), published by the Zionist World Organization (ZWO) headquartered in Jerusalem. We learn from it that the 1.8 million Jews of Israel in 1958 were equivalent to *one-eighth* of the Jewish world population.[16] In effect, this renowned Zionist source was estimating the number of Jews in the world at 14.4 million in 1958. Unfortunately, the ZWO did not provide more detailed figures on this subject and we are left guessing as to how many Soviet Jews were included in this estimate. Officially, the figure which was current in those days in Zionist literature on the Jews in the USSR was around 2.3 million; deducting it from the 14.4 million, we arrive at a Jewish population outside the USSR of 12.1 million for 1958. This estimate is very close to our own calcualtions of at least 12.3 million.

Henri Zoller, the Israel-correspondent of the magazine *Der Spiegel*, wrote in the summer of 1980 that 80% of the world Jewish population was still living in the diaspora.[17] Thus, if Israel's 3¼ million Jews[18] constituted 20% of world Jewry in early 1980, this one-time Jewish member of the French Resistance is putting the number of Jews in the world at 16.3 million in 1979/1980.

Now, Henri Zoller may not be exactly an expert on questions of Jewish demography, but Dr. Nahum Goldmann, the former president of the World Jewish Congress and one of the most prominent leaders of world Zionism, was one of the best-informed experts on the size of the world Jewish population. Dr. Goldmann, too, stated that 80% of world Jewry was living in the diaspora in early 1980;[19] in other words, only one-fifth was to be found in Israel. Dr. Goldmann rounded his figure for Israel to 3.5 million; official Israeli statistics mention only 3¼ million Jews for early 1980. On the basis of these 3¼ million, one arrives at 16.3 million

Jews in the world according to Dr. Goldmann.

Contacted by personal letter, Dr. Goldmann replied that Soviet Jews counted 3 to 3.5 million in 1980.[20] Deducting the upper end of his estimate, let us say 3.4 million, from the world Jewish population of 16.3 million, there remain 12.9 million Jews in the world outside the USSR.

It is noteworthy that Dr. Goldmann's admission is putting him squarely in the corner of the Jewish dissidents in the USSR with regard to the number of Jews in the Soviet Union. If he places the number of Soviet Jews at 3 to 3.5 million in 1980, he is saying in effect that in the early 1970's there were 3.5 to 4 million Jews in the Soviet Union; after all, one-quarter of a million Jews left the Workers' Paradise during the past decade and the excess of deaths over births may have reached up to one per cent per year for the Soviet-Jewish population during that period, or about 200,000.

Ostensibly, the development of world Jewry looked like this during the past forty years:

Purported World Jewish Population outside the USSR
– 1940, 1946, 1970, 1979 –

Year	Popu-lation	Changes	Period	Average Annual Changes in per cent since		
	(Mio.)	(Mio.)	(Years)	1940	1946	1970
1940	10.6	–	–	–	–	–
1946	9.0	–1.6	6	–2.7	–	–
1970	12.3	+3.3	24	0.5	1.3	–
1979	12.9	+0.6	9	0.5	1.1	0.5

We note that the entire increase for the last 9 years amounted to just 0.6 million (or even less); this is quite a contrast to the thirty years previous to that which were characterized by extremely large plus and minus changes but which, as the whole, recorded a most remarkable increase of 1.7 million. The suspicion is not unfounded that the contrary developments before and after 1946 are directly connected with each other. To be sure, one could blame the reduction between 1940 and 1946 on the German measures within the so-called "Final Solution", but there is no sensible explanation for the unheard of "fertility" between 1946 and 1970, namely, +1.3% p.a.!

The almost totally urbanized world Jewish population – which lived almost entirely in the large urban centers in the East and West and which not only recorded a birth rate that has been dropping for generations, but also suffered a relatively low net growth rate before the war already – would have demonstrated a fertility after the war close to the biological limit and nearly equivalent to the population growth in the developing countries.[21]This is pure fantasy!

There is only one reasonable conclusion: The figure published by the *Year Book* for the world Jewish population outside the USSR in 1946 did not conform to reality; political reasons were decisive for putting the number so low. Leaving aside the *Year Book's* obviously manipulated figure for 1946, the 40-year demographic development of world Jewry outside the Soviet Union begins to look much more realistic:

Probable World Jewish Population outside the USSR
– 1940, 1970, 1979 –

Year	Popu-lation	Changes	Period	Average Annual Changes in per cent since	
	(Mio.)	(Mio.)	(Years)	1940	1970
1940	10.6	–	–	–	–
1970	12.3	+1.7	30	0.5	–
1979	12.9	+0.6	9	0.5	0.5

The development evident from the above compilation shows no contrast between the time before and after 1970. The growth rate for the 30-year-period before 1970 was relatively large despite the losses in WWII because it also included the short-lived Jewish babyboom of the immediate post-war period. This growth of 0.5% per year until 1970 of the highly urbanized extra-Soviet world Jewish population is relatively large and represents conclusive evidence that the losses suffered in the war were relative small – at least as far as the Jews outside the Soviet Union are concerned.

At first glance it is surprising to see the growth rate maintain this level after 1970 as well, despite the reduction of the birth rate in all industrial countries since the early 1960's; this seemingly high rate of 0.5%, however, reflects also the quarter of a million Jews who emigrated from the USSR in the last decade. It is correct, of course, that Israel's immigrant population registered notable growth rates even after 1970, but all Zionist statements regarding the Jewish population in the rest of the Western World and in eastern Europe point to a drastic aging process and frequent negative net growth rates.[22]

The demographic development of the Jews in the Soviet Union was discussed before and there is no reason to repeat the statistical details at this point. Adding the 3½ million Soviet Jews – as confirmed by Soviet-Jewish dissidents, the *Encyclopaedia Judaica* and Dr. Goldmann – to the almost 13 million Jews outside the USSR, one obtains a total of 16.5 million for world Jewry; this is about half a million more than in 1940! The losses of at least one million during the war – mainly while serving in the Red Army, during the more or less forcible Soviet evacuation to Siberia and in the Siberian labor camps – caused the Jewish world population to drop below the 15-million-mark; since the end of WWII, it multiplied by at least 1.5 million and thus more than compensated for the losses incurred as a result of the war and Soviet barbarism. This is equivalent to a worldwide net growth of 0.4% p.a. since the end of the war.

Even today the world Jewish population figures still reflect the political interests of Zionism and estimating "mistakes" usually lead to too low figures for the post-war Jewish populations; nevertheless, the ever more frequent larger population statistics for the USSR represent a fundamental admission by Zionism that the original post-war figures were much too low. Slowly, but steadily, they are working themselves toward the real world Jewish population size – even though the means applied are implicit, unrealistic assumptions regarding Jewish fertility.

The purpose of this analysis was not to investigate the content of truth in the "Holocaust" story, but to outline the extent and the direction of the Jewish population movement before, during and after World War Two. If the developments as traced here are in conflict with the taboos of contemporary historians, it is their task to reconsider an untenable position.

Even though the well-known "Holocaust" figures are of only minor interest in this study it is necessary, nevertheless, to sketch the main controversial positions as far as the statistical data is concerned. Between 1939 and 1946, the *Year Book* found that the world Jewish population had been reduced by one-third from 16.64 million to 11 million (*Table 19*). Admittedly, the largest reduction was registered by today's Communist countries, but for the USSR itself the loss was put at "only" 1¼ million. In contrast, the countries beyond the former German sphere of influence recorded a plus of almost half a million Jews, obviously largely the result of migratory gains.

The fact that the political boundaries of 1946 in no way corresponded with those of 1939 – especially in the cases of Poland, Czechoslovakia, Rumania and the Soviet Union – was not mentioned at all by the *Year Book*, let alone taken into account in the determination of war losses. Only in the case of Rumania did the *Year Book* mention that the post-war borders excluded northern Bukovina and Bessarabia; yet this footnote was not reflected in the purported number of "missing" Ruma-

Table 20

Purported World Jewish Population: 1941 and 1946
1941: according to results of this analysis
1946: according to the American Jewish Year Book
(in 1,000)

	1941	1946	Difference
A. World *outside* the German sphere of influence 1939–1945:			
– North and South America	5,955 ('43)	5,757	− 198
– Asia, Africa, Australia	1,444	1,647	+ 203
– Non-occupied Europe	384	419	+ 35
	7,783	7,823	+ 40
B. German sphere of influence *outside* the Soviet Union:[x]			
– Poland	757	120	− 637
– Czechoslovakia	155	55	− 100
– Rumania	315	300	− 15
– Other European countries	1,511	670	− 841
	2,738	1,145	−1,593
C. World *excl.* the USSR	10,521	8,967	−1,554
D. Soviet Union, Baltic countries and Ruthenia	5,446	2,033	−3,413
E. World Jewish Population	15,967	11,000	−4,967
of which:			
F. Jewish population in the German sphere of influence in the years 1941–1945 (B+D)[y]	8,184	3,178	−5,006

Note: [x] For 1941, see *Table 11* excl. Ruthenia.

[y] In this table the entire Soviet Union was listed as having belonged to the German sphere of influence; in reality, in early 1941 only 3¾ million Jews lived in the area later occupied by German troops (disregarding the Ruthenian Jews).

nian Jews. The annexation of eastern Poland (1939) and Ruthenia (1945) by the USSR was completely disregarded. In short, a comparison of Jewish population statistics for 1939 and 1946 is incorrect in principle.

Certainly, this would make no difference as far as the total number of "missing" persons is concerned *if* the figures for 1939 and 1946 were correct. But the crucial question is precisely how reliable these figures are;

after all, it was the Soviet Union which acquired most of the Polish Jews in 1939/1940 besides hundreds of thousands of Rumanian and Baltic Jews. Any observer would immediately recognize the dubiousness of the "missing" figures if the comparison would depict the fact that the bulk of the "missing" Jews is ascribed to that country which with regard to falsification, lies, deception and statistical manipulation is in a class by itself, and whose inhuman "scorched earth" initiatives forced tens of millions of people from all walks of life to move from the embattled areas to Siberia during the war.

Adjusting the pre-war figures to take account of the border changes and population movements until 1941, an entirely different picture develops (*Table 20*). To be sure, this table too points to five million "missing" Jews and creates the erroneous impression that eight million Jews came within the German sphere of influence, but otherwise it presents a very different view.

First of all, we see that the Jewish population *outside* the former German sphere of influence in 1946 is too low by hundreds of thousands (point A). A reduction by 200,000 in the Western Hemisphere during the interim years when hundreds of thousands of Jews immigrated from Europe is hardly in conformity with reality.

Secondly, the table shows clearly that the vast bulk of the "missing" Jews must be sought in the Soviet Union.

Assuming that the Jewish population of the Western Hemisphere maintained its size between 1943 and the end of the war, that the losses on the Soviet side exceeded one million, that the surviving post-war Jewish population numbered more than four million in the Soviet Union and that the number of Jews who left Europe after the war – although "officially" unaccounted for – reached one million, the comparison with 1941 produces considerable differences with the current version of contemporary historians. These corrections were made on *Table 21*. There we see that the worldwide losses suffered by the Jews during the Second World War were in the neighborhood of 1¼ million – 8% of world Jewry – caused largely not by the direct impact of the war, i.e. those killed in action, but by Soviet barbarism. Over two hundred thousand remain unaccounted for. This latter worldwide figure agrees roughly with the missing figure of about 300,000 calculated for Europe in the Seventh Chapter.

Regardless of whether one traces the development of the Jewish population in Europe country by country or more generally for the world, the missing remainder seems to narrow to two or three hundred thousand. Even this figure has no claim on absolute certainty. Available data on population size, migration, flight and deportation, fertility and mortality rates, mixed marriages and assimilation tendencies often are so vague that it would not have been surprising to obtain a *statistically* unaccounted difference which is larger by several hundreds of thousands – or near zero.

Table 21
Probable World Jewish Population: 1941 and 1945
(in 1,000)

	1941	1945	Difference
A. World *outside* the German sphere of influence 1939–1945:			
– North and South America	5,955 ('43)	5,955	0
– Asia, Africa, Australia	1,444	1,647	+ 203
– Non-occupied Europe	384	419	+ 35
	7,783	8,021	+ 238
B. German sphere of influence *outside* the Soviet Union according to *Table 11* but excl. Ruthenia):			
– Poland	757	240	– 517
– Czechoslovakia	155	82	– 73
– Rumania	315	430	+ 115
– Other European countries	1,511	691	– 820
	2,738	1,443	–1,295
C. World *excl.* the USSR	10,521	9,464	–1,057
D. Soviet Union, Baltic states and Ruthenia	5,446*	4,301	–1,145
E. Number of Jews who left Europe during and shortly after World War Two and who could not be traced statistically		965	+ 965
F. Jewish World Population	15,967	14,730	–1,237
G. Jewish losses in the Red Army, in Siberian labor and concentration camps, etc.		1,030	
H. Statistically unaccounted for			– 207

Note: *Of the 5.5 million Jews approximately 700,000 Soviet Jews fell into German hands besides the roughly 100,000 Ruthenian Jews. On balance, no more than 3.5 million Jews were ever under German control during World War Two.

199

Today's dispersion of the Jews in all parts of the world is without precedent in Jewish history. What irony of fate that just in the age when a political force – Zionism – finally gave geographic substance to the old yearning "Next year in Jerusalem," assimilation in the diaspora became the driving force in a process of dissolution that may prove fatal in the end.

The Second World War destroyed Jewry in Europe as an important, geographically concentrated population group for all time. Other centers appeared in the place of Europe – the United States, Israel and the Soviet Union – and one may presume that these three countries include 80% of world Jewry within their borders today. Basically, the world's Jewish population never was as divided and dispersed throughout the world as it is at present.

But this process of dissolution did not start with the Jewish drama in World War Two, or with the growing anti-Semitism in the 1930's, or with the division of Eastern Jewry following the establishment of Soviet might on the ruins of Tsarist Russia; it began in the second half of the 19th Century with the swelling Jewish westward drive when literally millions of Eastern Jews poured into the melting pot across the ocean.

At the end of the 19th Century almost 90% of all Jews in the world lived in Europe[23] and within Europe almost exclusively in an area whose "borders" ran from Lithuania through Poland to Hungary, turning east to the Sea of Azov and from there, encompassing the Ukraine and White Russia, north towards the Baltic countries. In those days, world Jewry was concentrated in three European countries, but, nevertheless, occupied a relatively well-defined geographic core. More important, the Jewish population in this area was rather homogeneous with regard to language (Yiddish) and religion (little secularization).

The so-called dispersion of the Jews throughout the world was nothing but a fable until the end of the 19th Century; it became a reality only in the 20th Century. The emigration of millions of Jews to America, the accelerated migration to the east and north within the Soviet Union during the last war as well as the settlement of Palestine after World War One, brought about the dissolution of Eastern Jewry which seemed so stable just three generations ago, and dispersed them to all corners of the earth.

Today, four-fifths of the Jews live in regions where a hundred years ago not even three per cent of world Jewry could be found, i.e. the

Western Hemisphere, Israel, Russia proper (*excluding* the Ukraine and White Russia), Siberia, Africa and Australia. On the other hand, most of the historic regions of the traditional diaspora are almost entirely without Jews today; this applies especially to eastern Europe, the Balkans, North Africa and the Near East.[24]

This process continued uninterruptedly after the last war. It is, however, very difficult to obtain a rough outline of this development since 1945 because of a whole barrage of problems. Not only does the political character of Jewish population statistics make every "official" publication of relative data suspect, but the signs of disintegration in the course of accelerated secularization and assimilation tendencies in East and West, plus the difficulty in obtaining reliable data on Soviet Jewry, burden every attempt to trace the demographic development of world Jewry during the last 35 years.

Nevertheless, there is great unanimity that the USA, Israel and the Soviet Union together account for 80% of the world's Jews. The other fifth is composed of Jews in Europe, Latin America, South Africa, Australia and North African and Asian countries. No differences of opinion exist either on the generally largely urban character of world Jewry and its much lower fertility than the surrounding gentile population; only the Israelis register a healthy birth rate. In many countries – today probably in most – negative net growth rates replaced formerly small positive ones, and the trend toward assimilation and mixed marriages places a real question mark on the survival of the Jewish people outside Israel.

When looking into country-specific data, Zionist statistics suddenly become confused, even contradictory. Some Zionist experts insist on accepting the official Soviet statistics on Soviet Jewry (Schmelz), others are convinced that they underestimate the number of Jews in the USSR by 50% or more (Goldmann, Zand), while a third group prefers a figure somewhere in between (Shapiro); keep in mind, in just this one case millions of people are involved and the "Holocaust" story is affected directly by the final outcome of this controversy. As if this were not enough, some place the natural increase of post-war Soviet Jews at up to +1% p.a. (Shapiro), while others take it for granted that they actually suffered huge net growth deficits of up to -1% p.a. in part (Schmelz).

Similar inconsistencies could be listed for the United States where the Jewish population was unscrupulously "reduced" to 5.4 million (1971: 6.1 million, and at the end of the war: 5 million) even though half a million Jews immigrated meanwhile as a matter of record and the excess of births

Table 22
Purported World Jewish Population Development:
1945/46, 1970 and 1979
(in millions)
– according to the American Jewish Year Book –

Country/Region	1945/46	1970	1979	Changes in % p.a. 1945–1970	Changes in % p.a. 1970–1979
United States	5.0	5.9	5.6^x	+0.7	−0.6
Soviet Union	2.0	2.6	2.6	+1.1	0
Palestine/Israel	0.6	2.6	3.2	+1.6^y	+1.5^y
	7.6	11.1	11.4^x	+1.5	+0.3
Rest of the world	3.5	2.8	2.7	−0.9	−0.4
World Jewry	11.1	13.9	14.1^x	+0.9	+0.2
deduct: Soviet Union	2.0	2.6	2.6	+1.1	0
World Jewry *outside* the Soviet Union	9.1	11.3	11.5^x	+0.9	+0.2

Source: *AJYB*, 1946, Vol. 48, p. 603-608; 1971, Vol. 72, p. 475-479, and
  1980, Vol. 81, p. 285-289.
Notes: ^{x} Excluding the non-Jewish members in the so-called "Jewish"
  households in the United States.
  ^{y} Refers only to the natural increase.

over deaths in the late 1940's, in the 1950's and in the 1960's added almost another million.

The way the *Year Book* sees the development of world Jewry since 1945 can be seen on *Table 22*. For the United States, whose Jewish population was listed much too low for 1946 already, one finds a drastic drop since the early 1970's; for the Soviet Union, whose Jews suffered drastic negative birth rates throughout the entire post-war period, a positive growth rate of 1% per year was applied until 1970. The other countries of the world purportedly lost only 0.7 million Jews between 1945 and 1970; this contradicts the fact that Israel and the United States alone received more than one million Jewish immigrants from there and that the over-aged Jewish population remaining behind in Europe registered huge negative growth rates in part.

In an analysis published in the *Year Book*, the Israeli demographer Prof. U.O. Schmelz from the Hebrew University in Jerusalem listed annual rates of natural increase or decrease for the following countries:[25]

Jewish Net Fertility Rates

Country	Period	Per Cent
United States	1967–71	0
Canada	1967–71	+0.2
Brazil (Sao Paulo)	1965–69	+0.3
Argentina	1956–60	+0.1
France (Paris):		
– European Jews	1972–76	–0.3
– Oriental Jews	1972–76	+0.2
Belgium (Brussels)	1957–61	–0.2
Germany	1961–65	–1.8
Switzerland	1959–62	–0.5
Italy	1961–65	–0.5
Soviet Union (RSFSR)	1959–70	–0.9
Israel	1971–75	+1.7

Since then, a further drop in Jewish fertility rates occurred in almost all countries of the world; still, we should emphasize that at least in the United States and Canada the Jewish population developed more favorably in the first two decades after the war.

The above mentioned Jewish growth rates in the individual countries correspond much more closely with the population changes as traced in this study than with those utilized by the *Year Book*. Our investigation which is based largely on Zionist sources showed that world Jewry was clearly less than 15 million in 1945 but exceeded 16 million just as surely in 1980. The extremely low fertility rates of world Jewry – Israel excepted – just did not permit a faster growth. The probable development of the Jewish population and the factors behind it – migration or fertility – have been recorded in *Tables 23* and *24*.

Table 23 shows that the 14.7 million surviving Jews multiplied by 0.4% annually between 1945 and 1970; but the smallness of the rise was almost exclusively due to the decrease of the Soviet Union's post-war Jewish population whose losses of men in the ranks of the Red Army, untold deaths in Siberian labor camps and multitudes of mixed marriages effected a drastically dropping birth rate. In the last decade – signs of this were visible in the 1960's already – the Jewish population of the Western World had no further growth, Israel excepted. One might even say that from here on world Jewry will grow only as much as Israelis overcompensate for the net deficits in the USSR – and this, too, is becoming ever more questionable as Israel's excess of births over deaths begins to shrink and the deficit of the Jews in the USSR grows year by year.

Today, only Israel has a growing Jewish population and until two decades ago this was also true in the United States. The Soviet Union and

Table 23
Probable World Jewish Population Development: 1945, 1970 und 1979
(in millions)
– according to results of this study –

Country/Area	1945	Natural growth	Migration	1970	Natural growth	Migration	1979	Natural growth in per cent p.a.	
								1945–70	1970–79
USA	5.2	+0.9	+0.5	6.6	0	+0.1	6.7	+0.6	0
USSR	4.3	−0.4	0	3.9	−0.3	−0.2	3.4	−0.4	−0.8
Palestine or Israel	0.6	+0.8	+1.2	2.6	+0.4	+0.2	3.2	+1.6	+1.5
Subtotal	10.1	+1.3	+1.7	13.1	+0.1	+0.1	13.3	+0.4	+0.1
Rest of world	4.6	+0.2	−1.7	3.1	0	−0.1	3.0	+0.2	0
World Jewry	14.7	+1.5	0	16.2	+0.1	0	16.3	+0.4	+0.1
deduct: USSR	4.3	−0.4	0	3.9	−0.3	−0.2	3.4	−0.4	−0.8
World Jewry outside the Soviet Union	10.4	+1.9	0	12.3	+0.4	0.2	12.9	+0.7	+0.4

the group of the remaining countries in the world (within this group there were noticeable changes) registered a continually falling number of their Jewish population.

Table 24

Distribution of World Jewry: 1945 and 1979

(in per cent)

Country/Region	1945	1979
United States	35	41
Soviet Union	29	21
Palestine/Israel	4	20
Subtotal	69	82
Rest of the World	31	18
World Jewry	100	100
deduct: Soviet Union	29	21
World Jewry *outside* the Soviet Union	71	79

Source: *Table 23.*

The percentage distribution of world Jewry can be seen in *Table 24*. In 1945, the United States and Israel (Palestine) accounted for 40%, but today for more than 60%. In the Soviet Union – which contained more than one-third of world Jewry in 1940 – there were still almost 30% of the world's Jews in 1945 despite the huge wartime losses of men and among the internees in Siberian labor camps; by 1980, this share had fallen to about 20%. A similar reduction in the share of Jews was recorded by the rest of the countries of the world: From 30% at the end of the war to about 20% in 1979/80.

While 80% of world Jewry today may be found outside the USSR and of these, in turn, 80% in just two countries – USA and Israel – only time will tell whether or not this development really was a net gain for the once immensely fertile Eastern European Jewry. American Jews seem to have entered a phase of low, much too low fertility and assimilation tendencies and the rapidly rising phenomenon of mixed marriages promises large losses for the future. Only in Israel did a young Jewish population persist. But here it is essentially the Oriental Jews who provide a healthy birth rate and who finally may shape the future and culture of this island nation in an Arabian sea – if the dams don't break.

Bibliography

Adlerstein, Fanny R. "Foreign Department," *The Jewish Social Service Quarterly*, New York, Vol. XVII, No. 4, June 1941.

American Jewish Year Book, New York (various issues).

Annuaire Statistique Hongrois 1931, Nouveau Cours XXXIX, l'Office Central Royal Hongrois de Statistique, Budapest, 1933.

Aronson, Gregor. *Soviet Russia and The Jews*, New York, 1949.

Aschenauer, Rudolf. *Krieg ohne Grenzen: Der Partisanenkampf gegen Deutschland 1939-1945*, Leoni, 1982.

Baltimore Sun (The), "Willkie Urges Second Front At First Possible Moment," Baltimore, Md., September 27, 1942.

Blau, Bruno. "Schlussbilanz des deutschen Judentums," *Aufbau/Reconstruction*, New York, Vol. XIV, No. 33, August 13, 1948.

Brockhaus, Der Grosse, Leipzig, 1931.

Burg, J.G. *Schuld und Schicksal: Europas Juden zwischen Henkern und Heuchlern*, Munich, 1965.

Butz, A.R. *The Hoax of the Twentieth Century*, Los Angeles, 1977.

Centralnoye Statisticeskoye Upravlenie pri Sovete Ministrov SSSR, *Itogi Vsesojuznoi Perepnizi Nazeleniya 1959goda: Ukrainskaya SSR*, Moscow, 1963.

Ceturtā Tautas Skaitīšana Latvijā 1935.gadā, III: Vecums, Ģimenes Stāvoklis (*Quatrième Recensement de la Population en Lettonie en 1935*, III: Age, Etat Civil), Valsts Statistiskā Pārvalde, Riga, 1937.

Daily Express, "Your Questions about Russia – Answered by Paul Holt," London, (a few days before) May 26, 1943.

Dallin, Alexander. *German Rule in Russia, 1941-1945*, London, 1957.

Davies, Arthur Raymond. *Odyssey through Hell*, New York, 1946.

Département de la Jeunesse et du Hèhalouts de l'Organisation Sioniste Mondiale. *Israël Almanach 1958-1959*, Jerusalem.

Deutsche Ukraine-Zeitung, Lutsk/Wolhynia (various issues).

Deutsche Zeitung im Ostland, Riga/Latvia (various issues).

Die Bevölkerung des polnischen Staatsgebiets westlich der Demarkationslinie vom 21.9.1939 nach dem Bekenntnis auf Grund der polnischen Volkszählung von 1931, Koblenz: Bundesarchiv, Bestand R 153/287.

Die Bevölkerung des ehemaligen polnischen Staatsgebiets westlich der Grenzlinie vom 28.9.1939 nach dem Bekenntnis auf Grund der polnischen Volkszählung von 1931, Koblenz: Bundesarchiv, Bestand R 153/287.

Drugi Powszechny Spis Ludności Z Dn. 9.XII 1931, Głowny Urząd Statystyczny Rzeczypospolitej Polskiej, Statystyka Polski (*Deuxième Recensement Général de la Population du 9 Décembre 1931*, Office Central Statistique de la Republique Polonaise, Statistique de la Pologne), Warsaw (various issues).

Encyclopaedia Judaica, Jerusalem, 1972.

Encyclopaedia Judaica 1973 Year Book, Jerusalem, 1974.

Ettinger, S. "The Jews in Russia at the Outbreak of the Revolution," *The Jews in Soviet Russia since 1917*, (Lionel Kochan, Ed.), London, 1970.

Fischer, Dr. Ludwig and Dr. Friedrich Gollert. *Warschau unter deutscher Herrschaft*, Cracow, 1942.

Fortune, New York, 8/14/1978.

Goldmann, Dr. Nahum. "Aus Sorge um Israel," *Die Zeit*, No. 29, 7/11/1980.

–, "Israels Regierung hat das Volk betrogen," *Der Spiegel*, No. 34, August 28, 1982.

–, *Private letter* of February 13, 1981.

Grajdanzev, Andrew. "Asiatic Russia's War Potential," *Far Eastern Survey*, New York, Vol. X, No. 22, November 17, 1941.

Grayzel, Solomon. *A History of THE JEWS*, Philadelphia, 1948.

Gutachten des Instituts für Zeitgeschichte, Munich, 1958.

Haganov, Gédéon. *Le Communisme et les "Juifs"*, Supplèment de CONTACT, Paris, May 1951.

Halder, Franz. *Hitler als Feldherr*, Munich, 1949.

Hardach, Karl. *Wirtschaftsgeschichte Deutschlands im 20. Jahrhundert*, Göttingen, 1976.

Helmdach, Erich. *Überfall?* *Der sowjetisch-deutsche Aufmarsch 1941*, Neckargemünd, 1978.

Hilberg, Raul. *The Destruction of the European Jews*, New York, 1973.

Hoggan, David. *Der Unnötige Krieg*, Tübingen, 1977.

Immigration and Naturalization Systems of the United States (The). Report of the Committee on the Judiciary, U.S. Senate, 81st Congress, 2d Session, April 20, 1950.

Institute of Jewish Affairs. *Hitler's Ten-Year War on the Jews*, New York, 1943.

–, *Jews in Nazi Europe: February 1933 to November 1941*, Baltimore, Md., November 1941.

International Herald Tribune, "French Policies to Court the Jewish Vote," Paris, May 10, 1977.

–, "What Price a Soviet Jew?", Paris, March 6, 1981.

International WHO'S WHO (The), London, 43rd Edition, 1979.

Irving, David. *Hitler's War*, New York, 1977.

Israel. Central Bureau of Statistics. *Statistical Abstract of Israel*, (various issues).

Jacobsen, Hans-Adolf. *Kriegstagebuch des Oberkommandos der Wehrmacht (Wehrmachtführungsstab)*, Band 1: 1. August 1940 - 31. Dezember 1941, Frankfurt am Main, 1965.

Jüdisches Lexikon, Berlin (Jüdischer Verlag), 1930.

Kauener Zeitung, Kovno (Kaunas)/Lithuania (various issues).

Kempner, Dr. Robert M.W. "Briefe an den Herausgeber," *Frankfurter Allgemeine Zeitung*, Frankfurt am Main, No. 23, 1/28/1981, p. 9.

Kern, Erich. *Die Tragödie der Juden*, Preussisch Oldendorf, 1979.

Krakauer Zeitung, Cracow (various issues).

Lestschinsky, J. "National Groups in Polish Emigration," *Jewish Social Studies*, Vol. 5, 1943.

Lettl. Statistisches Amt. *Zahl der Einwohner Lettlands für das Jahr 1941* (*Stand 1.8.1941*), Riga; Koblenz: Bundesarchiv, Bestand R 92/1427.

Lorimer, Dr. Frank. *The Population of the Soviet Union: History and Prospects*, Geneva (League of Nations), 1946.

Magyar Statisztikai Évkönyv 1942, Új Folyam L, A Magyar Kir Központi Statisztikai Hivatal, Budapest, 1944.

Millman, Ivor. "Romanian Jewry: a Note on the 1966 Census," *Soviet Jewish Affairs*, London, No. 3, May 1972.

New York Times (*The*), "580,000 Refugees Admitted to United States in Decade," 12/11/1943.

–, "Willkie's Statement About Russia's Needs," 9/27/1942.

Niederreiter, Wilhelm. "Verbrannte Erde - Sowjetischer Wirtschaftskrieg im Zweiten Weltkrieg," *Deutschland in Geschichte und Gegenwart* (Wigbert Grabert, Ed.), Tübingen, 29th Year, No. 1, 1981, p. 18-21.

Oberkommando des Heeres, GenStdH/Attacheabteilung. Letter of February 10, 1942 to the Reichsminister for the occupied eastern territories, attn. Herrn Reg.Rat Disch, Berlin; Freiburg: Militärarchiv, Bestand RW 31/134.

Parming, Tönu. "Population Changes in Estonia, 1935 - 1970," *Population Studies*, London, Vol. 26, No. 1, March 1972.

Payne, Robert. *Stalin: Macht und Tyrannei*, Munich, 1981.

Pechenick, Rabbi Aaron. *Zionism And Judaism In Soviet-Russia*, New York, 1943.

Perspektiven zur Verpflegungsversorgung der U.d.S.S.R. im Winterfeldzug 1942/43, (Date unknown), Chef d.Vers.d.200.Schtz.Div. der 5. Armee, Freiburg: Militärarchiv, Bestand RW 31/232.

Publikationsstelle Berlin-Dahlem. *Bevölkerungsstatistik Lettlands* (Joh. Papritz and Wolfgang Kohte, Ed.), Berlin, 1942.

Publikationsstelle Wien. *Die Bevölkerungszählung in Rumänien 1941* (Geheim), Vienna, 1943.

Rachner, Dr. "Der Arbeitseinsatz in den besetzten Ostgebieten," *Reichsarbeitsblatt*, (Reichsarbeitsministerium), Berlin, 22nd Year, No. 7, March 5, 1942.

Rassinier, Paul. *Zum Fall Eichmann: Was ist Wahrheit?*, Leoni, 1963.

Recensământul General Al Populației României Din 29 Decemvrie 1930, Volumul II: Neam, Limbă, Maternă, Religie; Institutul Central de Statistică, Bukarest, 1938.

Reichswirtschaftsministerium. *Annähernde Angaben über die am 1. November 1942 besetzten Gebiete der UdSSR*, (Date unknown), Koblenz: Bundesarchiv, Bestand R 24/804.

–, *Die UdSSR Anfang 1942*, (Date unknown), Koblenz: Bundesarchiv, Bestand R 24/817.

–, *Gebiet und Bevölkerung der UdSSR*, (Date unknown), Koblenz: Bundesarchiv: Bestand R 24/804.

Reitlinger, Gerald. *The Final Solution*, New York, 1961.

Ringelblum, Emanuel. *Ghetto Warschau*, Stuttgart, 1967.

Rothenberg, Joshua. "Jewish Religion in the Soviet Union," *The Jews in Soviet Russia since 1917*, (Lionel Kochan, Ed.), London, 1970.

Ruppin, Arthur. *The Jewish Fate and Future*, London, 1940.

–, *The Jews in the Modern World*, London, 1934.

Schlag nach über Polen. Leipzig: Bibliographisches Institut, 1940 (?).

Schloss, Rolf W. *Die russischen Juden zwischen Sowjetstern und Davidstern,* Munich, 1971.

Schmelz, U.O. "A Guide to Jewish Population Studies," *Jewish Population Studies 1961-1968,* (U.O. Schmelz and P. Glickson, Ed.), London/Jerusalem, 1970.

–, "New Evidence on Basic Issues in the Demography of Soviet Jews," *The Jewish Journal of Sociology,* Vol. XVI, No. 2, December 1974.

Sčítání Lidu V Republice Československé Ze Dne 1. Prosince 1930 (Díl I.: Růst, Koncentrace A Hustota Obyvatelstva, Pohlaví, Věkové Rozvrstvení, Rodinný Stav, Státní Příslušnost, Národnost, Náboženské Vyznání), Vydal Státní Úřad Statistický, Československá Statistika - Svazek 98, Řada VI., Sešit 7, Prague, 1934.

Scott, John. *Jenseits des Ural,* Stockholm, 1944 (Engl. original: *Behind the Urals,* Boston, 1942).

Shapiro, Prof. Leon. *Private letter* dated January 3, 1980.

Statesman's Yearbook (The), New York, 1944.

Statistisches Bundesamt. *Statistisches Jahrbuch für die Bundesrepublik Deutschland,* Wiesbaden, 1962.

Statistisches Reichsamt. *Wirtschaft und Statistik,* Berlin (various issues).

Stegemann, Wilhelm. *Der Neue Weltkrieg,* First Volume 1939/40, Zurich, 1941.

–, *Der Neue Weltkrieg,* Second Volume 1940/41, Zurich, 1942.

Sykes, Christopher. *Kreuzwege nach Israel: Die Vorgeschichte des Jüdischen Staates,* Munich, 1967.

Tartakower, Arieh and Kurt R. Grossmann. *The Jewish Refugee,* New York, 1944.

Tat (Die), "Die erschütternde Bilanz zweier Weltkriege," Zurich/Switzerland, 1/18/1955.

Telpuchowski, Boris Semjonowitsch. *Die sowjetische Geschichte des Grossen Vaterländischen Krieges 1941-1945,* (Andreas Hillgruber and Hans-Adolf Jacobsen, Ed.) Frankfurt/Main, 1961.

Treatment of Jews by the Soviet. 17th Interim Report of Hearings before the Select Committee on Communist Aggression, House of Representatives, 83rd Congress, New York, September 22 and 23, 1954.

Universal Jewish Encyclopedia, New York, 1943.

U.S. Department of Commerce, Bureau of the Census. *Population Estimates and Projections,* Current Population Reports, Series P-25, No. 632, July 1976, Washington, D.C.

U.S. News and World Report, New York, April 7, 1980.

U.S. War Refugee Board. *Final Summary Report of the Executive Director, War Refugee Board,* Washington, D.C., 9/15/1945.

von Mende, Gerhard. "Die besetzten Ostgebiete," *Jahrbuch für Weltpolitik 1943,* Berlin (Deutsches Auslandswissenschaftliches Institut), 1943.

WER IST WER?, (Walter Habel, Ed.), Frankfurt, 1975.

WHO'S WHO in America, Chicago, Vol. 27, 1952-1953.

Werth, A. *Moscow '41,* London, February 1942.

Wirtschaftsstab Ost. *Bevölkerung in den besetzten Ostgebieten,* (Krüger, Chefgruppe W, Statistik), Berlin, 2/17/1943; Freiburg: Militärarchiv, Bestand RW 31/260.

–, *Vierzehntagesbericht Wi Stab Ost (3.8.-16.8.1941)*, 8/30/1941, Freiburg: Militärarchiv, Bestand RW 31/11.

–, *Halbmonatsbericht Wi Stab Ost (1.-15.11.1941)*, 12/8/1941, Freiburg: Militärarchiv, Bestand RW 31/68.

Wischnitzer, Mark. "The History of the Jews in Russia in Recent Publications," *The Jewish Quarterly Review*, Philadelphia, 1944-1945, Vol. XXXV.

World Almanac and Book of Facts, New York, (various issues).

Zentralblatt des Reichskommissars für die Ukraine, Rovno, No. 2, 2nd Year, 1/9/1943, Koblenz: Bundesarchiv, Bestand R 43 II/690c.

Zionist Year Book (The). London (various issues).

Zoller, Henri. "Dunkelheit umgibt uns," *Der Spiegel*, No. 20, 5/11/1981.

–, "Israel - Ein Nachtasyl?," *Der Spiegel*, No. 37, 9/8/1980.

References and Footnotes

First Chapter

1. Reitlinger, Gerald. *The Final Solution*, New York, 1961, p. 497.
2. *Universal Jewish Encyclopedia*, New York, Vol. 10., 1943, p. 33.
3. *Statesman's Yearbook (The)*. New York, 1944, p. 1196.
4. *Universal Jewish Encyclopedia*, Vol. 10, p. 36.
5. *ibid.*, p. 36. From 1930 to 1937 the mortality in Poland averaged 479,000 (*Schlag nach über Polen*. Leipzig: Bibliographisches Institut, 1940 [?] p. 15). The Jewish population accounted for 9.8% of Poland's population in 1931, but in the age group 50 years and over, where most of the natural deaths occurred, it was 10.9% (for source see *Graph 2*). Even conceding a smaller age-specific death rate for Jews than for the Polish or Ukrainian population, the average number of Jewish deaths in Poland in the 1930's must have been at least 45,000 per year.
6. *Drugi Powszechny Spis Ludności Z Dn. 9.XII 1931 R.* "Polska (Dane Skrócone): Mieszkania I Gospodarstwa Domowe, Ludność, Stosunki Zawodowe," Głowny Urząd Statystyczny Rzeczypospolitej Polskiej, Statystyka Polski, Seria C, Zeszyt 62 (*Deuxième Recensement Général de la Population du 9 Décembre 1931*. "Pologne (Données Abregées): Logements et Ménages, Population, Professions," Office Central Statistique de la Republique Polonaise, Statistique de la Pologne, Série C, Fascicule 62), Warsaw, 1937.
7. *Universal Jewish Encyclopedia*, Vol. 10, p. 33.
8. Ruppin, Arthur. *The Jewish Fate and Future*, London, 1940, p. 100.
9. Computed on the basis of information contained in *Table 12* of the *Drugi Powszechny Spis Ludności Z Dn. 9.XII 1931 R.* "Polska: Mieszkania I Gospodarstwa Domowe, Ludność," Seria C, Zeszyt 94a (*Deuxième Recensement Général de la Population du 9 Décembre 1931*, "Pologne: Logements et Ménages, Population," Série C, Fascicule 94a), Warsaw, 1938.
10. An indication of the validity of this conclusion can be found in the *Statistical Abstract of Israel*. According to issue no. 31 (1980), p. 133, 35,183 and 81,613 Jews immigrated in the years 1919/1923 and 1924/1931, respectively. Issue no. 2 (1950/51), p. 26, fixed the male share among the immigrants at 63.2 and 54%, respectively. This translates into an average share of 57% male Jewish immigrants in Palestine between the end of World War One and 1931, i.e. male Jews outnumbered Jewesses by one third. A large, probably the largest part of these immigrants hailed from Poland.
11. Lestschinsky, J. "National Groups in Polish Emigration," *Jewish Social Studies*, Vol. 5, 1943, p. 109.

12. *ibid.*, p. 109.
13. The figure of 68,000 Jewish immigrants in Palestine from Poland between 1934 and 1937 was computed as follows: The Jewish immigration in Palestine was listed by the *Encyclopaedia Judaica*, Jerusalem, 1972, Vol. 4, p. 534: 45,267 (1934), 66,472 (1935), 29,595 (1936), 10,629 (1937). The number of Jews coming from Poland according to Arieh Tartakower and Kurt R. Grossmann, *The Jewish Refugee*, New York, 1944, p. 345 was 43% (1934), 49% (1935), 41% (1936) und 35% (1937); the share of Jewish immigrants from Germany was listed as 16%, 11%, 27% und 34%, respectively, and the share of Jewish immigrants from all other countries as 41%, 40%, 32% und 31%, respectively. Inasmuch as the "other" Jewish immigrants could only have come from eastern Europe, the Jews coming from those "other" eastern European countries were almost as many in number as those from Poland. Because of the overwhelming size of the Polish Jews relative to the other eastern European Jews (excl. the USSR) this does not seem realistic; in all probability, the "other" Jewish immigrants in Palestine included many Jews who originally hailed from Poland as well. The Polish-Jewish group of immigrants in Palestine between 1934 and 1937 must have numbered far more than 68,000, possibly more than 80,000!
14. Adlerstein, Fanny R., "Foreign Department," *The Jewish Social Service Quarterly*, New York, Vol. XVII, No. 4, June 1941, p. 386. The figure of 100,000 also includes Jewish emigrants from Austria.
15. *Brockhaus (Der Grosse)*. Leipzig, 1931, Neunter Band, J-Kas, p. 473.
16. Reitlinger, *Final Solution*, p. 71.
17. Adlerstein, *Jewish Social Service Quarterly*, June 1941, p. 386.
18. *Gutachten des Instituts für Zeitgeschichte*, Munich, 1958, p. 79 and 80.
19. *Universal Jewish Encyclopedia*, Vol. 8, p. 574.
20. According to official Polish surveys, the birth rate fell in Poland between 1931 and 1937 from 3.02% to 2.49% (*Schlag nach über Polen*, p. 15). The Jewish rate reached 1.7% in 1931 already and it is not likely that it moved against the weakening Polish trend thereafter. A negative net growth rate is thus quite probable for Poland's Jewish population at the end of the 1930's.
21. *Universal Jewish Encyclopedia*, Vol. 8, p. 576.
22. *Sčítání Lidu V Republice Československé Ze Dne 1. Prosince 1930* (Díl I.: Růst, Koncentrace A Hustota Obyvatelstva, Pohlaví, Věkové Rozvrstvení, Rodinný Stav, Státní Příslušnost, Národnost, Náboženské Vyznání), Vydal Státní Úřad Statistický, Československá Statistika - Svazek 98, Řada VI., Sešit 7, Prague, 1934, Tab. 19, p. 156-164.
23. *Annuaire Statistique Hongrois 1931*, Nouveau Cours XXXIX, l'Office Central Royal Hongrois de Statistique, Budapest, 1933, Tab. 10, p. 11.
24. *ibid.*, Tab. 9, p. 10.
25. *ibid.*, Tab. 21, p. 28.
26. *Magyar Statisztikai Évkönyv 1942*, Új Folyam L, A Magyar Kir Központi Statisztikai Hivatal, Budapest, 1944, Tab. 21, p. 36.
27. *ibid.*, Tab. 14, p. 33 and Tab. 16, p. 34.
28. *Universal Jewish Encyclopedia*, Vol. 9, p. 265.
29. *Ceturtā Tautas Skaitīšana Latvijā 1935.gadā*, III: Vecums, Ģimenes Stāvoklis (*Quatrième Recensement de la Population en Lettonie en 1935*, III: Age, Etat

Civil), Valsts Statistiskā Pārvalde, Riga, 1937, Tab. 10, p. 217; Tab. 8, p. 206
   and pages 120-121.
30. *ibid.*, p. 297, 298 and 319.
31. *ibid.*, p. 216-217.

Second Chapter

1. *Universal Jewish Encyclopedia*, Vol. 8, p. 577.
2. *American Jewish Year Book* (AJYB), New York, 1946, Vol. 48, p. 324.
3. Fischer, Dr. Ludwig and Dr. Friedrich Gollert, *Warschau unter deutscher Herrschaft*, Cracow, 1942, p. 186.
4. *Encyclopaedia Judaica*, Vol. 15, p. 1214.
5. The Jewish population of the area between the Vistula and the Bug from which the Soviets withdrew after 9/28/1939 contained 386,600 Jews on 12/9/1931 according to the Bundesarchiv in Koblenz, Bestand R 153, Aktenband 287: *Die Bevölkerung des ehemaligen polnischen Staatsgebiets westlich der Grenzlinie vom 28.9.1939 nach dem Bekenntnis auf Grund der polnischen Volkszählung von 1931* as well as *Die Bevölkerung des polnischen Staatsgebiets westlich der Demarkationslinie vom 21.9.1939 nach dem Bekenntnis auf Grund der polnischen Volkszählung von 1931*.
6. *International WHO'S WHO (The)*. London, 43rd Edition, 1979, p. 93.
7. Rassinier, Paul. *Zum Fall Eichmann: Was ist Wahrheit?*, Leoni, 1963, p. 99.
8. *Encyclopaedia Judaica*, Vol. 11, p. 184.
9. –, Vol. 16, p. 201.
10. –, Vol. 11, p. 589.
11. –, Vol. 13, p. 543.
12. –, Vol. 14, p. 357.
13. *Treatment of Jews by the Soviet.* 17th Interim Report of Hearings before the Select Committee on Communist Aggression, House of Representatives, 83rd Congress, New York, September 22 and 23, 1954, p. 40.
14. *ibid.*, p. 46 and 47.
15. *ibid.*, p. 61.
16. *ibid.*, p. 25.
17. Haganov, Gédéon. *Le Communisme et les "Juifs"*, Supplément de CONTACT, Paris, May 1951, p. 9-15; see also Aronson, Gregor. *Soviet Russia and The Jews*, New York, 1949, p. 12.
18. *Pechenick*, Rabbi Aaron. *Zionism And Judaism In Soviet-Russia*, New York, p. 60.
19. *Universal Jewish Encyclopedia*, Vol. 6, p. 176.
20. Aronson, *Soviet Russia and The Jews*, p. 12.
21. Zoller, Henri. "Dunkelheit umgibt uns," *Der Spiegel*, No. 20, 5/11/1981, p. 31.
22. *Krakauer Zeitung*, Krakau, "Noch 1 Million Belgier in Frankreich," No. 195, 8/18-19/1940, p. 4.
23. *Universal Jewish Encyclopedia*, Vol. 6, p. 175.

24. *Krakauer Zeitung*, "Goralen in die Tucheler Heide verschoben," No. 157, 7/5/ 1940, p. 5.
25. *Kauener Zeitung*, Kovno (Kaunas)/Lithuania, "Die Bevölkerung des General-Gouvernements," No. 42, 2/19/1942, p. 7.
26. *Die Bevölkerung des polnischen Staatsgebiets westlich der Demarkationslinie vom 21.9.1939 nach dem Bekenntnis auf Grund der polnischen Volkszählung von 1931*, Bundesarchiv in Koblenz: Bestand R 153/287.
27. *Krakauer Zeitung*, "Kein Jude in Rumäniens Einheitspartei," No. 152, 6/29/ 1941, p. 3.
28. *Kauener Zeitung*, "Die jüdische Pest in Frankreich," No. 120, 5/23/1942, p. 3.
29. Reitlinger, *Final Solution*, p. 498.
30. *AJYB*, 1940, Vol. 42, p. 602.
31. –, 1941, Vol. 43, p. 330.
32. Ruppin, Arthur. *The Jews in the Modern World*, London, 1934, p. 26 and 27.
33. *AJYB*, 1944, Vol. 46, p. 501.
34. Lorimer, Dr. Frank. *The Population of the Soviet Union: History and Prospects*, Geneva (League of Nations), 1946, p. 138.
35. Dr. Lorimer mentioned a Jewish population of 2,672,499 ; this figure is 6,742 smaller than Zionist sources usually mention.
36. Lorimer, *Population of the Soviet Union*, p. 95 and 96.
37. *ibid.*, p. 94 and 97.
38. *AJYB*, 1939, Vol. 41, p. 588.
39. *Universal Jewish Encyclopedia*, Vol. 10, p. 24.
40. *Encyclopaedia Judaica*, Vol. 11, p. 17 and Vol. 12, p. 365.
41. *Kauener Zeitung*, "Juden-Metropole Moskau," No. 130, 6/4/1943, p. 2, mentions the same statistics for the years 1920, 1923 and 1926, but none for 1940. On the other hand, this newspaper wrote that the latest published statistical material placed the number of Moscow's Jewish inhabitants in 1937 already at over 450,000.
42. *Universal Jewish Encyclopedia*, Vol. 10, p. 24.
43. Institute of Jewish Affairs. *Hitler's Ten-Year War on the Jews*, New York, 1943, p. 184.
44. *Universal Jewish Encyclopedia*, Vol. 9, p. 670.
45. *AJYB*, 1941, Vol. 43, p. 319.

Third Chapter

1. Helmdach, Erich. *Überfall? Der sowjetisch-deutsche Aufmarsch 1941*, Neckargemünd, 1978, p. 31.
2. Scott, John. *Jenseits des Ural: Die Kraftquellen der Sowjetunion*, Stockholm, 1944, p. 301-302.
3. Helmdach, *Überfall?*, p. 10.
4. *ibid.*, p. 30.

5. Irving, David. *Hitler's War*, New York, 1977, p. 238.
6. *ibid.*, p. 234.
7. Helmdach, *Überfall?*, p. 30.
8. Irving, *Hitler's War*, p. 236.
9. *Kauener Zeitung*, "'Rote Professoren' wussten längst vom Krieg," No. 172, 7/25/1942, p. 5.
10. Helmdach, *Überfall?*, p. 35.
11. Irving, *Hitler's War*, p. 236.
12. Helmdach, *Überfall?*, p. 35.
13. Halder, Franz. *Hitler als Feldherr*, Munich, 1949, p. 36 - 37.
14. Hoggan, David. *Der Unnötige Krieg*, Tübingen, 1977, p. 438 and 486 f.
15. Payne, Robert. *Stalin: Macht und Tyrannei*, Munich, 1981, p. 507 f.
16. Irving, *Hitler's War*, p. 235.
17. Helmdach, *Überfall?*, p. 38.
18. *ibid.*, p. 75.
19. Irving, *Hitler's War*, p. 237.
19a. Aschenauer, Rudolf. *Krieg ohne Grenzen*, Leoni, 1982, p. 115.
20. Publikationsstelle Wien. *Die Bevölkerungszählung in Rumänien 1941* (Geheim), Vienna, 1943: In 1930, Bessarabia and the northern Bukovina had a population of 3.41 million (p. 17); assuming a natural increase of maybe 1.5% p.a., there should have been 4.02 million people in 1941. Deducting the 137,000 resettled ethnic Germans (p. 27), there remain 3.88 million; however, only 3.22 million were found (p. 17) – a decrease by 20%. Kishinev had 140,000 inhabitants before the war (1930: 114,896), but the Rumanians found only 52,962 – a reduction by 62%; Chernovitsy's population of roughly the same size before WWII (1930: 112,427) was down to 78,825 in August 1941 – a minus of 42% (p. 70-73).
21. Helmdach, *Überfall?*, p. 30.
22. Irving, *Hitler's War*, p. 238 - 240.
23. *ibid.*, p. 265.
24. Helmdach, *Überfall?*, p. 58.
25. *ibid.*, p. 99.
26. *ibid.*, p. 42.
27. *Krakauer Zeitung*, "Die Sowjetflugplätze viel zu dicht belegt," No. 151, 7/1/1941, p. 2.
28. –, "Entscheidung von weltgeschichtlichen Ausmaßen," No. 153, 7/3/1941, p. 1.
29. Telpuchowski, Boris Semjonowitsch. *Die sowjetische Geschichte des Grossen Vaterländischen Krieges 1941-1945*, (Andreas Hillgruber and Hans-Adolf Jacobsen, Ed.) Frankfurt am Main, 1961, p. 27E and 28E.
30. Scott, *Jenseits des Ural*, p. 76, 79, 105, 304-305.
31. *ibid.*, p. 307 and 312.
32. Lorimer, *Population of the Soviet Union*, p. 195.
33. Telpuchowski, *Die sowjetische Geschichte*, p. 84.
34. Reichswirtschaftsministerium. *Die UdSSR Anfang 1942*, (Date unknown), Bundesarchiv Koblenz, Bestand R 24/817.
35. Scott, *Jenseits des Ural*, p. 312-313.
36. Telpuchowski, *Die sowjetische Geschichte*, p. 28E.

37. Scott, *Jenseits des Ural*, p. 301 and 303.
38. *ibid.*, p. 310.
39. Niederreiter, Wilhelm. "Verbrannte Erde - Sowjetischer Wirtschaftskrieg im Zweiten Weltkrieg," *Deutschland in Geschichte und Gegenwart* (Wigbert Grabert, Ed.), Tübingen, 29th Year, No. 1, 1981, p. 20.
40. Telpuchowski, *Die sowjetische Geschichte*, p. 81-83, 86.
41. The economic administration of the occupied Soviet areas was in the hands of the so-called Wirtschaftsstab Ost (Economy Staff East).
42. Wirtschaftsstab Ost. *Vierzehntagesbericht Wi Stab Ost (3.8.-16.8.1941)*, 8/30/ 1941, Militärarchiv Freiburg, Bestand RW 31/11.
43. –, *Halbmonatsbericht Wi Stab Ost (1.-15.11.1941)*, 12/8/1941, Militärarchiv Freiburg, Bestand RW 31/68.
44. Scott, *Jenseits des Ural*, p. 262, 281, 301.
45. Telpuchowski, *Die sowjetische Geschichte*, p. 82 and 88.
46. Irving, *Hitler's War*, p. 272.
47. Institute of Jewish Affairs. *Hitler's Ten-Year War*, p. 184.
48. *AJYB*, 1947, Vol. 49, p. 395.
49. Lorimer, *Population of the Soviet Union*, p. 138.
50. Statistisches Reichsamt. *Wirtschaft und Statistik*, Berlin, 20th Year, No. 14, 2nd July-issue 1940, p. 290.
51. For 1926, *Wirtschaft und Statistik* provided figures for the age groups 1897/ 1906, 1907/1911, 1912/1918; for 1939, the age groups 1899/1908, 1909/1918. In order to match the age groups of 1926 and 1939 censuses three average years were deducted from the group 1907/1911 and added to the group 1909/1918. The group 1899/1908 for 1926 was calculated in a similar fashion.
52. The sum does not add up to the final census figure for 1939; the difference applies to the extreme North of the Soviet Union where the census was taken somewhat later.
53. Normally, this young age group should have had a mortality of maybe 1% for a 12-year-period; in order to take account of the worse hygienic and social environment in the Soviet Union of the 1920's and 1930's, a mortality of 2% was presumed even though this is probably too high.
54. *Wirtschaft und Statistik*, 2nd July-issue 1940, p. 288.
55. *AJYB*, 1940, Vol 42, p. 602.
56. Lorimer, *Population of the Soviet Union*, p. 194.
57. *ibid.*, p. 241 and 242.
58. *ibid.*, p. 194.
59. Telpuchowski, *Die sowjetische Geschichte*, p. 78.
60. Reichswirtschaftsministerium. *Annähernde Angaben über die am 1. November 1942 besetzten Gebiete der UdSSR*, (Date unknown), Bundesarchiv Koblenz: Bestand R 24/804.
61. Lorimer, *Population of the Soviet Union*, p. 194.
62. Reichswirtschaftsministerium. *Gebiet und Bevölkerung der UdSSR*, (Date unknown), Bundesarchiv Koblenz: Bestand R 24/804. The urban population for the areas annexed by the Soviet Union in the years 1939 and 1940 (Baltic countries, eastern Poland, northern Bukovina and Bessarabia) is given as 3.42 million. In order to estimate the urban population before the outbreak of the war in the subsequent German-occupied Soviet territories, one has to add part

of the urban population of those Soviet areas which were not fully occupied by German troops like the oblasts of Stalingrad, Leningrad, Moscow and Tula; we also have to take into account that since the last census in 1939 continued war preparations and industrialization measures may have forced at least another two million people into the cities.

63. Lorimer, *Population of the Soviet Union*, p. 195-197.
64. Reitlinger, *Final Solution*, p. 228.
65. Institute of Jewish Affairs, *Hitler's Ten-Year War*, p. 184.
66. *Wirtschaft und Statistik*, 2nd July-issue, p. 290.
67. Lorimer, *Population of the Soviet Union*, p. 196, 250-252.
68. Reitlinger, *Final Solution*, p. 228.
69. Rachner, Dr. "Der Arbeitseinsatz in den neu besetzten Ostgebieten," *Reichsarbeitsblatt* (published by the Reichsarbeitsministerium), Berlin, 22nd Year, No. 7, March 5, 1942, p. V 131.
70. Letter of February 10, 1942 from the Oberkommando des Heeres, GenStdH/Attacheabteilung, to the Reichsminister für die besetzten Ostgebiete, attn. Reg.Rat Disch, Berlin; Militärarchiv Freiburg, Bestand RW 31/134.
71. Wirtschaftsstab Ost (Krüger, Chefgruppe W, Statistik). *Bevölkerung in den besetzten Ostgebieten*, Berlin, 2/17/1943, Militärarchiv Freiburg, Bestand RW 31/260.
71a. The 1930 census recorded a total population of 2,864,402 in Bessarabia. Natural growth of this largely agricultural population probably was at least 1.2% p.a. Thus, until mid-1941 there should have been an increase by over 380,000 to at least 3,245,000. But the Rumanian census of August 1941 taken immediately after that region's liberation from the Soviet yoke found only 2,733,565 inhabitants (Publikationsstelle Wien, *Die Bevölkerungszählung in Rumänien*, p. 51) – more than half a million persons including almost the entire Jewish population was missing. This amounts to a loss of more than 15%.
72. *Deutsche Zeitung im Ostland*, "Die wehrwirtschaftlichen Verluste der Sowjetunion," No. 14, 1/14/1943, p. 6.
73. *Perspektiven zur Verpflegungsversorgung der U.d.S.S.R. im Winterfeldzug 1942/43*, (Date unknown), Chef d.Vers.d.200.Schtz.Div. der 5. Armee, Militärarchiv Freiburg, Bestand RW 31/232.
74. *WHO'S WHO in America*, Chicago, Vol. 27, 1952-1953, p. 403.
75. Grajdanzev, Andrew. "Asiatic Russia's War Potential," *Far Eastern Survey*, New York, Vol. X, No. 22, 11/17/1941, p. 25.
76. Dallin, Alexander. *German Rule in Russia, 1941-1945*, London, 1957, p. 365.
77. *New York Times (The)*, 9/29/1942, front page.
77a. *Baltimore Sun (The)*, "Willkie Urges Second Front At First Possible Moment" (An Associated Press report), September 27, 1942, p. 1; also see *New York Times (The)*, "Willkie's Statement About Russia's Needs," 9/27/1942, p. 3.
78. Rachner, *Reichsarbeitsblatt*, 3/5/1942, p. V 131 - V 132.
79. *Deutsche Ukraine-Zeitung*, "Ukraine auf dem Weg nach Europa," 2/22/1942, p. 3.
80. Scott, *Jenseits des Ural*, p. 63.
81. *Deutsche Ukraine-Zeitung*, 2/15/1942, p. 3; 2/25/42, p. 3; 3/29/42, p. 3; 5/17/42,

p. 3; 7/10/42, p. 3.

82. Publikationsstelle Berlin-Dahlem. *Bevölkerungsstatistik Lettlands* (Joh. Papritz and Wolfgang Kohte, Ed.), Berlin, 1942, p. 10/11, 42/43, 46/47.

83. *Zentralblatt des Reichskommissars für die Ukraine*, Rovno, No. 2, 2nd Year, 1/9/1943, p. 8-20, Bundesarchiv Koblenz: R 43 II/690c.

84. von Mende, Gerhard. "Die besetzten Ostgebiete," *Jahrbuch der Weltpolitik 1943*, Berlin (Deutsches Auslandswissenschaftliches Institut), 1943, p. 231.

85. Wirtschaftsstab Ost (Krüger, Chefgruppe W, Statistik). *Bevölkerung in den besetzten Ostgebieten*, Berlin, 2/17/1943, Militärarchiv Freiburg, Bestand RW 31/260.

86. Centralnoye Statisticeskoye Upravlenie pri Sovete Ministrov SSSR. *Itogni Vsesojuznoy Perepnizi Nazeleniya 1959goda: Ukrainskaya SSR*, Moscow, 1963, p. 12-17.

87. The figure of 18.25 million contains the oblast Vinnitsa with a population of 2.28 million. In part, this oblast stretched onto the area west of the Bug which came under Rumanian administration during World War Two (northern Transdniestria). It is possible that up to one third of the population of the oblast Vinnitsa should be allocated to Rumanian Transdniestria and not to the RK Ukraine. On the other hand, we should also take account of the natural increase of 4-5% for the 2½ years until mid-1941. Both corrections amount to about 750,000 persons and offset each other.

Fourth Chapter

1. Institute of Jewish Affairs, *Hitler's Ten-Year War*, p. 186.

2. *ibid.*, p.186.

3. *ibid.*, p. 186; the census of January 1939 found a total population of 95,090 in Shitomir. Until mid-1941 the city must have grown by at least another 10,000. Inasmuch as the German administration found only 42,000, at least 63,000 inhabitants must have been deported; of these, 44,000 were Jews. Thus the Jewish share among the evacuees probably was closer to 70% than 80%.

4. Reitlinger, *Final Solution*, p. 223.

5. Institute of Jewish Affairs, *Hitler's Ten-Year War*, p. 186.

6. *Encyclopaedia Judaica*, Vol. 11, p. 57.

7. Rothenberg, Joshua. "Jewish Religion in the Soviet Union," *The Jews in Soviet Russia since 1917*, (Lionel Kochan, Ed.), London, 1970, p. 172.

8. *Encyclopaedia Judaica*, Vol. 11, p. 232.

9. Institute of Jewish Affairs, *Hitler's Ten-Year War*, p. 186.

10. Aronson, *Soviet Russia and The Jews*, p. 19.

11. Reitlinger, *Final Solution*, p. 498.

12. Publikationsstelle Wien. *Die Bevölkerungszählung in Rumänien 1941* (Geheim), Vienna, 1943, p. 73.

13. *ibid.*, p. 51.

14. Institute of Jewish Affairs, *Hitler's Ten-Year War*, p. 186.

15. *ibid.*, p. 177.
16. *Encyclopaedia Judaica*, Vol. 11, p. 385-386.
17. *AJYB*, 1942, Vol. 44, p. 240.
18. *Kauener Zeitung*, "Fünftausend Tote klagen an," No. 138, 6/15/1942, p. 1; as well as the *Deutsche Zeitung im Ostland*, "Das Schicksal der Verschleppten," No. 161, 6/13/1943, p. 5.
19. *Encyclopaedia Judaica*, Vol. 6, p. 141.
20. *Deutsche Ukraine-Zeitung*, 2/6/1942, p. 3, reported that the population count found only 702 Jews.
21. Hilberg, Raul. *The Destruction of the European Jews*, New York, 1973, p. 192.
22. *Encyclopaedia Judaica*, Vol. 15, p. 1515.
23. Institute of Jewish Affairs, *Hitler's Ten-Year War*, p. 185.
24. Aronson, *Soviet Russia and The Jews*, p. 18.
25. *ibid.*, p. 18.
26. *Zentralblatt des Reichskommissars für die Ukraine*, Rovno, No. 2, 2nd Year, 1/9/1943, p. 8-20, Bundesarchiv Koblenz: R 43 II/690c.
27. *Drugi Powszechny Spis Ludności Z Dn. 9.XII 1931 R.*; Województwo Wołyńskie: Mieszkania I Gospodarstwa Domowe, Ludność, Stosunki Zawodowe; Głowny Urząd Statystyczny Rzeczypolitej Polskiej, Seria C, Zeszyt 70 (*Deuxième Recensement Général de la Population du 9 Décembre 1931*; Voievodie de Wolyn: Logements et Ménages, Population, Professions), Warsaw, 1938, Table 13.
28. *Zentralblatt*, 1/9/1943, p. 8 - 11.
29. *Bevölkerung in den besetzten Ostgebieten*, 2/17/1943, Militärarchiv Freiburg, Bestand RW 31/260.
30. Reitlinger, *Final Solution*, p. 241.
31. *ibid.*, p. 237.
32. See *Table 6*. Reitlinger, however, arrived at only 175,000.
33. Reitlinger, *Final Solution*, p. 240: He says that two-thirds of the Odessan Jews left *by train* for the eastern Soviet Union before the city was encircled by Rumanian troops on 8/13/1941. It was not captured by German and Rumanian troops until 10/16/1941. In the meantime, the Soviets deployed their Black Sea Fleet to deport tens of thousands of civilians, including many Jews.
34. *Encyclopaedia Judaica*, Vol. 10, p. 994.
35. Reitlinger, *Final Solution*, p. 227, writes that the number of those remaining behind in Vinnitsa, Kiev, Uman und Berdichev was about one-fourth or one-fifth.
36. *Encyclopaedia Judaica*, Vol. 10, p. 1049.
37. Reitlinger, *Final Solution*, p. 227 - 228.
38. Hilberg, *Destruction of the European Jews*, p. 190.
39. Reitlinger, *Final Solution*, p. 240.
40. Davies, Arthur Raymond. *Odyssey through Hell*, New York, 1946, p. 142.
41. *Treatment of Jews by the Soviet*, 1954, p. 40.
42. Burg, J.G. *Schuld und Schicksal: Europas Juden zwischen Henkern und Heuchlern*, Munich, 1965, p. 50.
43. Most of the Jewish publications mention with pride a strong Jewish participation in partisan activities during the last war; examples may be found in almost all volumes of the *Encyclopaedia Judaica*.

44. Telpuchowski, *Die sowjetische Geschichte*, p. 284, asserts that White Russian partisans alone murdered about 500,000 German soldiers and officers and 47 generals.

45. *WER IST WER?* (Walter Habel, Ed.), Frankfurt, 1975, describes this gentleman, inter alia, as follows: "after the war dept.head of chief prosecutor (Jackson) at Intern. Mil. Tribunal Nuremberg, asst. prosec. against Reichs Interior Min. Frick, beg. 1947 American dep. chief prosec. Wilhelmstr.-Process against cabinet members and diplomats of the III. Reich." The American professor A.R. Butz, *The Hoax of the Twentieth Century*, Los Angeles, however, arrived at vastly different conclusions in 1977; see in particular pages 29, 160-161, 163-169, 194, 195, and 244.

46. Kempner, Dr. Robert M.W. "Briefe an den Herausgeber," *Frankfurter Allgemeine Zeitung*, Frankfurt am Main, No. 23, 1/28/1981, p. 9.

47. Aronson, *Soviet Russia and The Jews*, p. 23.

48. Reitlinger, *Final Solution*, p. 500.

49. compare Institute of Jewish Affairs, *Hitler's Ten-Year War*, p. 186.

50. The Jewish mortality rate in the Soviet Union must have been greater than 1.2%. Since natural deaths occur primarily in the age groups 50 years and over and these age groups accounted for roughly 30% of the population, it may be presumed that at least 3.5% of the population over 49 years of age died annually of natural causes. We based our calculations on a rate of 3% because the exact composition of the remaining Jews is not known, but the older age groups nevertheless constituted the vast majority.

51. *Universal Jewish Encyclopedia*, Vol. 9, p. 681.

52. Aronson, *Soviet Russia and The Jews*, p. 12.

53. Reitlinger, *Final Solution*, p. 499.

54. Understandably, there are no exact figures on the extent of this vast number of deaths. But the fact that post-war literature contains no hints to the effect that a considerable number of former Polish-Jewish refugees remained behind in the Soviet Union after the war, allows us to conclude that except those 157,500 returnees almost all the others died in Siberia. The Jewish economist Jacob Lestschinsky (*AJYB*, Vol. 49, p. 397) puts the number of those who died in Siberia and central Asia at 500,000 Jews, while Gédéon Haganov (*Le Communisme et le "Juifs"*, Supplément de CONTACT, Paris, May 1951) arrived at about 450.000. The American Jewish Committee noted that only 200,000 had died in Sibiria (*AJYB*, Vol. 49, p. 394).

55. Telpuchowski, *Die sowjetische Geschichte*, p. 82 and 88.

56. *Encyclopaedia Judaica*, Vol. 11, p. 385 - 386.

57. *Deutsche Zeitung im Ostland*, "30.000 Verschleppte nachgewiesen," No. 5, 8/5/1941, p. 4 as well as "Die Schreckensnacht zum 14. Juni," No. 12, 8/16/1941, p. 5; *Kauener Zeitung*, "Die Sonne Stalins über Litauen," No. 6, 10/17/1941, p. 2 as well as "So fuhren sie in die Verbannung," No. 140, 6/17/1942, p. 5.

58. *Kauener Zeitung*, "Schicksale, die ganz Europa angehen," No. 88, 4/14/1943, p. 5.

59. *Treatment of Jews by the Soviet*, 1954, p. 86.

60. *Universal Jewish Encyclopedia*, Vol. 10, p. 23.

61. *Encyclopaedia Judaica*, Vol. 14, p. 479.

62. see *Sixth Chapter*.

Fifth Chapter

1. *AJYB*, 1948, Vol. 49, p. 740.
2. –, 1942, Vol. 44, p. 234. Other Jewish sources provide somewhat lower figures for Jewish Red Army soldiers; Solomon Grayzel mentions only 500,000 Jews in the Red Army in his book *A History of THE JEWS* (Philadelphia, 1948, p. 766). Unfortunately, Grayzel does not indicate the source where his figure originated; the *AJYB* however refers expressly to Soviet reports. It is interesting that Grayzel also mentions 550,000 and 17,000 Jews, respectively, in the armed forces of the United states and Canada. Relative to the entire Jewish population in those two countries (for more details see the Seventh Chapter), this is equivalent to a rate of about 10%. The same applies to South Africa. In the case of Great Britain 60,000 Jews are said to have served in Her Majesty's armed forces; this is an excellent indicator that the actual size of the Jewish population in England during the war was not 350,000 as Zionist sources maintain but probably around 600-700,000. Inasmuch as the Soviet Union had a somewhat larger Jewish population at the beginning of the war than the USA and as the Soviets mobilized a relatively larger share of the male population, even the figures published in Moscow seem to be on the low side. But Grayzel's figure is lower yet and thus even less likely.
3. *Drugi Powszechny Spis Ludności Z Dn. 9.XII 1931 R.*, "Polska: Mieszkania I Gospodarstwa Domowe, Ludność," Głowny Urząd Statystyczny Rzeczypospolitej Polskiej, Statystyka Polski, Seria C, Zeszyt 94A (Deuxième Recensement Général de la Population du 9 Décembre 1931, "Pologne: Logements et Ménages, Population," Office Central de Statistique de la Polonaise, Statistique de la Pologne, Série C, Fascicule 94A), Warsaw, 1938, Table 13.
4. see *Second Chapter.*
5. *AJYB*, 1964, Vol. 65, p. 268.
6. –, 1976, Vol. 77, p. 165.
7. Schmelz, U.O. "New Evidence on Basic Issues in the Demography of Soviet Jews," *The Jewish Journal of Sociology*, Vol. XVI, No. 2, December 1974, p. 210-214.
8. Statistisches Bundesamt. *Statistisches Jahrbuch für die Bundesrepublik Deutschland*, Wiesbaden, 1962, p. 29 .
9. *AJYB*, 1971, Vol. 72, p. 402 - 405.
10. Israel. The Central Bureau of Statistics and Economic Research. *Statistical Abstract of Israel 1951/52*, No. 3, Table 9, p. 27: Between May 15, 1948 and 12/31/1951 77,536 Jewish immmigrants aged 50-64 were registered; of these, 49% were male.
11. –, Central Bureau of Statistics. *Statistical Abstract of Israel 1977*, Tables V/5 in (No. 28, p. 125), *1978* (No. 29, p. 139), *1979* (No. 30, p. 138) and *1980* (No. 31, p. 136).
12. *AJYB*, 1947, Vol. 49, p. 393 - 397.
13. –, 1949, Vol. 50, p. 696.
14. –, 1961, Vol. 62, p. 284.
15. –, 1971, Vol. 72, p. 403.
16. –, 1972, Vol. 73, p. 536.
17. –, 1977, Vol. 78, p. 432.

18. *New York Times*, 1/22/1975, quoted in *AJYB*, 1976, Vol. 77, p. 460.
19. *Private letter* dated January 3, 1980 from Prof. Leon Shapiro who is in charge of population statistics at the *American Jewish Year Book*.
20. *Encyclopaedia Judaica*, Vol. 9, p. 542.
21. Kern, Erich. *Die Tragödie der Juden*, Preussisch Oldendorf, 1979, p. 260. With letter dated 8/15/1980 Prof. Zand (Hebrew University of Jerusalem) was requested to confirm the figure of 4.5 million in the Soviet Union ascribed to him; since no answer was forthcoming, another letter was sent to him on 1/2/1981. Thereupon, Prof. Zand answered with letter dated 2/13/1981 asking to have the question sent to him on 8/15/1980 repeated; he promised to reply if at all possible. Unfortunately, he failed to to do so in spite of repeated reminders (letters dated 2/25/1981 and 6/18/1981).
22. *Fortune*, New York, 8/14/1978, p. 158.
23. Rabinovich, Solomon. *Jews In The Soviet Union*, Moscow, 1967, p. 45 in: S. Ettinger, "The Jews in Russia at the Outbreak of the Revolution," *The Jews in Soviet Russia since 1917* (Lionel Kochan Ed.), London, 1970, p. 32.
24. *Encyclopaedia Judaica* Research Foundation: Ambassador Arthur J. Goldberg, Hon. Chairman; Dr. Nahum Goldmann, Hon. President; Dr. Joseph J. Schwartz; Prof. Salo W. Baron, Consulting Editor.
25. *Encyclopaedia Judaica*, Vol. 14, p. 482.
26. *AJYB*, 1962, Vol. 63, p. 350.
27. see *Second Chapter*.
28. Ettinger, S. "The Jews in Russia at the Outbreak of the Revolution," *The Jews in Soviet Russia since 1917*, (Lionel Kochan, Ed.), London, 1970, p. 35.
29. *AJYB*, 1976, Vol. 77, p. 472.
30. *Universal Jewish Encyclopedia*, Vol. 9, p. 670.
31. *AJYB*, 1973, Vol. 74, p. 481.
32. i.e. 700,000 (see *Table 8*) of about 3-4,000,000 (see footnote no. 20).
33. Schmelz, U.O. "New Evidence on Basic Issues in the Demography of Soviet Jews," *The Jewish Journal of Sociology*, London, Vol. XVI, No. 2, December 1974, p. 214.
34. *New York Times (The)*. "What Price a Soviet Jew?" in *International Herald Tribune*, Paris, March 6, 1981, p. 2.
35. *Encyclopaedia Judaica 1973 Year Book*, Jerusalem, 1974, p. 190.
36. In reply to a personal letter dated 2/5/1981 Dr. Nahum Goldmann replied in writing through his secretary on 2/13/1981 that "the Jewish population of the Soviet Union counted approximately three to three-and-one-half million persons."
37. Scott, John. *Jenseits des Ural*, Stockholm, 1944, p. 12 (Engl. original: *Behind the Urals*, Boston, 1942).
38. *Deutsche Zeitung im Ostland*, Riga/Latvia, "Neuer Stalin-Terror," No. 77, 3/18/1943, p. 7.
38a. *New York Times (The)*, "Willkie's Statement About Russia's Needs," 9/27/1942, p. 3.
39. *Daily Express*, "Your Questions about Russia – Answered by Paul Holt," London, (a few days before) May 6, 1943.
40. *Kauener Zeitung*, "18 Millionen Gesamtverluste der Sowjets," No. 149, 6/28/1943, p. 1.

41. *Die Tat*, Zürich, "Die erschütternde Bilanz zweier Weltkriege," No. 18, 1/18/ 1955, p. 2.

Sixth Chapter

1. *AJYB*, 1940, Vol. 42, p. 595.
2. Reitlinger, *Final Solution*, p. 71.
3. *AJYB*, 1941, Vol. 43, p. 324.
4. *ibid.*, p. 325.
5. Institute of Jewish Affairs, *Hitler's Ten-Year War*, p. 265.
6. *AJYB*, 1939, Vol. 41, p. 585.
7. Reitlinger, *Final Solution*, p. 349 and 351.
8. *AJYB*, 1940, Vol. 42, p. 602.
9. –, 1939, Vol. 41, p. 585.
10. Reitlinger, *Final Solution*, p. 352.
11. *ibid.*, p. 329.
12. *ibid.*, p. 494.
13. *ibid.*, p. 87 and 494.
14. *ibid.*, p. 328.
15. *ibid.*, p. 349 and 351.
16. *ibid.*, p. 495.
17. *ibid.*, p. 329.
18. *ibid.*, p. 494.
19. *ibid.*, p. 328.
20. *ibid.*, p. 495.
21. *ibid.*, p. 329.
22. *ibid.*, p. 342 and 344.
23. *ibid.*, p. 494.
24. *ibid.*, p. 328.
25. *ibid.*, p. 352 and 495.
26. Reitlinger, *Final Solution*, p. 501.
27. *Universal Jewish Encyclopedia*, Vol. 10, p. 36.
28. Reitlinger, *Final Solution*, p. 496.
29. Butz, *Hoax of the Twentieth Century*, 1977, p. 137.
30. Hilberg, *Destruction of European Jews*, p. 737.
31. *ibid.*, p. 737.
32. Reitlinger, *Final Solution*, p. 495-496.
33. Hilberg, *Destruction of European Jews*, p. 670.
34. Reitlinger, *Final Solution*, p. 496.
35. *AJYB*, 1940, Vol. 42, p. 595-596.
36. *ibid.*, p. 600.
37. Reitlinger, *Final Solution*, p. 492.
38. According to *Statistisches Jahrbuch für die Bundesrepublik Deutschland*, for example, the mortality rate (in West Germany) for 1977 was 3% p.a. for those

aged 47 years and more.

39. Reitlinger, *Final Solution*, p. 492.
40. *AJYB*, 1940, Vol. 42, p. 595.
41. –, 1941, Vol. 43, p. 663.
42. Reitlinger, *Final Solution*, p. 492.
43. *Annuaire Statistique Hongrois 1931*, Nouveau Cours XXXIX, l'Office Central Royal Hongrois de Statistique, Budapest, 1933, Tab. 10, p. 11.
44. *Magyar Statisztikai Évkönyv 1942*, Új Folyam L, A Magyar Kir Központi Statisztikai Hivatal, Budapest, 1944, Tab. 11, p. 17.
45. *Annuaire Statistique Hongrois 1931*, Tab. 10, p. 11.
46. *Magyar Statisztikai Évkönyv 1942*, Tab. 11, p. 14-17.
47. *Universal Jewish Encyclopedia*, Vol. 10, p. 24, estimated Hungary's Jewish population at the end of 1939 at 403,000.
48. *ibid.*, p. 25; the *Universal* mentions 5,250 Jewish emigrants until 1939.
49. Reitlinger, *Final Solution*, p. 415.
50. Publikationsstelle Wien. *Die Bevölkerungszählung in Rumänien 1941* (Geheim), Vienna, 1943, p. 20.
51. Butz, *Hoax of the Twentieth Century*, p. 149.
52. *ibid.*, p. 133.
53. *ibid.*, p. 138.
54. *ibid.*, p. 138-139.
55. *ibid.*, p. 144.
56. Hilberg, *Destruction of the European Jews*, p. 517.
57. *Encyclopaedia Judaica*, Vol. 8, p. 1098.
58. *Treatment of Jews by the Soviet*, 1954, p. 85-86.
59. *Universal Jewish Encyclopedia*, Vol. 10, p. 36.
60. Butz, *Hoax of the Twentieth Century*, p. 141.
61. *Treatment of Jews by the Soviet*, 1954, p. 72.
62. Butz, *Hoax of the Twentieth Century*, p. 139.
63. U.S. War Refugee Board. *Final Summary Report of the Executive Director, War Refugee Board*, Washington, D.C., 9/15/1945, p. 42.
64. Hilberg, *Destruction of European Jews*, p. 729.
65. Reitlinger, *Final Solution*, p. 497.
66. *Sčítání Lidu V Republice Československé Ze Dne 1. Prosince 1930* (Díl I.: Růst, Koncentrace A Hustota Obyvatelstva, Pohlaví, Věkové Rozvrstvení, Rodinný Stav, Státní Příslušnost, Národnost, Náboženské Vyznání), Vydal Státní Úřad Statistický, Československá Statistika - Svazek 98, Řada VI., Sešit 7, Prague, 1934, p. 156-190.
67. *Reitlinger*, p. 492.
68. Institute of Jewish Affairs, *Hitler's Ten-Year War*, p. 304.
69. *AJYB*, 1940, Vol. 42, p. 597.
70. –, 1941, Vol. 43, p. 663.
71. Reitlinger, *Final Solution*, p. 492-493.
72. *ibid.*, p. 492.
73. Butz, *Hoax of the Twentieth Century*, p. 208.
74. *ibid.*, p. 137.
75. Reitlinger, *Final Solution*, p. 493.
76. *Recensământul General Al Populaţiei României Din 29 Decemvrie 1930,*

Volumul II: Neam, Limbă, Maternă, Religie; Institutul Central de Statistică, Bukarest, 1938, p. XXIV.

77. *Wirtschaft und Statistik*, October 2, 1941, No. 20, p. 392.
78. Publikationsstelle Wien. *Die Bevölkerungszählung in Rumänien 1941* (Geheim), p. 20.
79. *Recensământul General Al Populaţiei României Din 29 Decemvrie 1930*, Volumul II: Neam, Limbă, Maternă, Religie; Institutul Central de Statistică, Bukarest, 1938, p. LXXXV.
80. In early 1938, the Rumanian Jews numbered 692,244 (see footnote no. 81) compared to 756,930 at the end of 1930; this amounts to an averagxe of 724,600 for the years 1931 to 1937.
81. The Institute of Jewish Affairs (*Hitler's Ten-Year War*, p. 83) wrote that under the law of January 21, 1938 all Jews in Rumania had to submit proof of citizenhsip if they wanted to keep it. 617,396 registered, 44,848 abstained and 30,000 were not qualified to register. This adds up to 692,244 for early 1938.
82. Publikationsstelle Wien. *Die Bevölkerungszählung in Rumänien 1941* (Geheim), p. 23.
83. *Wirtschaft und Statistik*, 10/2/1941, p. 392.
84. Publikationsstelle Wien. *Die Bevölkerungszählung in Rumänien 1941* (Geheim), p. 20.
85. *Jüdisches Lexikon*, Berlin (Jüdischer Verlag), 1930, Vol. IV/2, S-Z, p. 650-651.
86. Reitlinger, *Final Solution*, p. 497.
87. *AJYB*, 1941, Vol. 43, p. 330.
88. Reitlinger, *Final Solution*, p. 405.
89. *ibid.*, p. 409.
90. *Universal Jewish Encyclopedia*, Vol. 9, p. 265.
91. Millman, Ivor. "Romanian Jewry: a Note on the 1966 Census," *Soviet Jewish Affairs*, No. 3, May 1972, p. 105; this Jewish author asserts that the Communist census authorities of post-war Romania put the size of the Jewish population within today's borders at 452,000 for the time of the 1930 census. If this estimate were correct, our figure of 451,000 Romanian Jews in 1939 (in today's borders) would be too large by at least 20,000!
92. Reitlinger, *Final Solution*, p. 497.
93. *Treatment of Jews by the Soviet*, p. 53.
94. Hilberg, *Destruction of European Jews*, p. 737.
95. *AJYB*, 1941, Vol. 43, p. 668.
96. –, 1947, Vol. 49, p. 740.
97. Reitlinger, *Final Solution*, p. 379.
98. *AJYB*, 1971, Vol. 72, p. 476.
99. –, 1947, Vol. 49, p. 740.

Seventh Chapter

1. Hilberg, *Destruction of European Jews*, p. 729-730.
2. Butz, *Hoax of the Twentieth Century*, p. 232.
3. *The Immigration and Naturalization Systems of the United States*, Report of the Committee on the Judiciary, U.S. Senate, 81st Congress, 2d Session, April 20, 1950, p. 843.
4. *AJYB*, 1976, Vol. 77, p. 268
5. *ibid.*, p. 271-274.
6. *The Immigration and Naturalization Systems*, p. 21.
7. U.S. Department of Commerce, Bureau of the Census. *Population Estimates and Projections*, Current Population Reports, Series P-25, No. 632, July 1976, Washington, D.C., p. 1.
8. *AJYB*, 1947, Vol. 49, p. 749.
9. *Encyclopaedia Judaica*, Vol. 16, p. 554-555.
10. Wischnitzer, Mark. "The History of the Jews in Russia in Recent Publications," *The Jewish Quarterly Review*, Philadelphia, 1944-1945, Vol. XXXV, p. 393.
11. Sykes, Christopher. *Kreuzwege nach Israel: Die Vorgeschichte des Jüdischen Staates*, Munich, 1967, p. 414.
12. *The New York Times*. "580,000 Refugees Admitted to United States in Decade," 12/11/1943, p. 1; see also footnote no. 11.
13. *AJYB*, 1947, Vol. 49, p. 749.
14. Ruppin, Arthur. *The Jewish Fate and Future*, London, 1940, p. 46.
15. *The New York Times*. "580,000 Refugees Admitted to United States in Decade," 12/11/1943, p. 6.
16. *AJYB*, 1974, Vol. 75, p. 300 and 1977, Vol. 78, p. 262-263.
17. It must be assumed that the Jewish natural rate of increase fell below zero in the USA in the 1970's. The *AJYB*, 1976, Vol. 77, p. 310 wrote for instance: "... the current Jewish fertility is 6 points below the rate that prevails in even the most intensely urbanized areas." The urban population, especially in the large cities, in the United States like in all industrial countries recorded natural increases far below that of the general population. But if, as the publication "Population Estimates and Projections" of the U.S. Department of Commerce notes, the average American net growth rate was below 0.6% after 1972, the logical conclusion must be that the American-Jewish population is confronted with a serious demographic crisis since the early 1970's.
18. *AJYB*, 1973, Vol. 74, p. 276.
19. The *Statistical Abstract of Israel* does not list the immigrant Jews from America and Europe separately; but the Jewish immigrants from America represent only a tiny fraction of this group.
20. *Statistical Abstract of Israel 1955/56*, Table 16, p. 14.
21. –, 1980, Table V/1, p. 133.
22. –, 1954/55, Table 5, p. 33.
23. –, 1955/56, Table 3, p. 7.
24. *1958 World Almanac and Book of Facts*, New York, p. 270.
25. The excess of births over deaths numbering 865,000 for the years 1946-1970 was calculated on the basis of the age structure as published by NJPS.

26. The immigration of 490,000 for the years 1946-1970 was computed as follows:
    a) The Jewish population born in 1946-1950 is 8.7% of 6,600,000, or 574,000.
    b) Of these 574,000 8.6%, or 49,000 were born abroad. c) These 49,000
    represent about 10% of the immigrants.
27. *U.S. News & World Report*, New York, April 7, 1980, p. 41.
28. *AJYB*, 1947, Vol. 49, p. 742.
29. *Statistical Abstract of Israel 1971*, No. 22, Table B/2, p. 22.
30. *Encyclopaedia Judaica*, Vol. 9, p. 534.
31. *ibid.*, p. 541.
32. *AJYB*, 1944, Vol. 46, p. 501.
33. *1972 World Almanac*, p. 156.
34. *Encyclopaedia Judaica*, Vol. 9, p. 533.
35. *AJYB*, 1945, Vol. 47, p. 638.
36. *Universal Jewish Encyclopedia*, Vol. 10, p. 36.
37. *AJYB*, 1946, Vol. 48, p. 609.
38. *1972 World Almanac*, p. 156.
39. Butz, *Hoax of the Twentieth Century*, p. 227.
40. *AJYB*, 1944, Vol. 46, p. 501.
41. –, 1951, Vol. 52, p. 199.
42. It is not known whether the Jews coming to Israel from Tunesia belonged to
    the Oriental or to the immigrated (eastern) European part. We assumed them
    to belong to the European Jews; consequently, the Jews migrating to France
    from Tunesia were grouped among the Orientals.
43. *Statistical Abstract of Israel 1971*, Table B/2, p. 22.
44. Tartakower, Arieh and Kurt R. Grossmann. *The Jewish Refugee*, New York,
    1944, p. 343; also, *AJYB*, 1944, Vol. 46 (p. 500-501), 1951 Vol. 52 (p. 196-198)
    and 1971 Vol. 72 (p. 477-479).
45. According to *AJYB*, 1969, Vol. 70, p. 276, the estimated number of Jews in
    Great Britain rose to 450,000 in 1950 "and has stood at this figure ever since."
    In the issue of 1977, Vol. 78, p. 339-340 the *AJYB* wrote again:
    > An outstanding feature [of British Jews] is a demographic decline.
    > ... demographers forecast that, in the foreseeable future, the
    > Jewish population may fall to 225,000 compared with the 410,000
    > currently [in 1971] estimated. The primary cause is the low birth
    > rate. ... Jewish families [showed] only an average of 1.72 children
    > per familiy [compared to] to the general population, which had an
    > average of 2.16 children. ... intermarriage unmistakably emerges
    > as the greatest single threat to the future of British Jewry. ... the
    > true level of assimilation ... is approximately 20 per cent ...

    The reduction since 1950 thus may be explained by both of these factors –
    intermarriage and too few births.
46. Tartakower and Grossmann, *Jewish Refugee*, p. 343.
47. *AJYB*, 1971, Vol. 72, p. 476.
48. *Encyclopaedia Judaica*, Vol. 9, p. 538-539.
49. *International Herald Tribune*. "French Policies to Court the Jewish Vote," May
    10, 1977, p. 2.
50. *AJYB*, 1971, Vol. 72, p. 476. The Jewish population figures (1970) given for
    European countries (excl. France) are not necessarily identical with reality as

Table 15 shows. According to *AJYB*, 1969, Vol. 70, p. 285, the frequent intermarriages of European Jews and the withdrawal from the Jewish community which often results therefrom, caused considerable but, unfortunately, not ascertainable losses to the European Jewish population.

51. Institute of Jewish Affairs, *Hitler's Ten-Year War*, p. 306.
52. U.S. War Refugee Board, *Final Summary Report*, p. 4-5.
53. *ibid.*, p. 34.
54. *ibid.*, p. 7.
55. *ibid.*, p. 20-21.
56. *ibid.*, p. 9.
57. *ibid.*, p. 19-20.
58. *ibid.*, p. 18.
59. *ibid.*, p. 21-23.
60. *ibid.*, p. 26.
61. *ibid.*, p. 64.
62. *ibid.*, p. 61-62.
63. *ibid.*, p. 32-33.

Eighth Chapter

1. *AJYB*, 1932, Vol. 34, p. 251.
2. U.S. Department of Commerce, *Population Estimates*, p. 1.
3. *AJYB*, 1946, Vol. 48, p. 603.
4. *Statistical Abstract of Israel 1971*, Table B/3.
5. U.S. Department of Commerce, *Population Estimates*, p. 1.
6. Hardach, Karl. *Wirtschaftsgeschichte Deutschlands im 20. Jahrhundert*, Göttingen, 1976, p. 246.
7. see Seventh Chapter.
8. *AJYB*, 1945, Vol. 47, p. 637.
9. –, 1940, Vol. 42, p. 604.
10. –, 1947, Vol. 49, p. 741-744.
11. *ibid.*, p. 740.
12. In 1939 (before the oubreak of the German-Polish war), 5,044,000 Jews lived in those European countries later occupied by Germany (excl. USSR and Baltic countries) according to *Table 11*. Of these, 1,867,000 Polish and 225,000 Rumanian Jews came within the Soviet empire before the start of the war; there remain 2,952,000.
13. *AJYB*, 1946, Vol. 48, p. 603-607.
14. –, 1971, Vol. 72, p. 475-476.
15 –, 1975, Vol. 76, p. 251.
16 Département de la Jeunesse et du Héhalouts de l'Organisation Sioniste Mondiale. *Israël Almanach 1958-1959*, Jerusalem, p. 282.
17. Zoller, Henri. "Israel - Ein Nachtasyl?", *Der Spiegel*, No. 37, 9/8/1980, p. 148-149.

18. *Statistical Abstract of Israel 1980*, Table II/2.
19. Goldmann, Dr. Nahum. "Aus Sorge um Israel," *Die Zeit*, No. 29, 7/11/1980, p. 13 f. A short time before his death, Dr. Goldmann was still more specific: in *Der Spiegel* ("Israels Regierung hat das Volk betrogen," No. 34, August 28, 1982, p. 9); he narrowed Israel's share of the world Jewish population down to *less than 20%*; applying this rate to Israel's Jewish population of 3.2 million, Dr. Goldmann, in effect, placed world Jewry at over 16.5 million.
20. Goldmann, Dr. Nahum. *Private letter* dated 2/13/1981.
21. *AJYB*, 1980, Vol. 81, p. 61f.: Since the middle of the 1960's at the latest, there has been a drastic drop in births.
22. –, 1969, Vol. 70, p. 275:

> In all diaspora Jewish communities for which we have data, the proportion of elderly and old people is greater than in the surrounding general population. This is basically due to low fertility over the last few decades. ... Contributory factors may be the differential impact of withdrawals and a recent negative migration balance, involving particularly younger adults. ... more than half of some European Jewish populations are above the age of 40. In Europe and America the aging of the Jewish populations has led to an exaggerated proportion of persons no longer participating in reproduction while being subject to the comparatively high age-specific mortality of the elderly.

The *AJYB* (p. 274-275) goes on:

> The population dynamics of the Jews in Europe, the Americas, South Africa, Australia, and New Zealand should be viewed in the context of their socio-economic position. These Jews have a strong tendency toward urbanization, educational attainment, and concentration in white-collar occupations and higher income brackets. In most of these countries, the relatively small or highly dispersed Jewish communities are strongly affected by environmental influences, secularization and assimilation. ... The keynote is the very low level of Jewish fertility. In all countries for which data are available, including the United States, the fertility of the Jews is below that of the general population. In several countries it has fallen below replacement level. After a short-lived post-World War II baby boom, Jewish birth figures declined in the 1950s.

23. Schmelz, U.O. "A Guide to Jewish Population Studies," *Jewish Population Studies 1961-1968*, (U.O. Schmelz and P. Glickson, Ed.), London/Jerusalem, 1970, p. 34.
24. *AJYB*, 1980, Vol. 81, p. 61 and 62.
25. *ibid.*, p. 68 and 69.

Index

235

238

Z

Zand, Michael 118, 201
Zaporoshye 63, 70, Table 6, Chart 1
Zaslavsky, D. 94
Zhukov, Georgi K. 53

Zinger, Lev K. 104, 105
Zionist Jewish population estimates for post-war Soviet cities 118, 119, Table 10
Zionist Organization in Hungary 140
Zionist World Organization 193
Zoller, Henri 193
Zukerman, Jacob T. 42